PROVINCIAL SOLIDARITIES

Working Canadians: Books from the CCLH
Series editors: Alvin Finkel and Greg Kealey

The Canadian Committee on Labour History is Canada's organization of historians and other scholars interested in the study of the lives and struggles of working people throughout Canada's past. Since 1976, the CCLH has published *Labour/Le Travail*, Canada's pre-eminent scholarly journal of labour studies. It also publishes books, now in conjunction with AU Press, that focus on the history of Canada's working people and their organizations. The emphasis in this series is on materials that are accessible to labour audiences as well as university audiences rather than simply on scholarly studies in the labour area. This includes documentary collections, oral histories, autobiographies, biographies, and provincial and local labour movement histories with a popular bent.

SERIES TITLES

Champagne and Meatballs: Adventures of a Canadian Communist
    Bert Whyte, edited and with an introduction by Larry Hannant

Working People in Alberta: A History
    Alvin Finkel, with contributions by Jason Foster, Winston Gereluk, Jennifer Kelly and Dan Cui, James Muir, Joan Schiebelbein, Jim Selby, and Eric Strikwerda

Union Power: Solidarity and Struggle in Niagara
    Carmela Patrias and Larry Savage

The Wages of Relief: Cities and the Unemployed in Prairie Canada, 1929–39
    Eric Strikwerda

Provincial Solidarities: A History of the New Brunswick Federation of Labour/ Solidarités provinciales: Histoire de la Fédération des travailleurs et travailleuses du Nouveau-Brunswick
    David Frank

PROVINCIAL SOLIDARITIES

A History of the
New Brunswick Federation of Labour

DAVID FRANK

AU PRESS   CANADIAN COMMITTEE ON LABOUR HISTORY

Published by AU Press, Athabasca University
1200, 10011 – 109 Street, Edmonton, AB T5J 3S8
ISBN 978-1-927356-23-4 (print)   978-1-927356-24-1 (PDF)   978-1-927356-25-8 (epub)
A volume in Working Canadians: Books from the CCLH
ISSN 1925-1831 (print)   1925-184X (digital)

Cover and interior design by Natalie Olsen, Kisscut Design.
Printed and bound in Canada by Marquis Book Printers.

Library and Archives Canada Cataloguing in Publication
Frank, David
Provincial solidarities : a history of the New Brunswick Federation of Labour / David Frank.

(Working Canadians, ISSN 1925-1831 ; 5)
Includes bibliographical references and index.
Issued also in electronic formats.
Co-published by: Canadian Committee on Labour History.
ISBN 978-1-927356-23-4

1. New Brunswick Federation of Labour — History. 2. Labor unions — New Brunswick
— History. 3. Labor movement — New Brunswick — History. I. Canadian Committee
on Labour History II. Title. III. Series: Working Canadians (Edmonton, Alta.) ; 5

HD6529.N4F73 2013   331.88097151   C2012-905866-1

Publication of this book was supported by a Community-University Research Alliance
grant provided by the Social Sciences and Humanities Research Council of Canada.

Social Sciences and Humanities
Research Council of Canada

Conseil de recherches en
sciences humaines du Canada

Canadä

We acknowledge the financial support of the Government of Canada through the Canada
Book Fund (CBF) for our publishing activities.

Canadian   Patrimoine
Heritage   canadien

Assistance provided by the Government of Alberta, Alberta Multimedia Development Fund.

Government

CONTENTS

CONTENTS

ABBREVIATIONS

ACCL	All-Canadian Congress of Labour
ARLEC	Atlantic Region Labour Education Centre
CBRE	Canadian Brotherhood of Railroad (later Railway) Employees
CCF	Co-operative Commonwealth Federation
CCL	Canadian Congress of Labour
CEP	Communications, Energy and Paperworkers Union of Canada
CIO	Committee for (later Congress of) Industrial Organization(s)
CLC	Canadian Labour Congress
CPU	Canadian Paperworkers Union
CSU	Canadian Seamen's Union
CUPE	Canadian Union of Public Employees
IAM	International Association of Machinists
IBEW	International Brotherhood of Electrical Workers
ILA	International Longshoremen's Association
MFU	Maritime Fishermen's Union
MLA	Member of the Legislative Assembly
MP	Member of Parliament
NBCL	New Brunswick Council of Labour
NBFL	New Brunswick Federation of Labour
NBPEA	New Brunswick Public Employees Association
NBU	New Brunswick Union of Public and Private Employees
NDP	New Democratic Party
NUPE	National Union of Public Employees
RWDSU	Retail, Wholesale and Department Store Union
SIU	Seafarers' International Union
TLC	Trades and Labour Congress of Canada
UMWA	United Mine Workers of America

ACKNOWLEDGEMENTS

Many individuals and institutions helped in the preparation of this book, which has been one of the major undertakings of the Labour History in New Brunswick Project, a Community-University Research Alliance supported by the Social Sciences and Humanities Research Council of Canada. The council's generous support made it possible to undertake several initiatives in the field, including this book. For a project functioning in both official languages of the province and based on collaboration between researchers at the two provincial universities, the Université de Moncton and the University of New Brunswick provided essential support. Members of the project team have made their own research contributions in the field and have also assisted in the preparation of this book. At the University of New Brunswick, Linda Kealey, Greg Kealey, and Bill Parenteau were always ready to provide advice and assistance. Nelson Ouellet developed the project website (http://www.lhtnb.ca) and coordinated work in Moncton, with the assistance of Denise Paquette. At the Université de Moncton in Edmundston, Nicole Lang was a model of efficiency and cooperation at all times; in the production of this book, she provided expert editorial help in working with our excellent translator, Réjean Ouellette. Throughout the life of the project, our Fredericton project officer, Carol Ferguson, was indispensable in coordinating the work of the research team and our institutional partners. Student assistants participated in several phases of the work on this book, including the archival research and oral history. At the University of New Brunswick they included Christo Aivalis, Matt Baglole, Jazmine Belyea, Dana Brown, Kim Dunphy, Kelly Flinn, Steven Hansen, Courtney MacIsaac, Patrick Marsh, Mark McLaughlin, Don Nerbas, Lisa Pasolli, Amy Wallace, Leta Waugh, and Michael Wilcox; at the Université de Moncton they included Zoé Lessard-Couturier, Valerie McLaughlin, and Philippe Volpé. The responsibility for insisting that I undertake work in New Brunswick labour history belongs to Raymond Léger, who was already making notable contributions to the field as a researcher, educator, and activist long before this project was initiated; he has been a source of encouragement and advice for many years. Jean-Claude Basque, Education Representative for the Canadian Labour Congress in Moncton, was also an early advocate for this project. I am very grateful to George Vair, a former president of the Saint John and District Labour Council and a pioneer in Saint John labour history, who has always been ready to provide practical assistance. In the preparation of this book, the Provincial Archives of New Brunswick, under the direction of Marion Beyea, made a home for the records of the New Brunswick Federation of Labour as well as for the oral history and administrative files produced by the project. When the idea of this history was discussed in the 1990s, Federation president Tim McCarthy provided support and encouragement, as did members of the Federation's Education Committee. The late Blair Doucet, president of the Federation of Labour at the time the project was organized, understood the importance of sharing labour's story with union members and the wider public. His successor, Michel Boudreau, has continued to provide cooperation and assistance. In the final stages of editorial work, the Busteed Fund at the University of New Brunswick assisted in securing illustrations. I am grateful to Athabasca University Press for undertaking to publish this book, in both English and French editions; a special thank-you is extended to Pamela MacFarland Holway, for supervising the editorial process, and to Natalie Olsen, for the handsome design.

PROVINCIAL SOLIDARITIES

THE BELL In 1929, delegates to the Trades and Labour Congress of Canada meetings in Saint John were reminded that labour had deep roots in New Brunswick history. In 1849, the Saint John longshoremen, organized as the Labourers' Benevolent Association, petitioned the city to place a bell on the waterfront to enforce the ten-hour day. Eighty years later it was celebrated as "the bell which had first rung out the message of hope for the workers and marked the beginning of the struggle for the shorter work day." Source: Rare Books and Special Collections, University of British Columbia.

"Makers *of* History"

When you enter the crowded conference room, your credentials are examined by one of the sentinels at the door. Are you a delegate? A guest? An observer? Everyone is here with a mandate, and the men and women in attendance are seated at tables according to the constituencies they represent. The walls are decorated with banners, and the tables are covered with reports and resolutions. At the front, the president is addressing the meeting, speaking in both English and French, and translations are flowing from a booth at the back of the hall. There are some comments and questions from the floor microphones, followed by a vote. Then everyone is standing, and they are singing. Not everybody knows the verses, but they do know the chorus of this anthem that is almost as old as their own organization: "Solidarity forever, Solidarity forever, Solidarity forever, for the union makes us strong."

When the chanting and clapping are over and everyone is again seated, the agenda continues, and for the next several days the big hotel ballroom is transformed into a chamber of discussion for what is in effect a provincial parliament of labour.

The meetings of this assembly have been taking place for a full century now, a longer record of continuity than in almost any other province in Canada. The New Brunswick Federation of Labour is far from the largest provincial federation in Canada, but it is one of the oldest and has shown the power of persistence — what the poet Fred Cogswell has called the "stubborn strength"— that is one of the features of the provincial identity. The affiliated membership has never exceeded 50,000 people, and not all labour organizations have been participants, but in a relatively small province whose total population is little more than 750,000 people, the Federation of Labour has had a long and influential presence. These kinds of "union centrals," as they are called in industrial relations terminology, are labour organizations that have no direct control over their affiliates and do not represent them in matters such as collective bargaining. Instead, they speak for the more general interests that union members have in common with one another, and their power depends on their ability to inspire solidarity around these causes. When we look back over the past century, the history of this organization is filled with examples of working people taking up their responsibilities as members of their unions and as citizens of the province. The mission of the Federation of Labour has been to assist the unions in raising the status and strengthening the rights of all workers in the province. In addition to the ambitions and achievements, there have been disappointments and divisions, but the long history of the Federation reminds us that the search for a greater measure of social justice is a significant theme in the history of the province.

In beginning the story of the Federation of Labour in 1913, we also need to remember that organized labour has deep roots in New Brunswick history. Social inequalities and the exploitation of labour are as old as the earliest staple trades in the region, but the emergence of trade unions as a form of resistance can be traced back to the early nineteenth century. Unions existed for about a century before the founding of the Federation of Labour. They were established in towns and cities by small local groups of workers and often called themselves "benevolent associations"; they demanded better wages, hours, and conditions for members and provided benefits for their families in cases of illness, injury, and death. Eugene Forsey has pointed out that before Confederation, New Brunswick was one of the birthplaces of the union movement in British North America, and he often singled out the example of the Saint John longshoremen, whose history began in the struggle for the ten-hour day in 1849, making them today one of the oldest continuously existing unions in Canada. Local unions such as these also went on to link up with regional, national, or international organizations in the same trade or industry, as the longshoremen did when they joined the International Longshoremen's Association in 1911; this helped them to achieve higher standards and, when necessary, receive assistance and support from the larger bodies. In the case of the Canadian Brotherhood of Railroad Employees, the organization was founded at Moncton in 1908 as a regional body before going on to expand across the country and become one of the most important unions in twentieth-century Canada; by the time of their centennial year, they had joined the Canadian Auto Workers. This pattern of accelerating solidarities was also visible at the community level when workers from varied occupations organized themselves into local trades and labour councils. By the 1890s, such bodies were marching in large numbers in Labour Day parades in Saint John and Moncton and making their presence felt within the social and political life of the province's two largest cities. These workers in turn took the lead in establishing the Federation of Labour. In short, the construction of a provincial "house of labour" in 1913 was not the beginning of labour history in New Brunswick but the latest stage in a longer history of solidarities among workers of the province.[1]

A historical perspective also reminds us of the importance of all workers in building the provincial economy. "True history is the record of the workers," wrote the carpenter, poet, and socialist agitator Wilfrid Gribble in "Makers of History," around the time he took up residence in Saint John and the Federation of Labour was coming into existence:

> True history is the record
> Of the workers. It was they
> Who wrote its page in every age,
> They're writing it today.[2]

New Brunswick workers laboured in the woods, on the rivers, in the fisheries, and on the farms; they prepared fish, potatoes, apples, and other foods for market; they toiled in sawmills, shipyards, and pulp and paper mills; they worked hard rock and coal mines; they manufactured boots and shoes, boilers and machines, textiles and clothing, windows and furniture; they opened roads and trails, raised towers, and built dams and bridges; they loaded deals of lumber and shipped freight and cargo; they operated trains, buses, trucks, and taxis; they sweated in laundries and restaurants, hotels, and kitchens; they ran stores, offices, and telephone exchanges; they cleaned floors, served meals, and guided visitors; they fought fires, generated power, delivered mail, and cleared snow; they cared for the young, educated the students, assisted the seniors, and protected our health.

The list is as endless as the occupations in the province, but when we read about labour history, we also need to think about the economic relationships that define the world of work. In the eighteenth century, Adam Smith originally defined the working class as "those who live by wages," setting this category aside from the unpaid labour of slaves and servants and the apparent independence of many artisans and small producers. Over the next two centuries, however, paid employment became the most common way of making a living. The industrial revolution of the nineteenth century and the waves of economic transformation that followed drew large numbers of people out of independent production and household economies and brought them into the labour market as earners of wages and salaries. As such, they became dependent on the decisions of employers who were not necessarily or even primarily committed to the welfare of the individual worker or the community. Workers who depended for their lving on daily or weekly wages had much less bargaining power than their employers in determining how to distribute the risks and rewards of economic life. In 1898, a New Brunswick professor of political economy and moral philosophy, John Davidson, made a notable observation about the contemporary Labour Question, as it was called in the late nineteenth century: "Labor, in spite of sentimental objections is undoubtedly a commodity which is bought and sold," he reasoned. However, he went on to explain, this was not an ordinary economic proposition because labour was a unique commodity and market conditions could never be a sufficient guide to its value: "Labor differs from most, if not all, other commodities in retaining, even under modern industrial conditions, its subjective value to the seller. We cannot separate the labor and the laborer. It is labor that is bought and sold but, with the labor, goes the laborer. Therefore instead of a great simplification we have a great complication."[3]

Every chapter in history has its own complications. To take one example, in the 1880s a famous investigation documented some of the worst effects of industrial capitalism in Canada. The Royal Commission on the Relations of Labor and Capital held hearings in the four original provinces of the Confederation, including New Brunswick, and their findings documented the conditions of the time. Among other things, the commissioners recommended the payment of wages regularly, and in cash; they also called for an end to fines and beatings, the prohibition of convict labour and child labour, the inspection of workplaces for safety and sanitation, the payment of compensation for workplace injuries, and more attention to literacy and training. They even recommended a statutory Labour Day holiday, the only one of their recommendations that was actually implemented by the federal government at the time, enacted by Parliament in 1894. It is also important to note their comments on the value of labour organizations. The commissioners concluded that the unions were a positive force that promoted social progress and encouraged self-respect and good citizenship among their members. Most of all, they explained, the unions were there to correct the unequal power of workers and their employers within the existing economic system: "Labour organizations are necessary in order to enable workingmen to deal on equal terms with their employers."[4]

When the claim is made that the working class today has disappeared and has been replaced by a universal middle class, it is worth remembering that most citizens continue to earn their living in the form of paid employment and are thus associated with the classic definition of the working class. There are great differences in incomes and security and bargaining power among workers, but those who are organized in unions are best able to defend their interests. The improved conditions they achieve in wages, hours, benefits, pensions, and other forms of security are often described as "the union advantage." While their critics argue that unions have created a "two-tier" economic system that favours some workers to the detriment of others, the unions argue that all workers should be entitled to higher standards and that unions generally succeed in "levelling-up" the prevailing conditions in society. Certainly, the ability to overcome differences and to share the influence of their power with other citizens is one of the attractive legacies of the union movement in New Brunswick. To take another historical example, the long campaign against child labour was led by an alliance of labour unions, social reformers, and early feminists. None of these groups was strong enough to achieve this reform alone, but their success came from working together. Despite objections that their demands would make too many New Brunswick businesses unprofitable, the provincial government in 1905 finally enacted a law to limit the employment of children less than fourteen years of age. This reform was soon followed by the school attendance laws, another advance in the social progress in the province.[5]

Although much has changed in the structure and influence of the labour movement over the years, the place of unions within society has stood the test of time. As students of the nineteenth-century Labour Question understood, by strengthening the bargaining position of workers within society, the unions were taking on an ambition to achieve a more balanced, even a more just, distribution of the wealth produced in the economy by directing a larger share of it to the working class. Although union membership in Canada as a whole has rarely exceeded more than one-third of the work force — and the same is true in New Brunswick — the unions have helped to set standards that improve conditions and raise incomes for all workers. Through organizations such as the Federation of Labour, the unions have defended the rights of workers in their places of employment and have also helped to lead the struggle for a more equitable distribution of the "social wage" in the form of public services that benefit all citizens.

In the writing of Canadian labour history, provincial stories are generally overlooked, and there have been few general histories of provincial labour movements or federations.[6] Nonetheless, labour history in Canada is very much a provincial experience, in part for the simple constitutional reason that most Canadian workers have lived and worked under labour and employment regimes enacted and administered by the provinces. As a result, the various local, occupational, national, and international affiliations of union members have been supplemented by bonds of solidarity based on the political and spatial realities of the provincial communities within Canada. From this perspective, the emergence of provincial federations of labour was an additional expression of emerging solidarities within the twentieth-century labour movement in Canada. When the Trades and Labour Congress of Canada in 1910 encouraged member unions to create provincial federations, British Columbia (in 1910) and Alberta (in 1912) were the first to do so, and New Brunswick was the only other province to join them prior to the First World War. Not all provinces are the same, however, and in the fractious labour climate of the times, British Columbia's federation did not survive its first decade and was not reorganized until 1944. In working to achieve recognition as the provincial voice of labour, the New Brunswick Federation may well have benefited from a greater sense of provincial solidarity as well as the moderate goals of the founders.

It is also the case that the Federation has grown unevenly and has often fallen short of its goal of attracting the majority of unions and union members in the province. In part this has been due to its constitutional status as a subordinate body within the Trades and Labour Congress and later the Canadian Labour Congress, bodies that have discouraged or even precluded the affiliation of unions to which they objected. In the 1930s and 1940s, for instance, some rival unions, pursuing more nationalist and industrial forms of organization, even established a separate federation, known as the New Brunswick Council of Labour. The province's workers have also been divided by the economic geography of New Brunswick — north against south, urban centres against rural regions, temporary workers against permanent employees. And the ideals of solidarity have been undermined by perceived hierarchies of status and stature based on differences of skill, language, ethnicity, and gender. Although the Federation elected an Acadian as president as early as 1919, fuller partnerships between French-speaking and English-speaking workers developed more slowly. There were similar challenges in the Federation's ability to address the needs of women workers and of public employees, two major groups who entered the labour force in rapidly increasing numbers in the second half of the twentieth century. Moreover, in New Brunswick, as in other less powerful and less populous parts of Canada, the political economy of underdevelopment has cut deeply into the social, human, and environmental stability of the provincial economy. This has contributed to a constant concern about the ravaged resource base of the province, the unforgiving cycles of capitalist investment and disinvestment, the push and pull of labour markets from beyond the provincial borders, and the recurring fiscal crises of the provincial state. The unions on their own have not had the capacity to solve these questions, but the quest for social and economic democracy has nonetheless been a continual theme in the history of the Federation of Labour.

"Honour the Past. Build the Future." Back in the hotel ballroom where the Federation of Labour is meeting, these are the announced watchwords for the convention. Looking around the tables, it is apparent that many delegates are wearing gold pins that celebrate the latest milestone in the Federation's history. As the opening evening proceeds, there are tributes to veteran activists for their decades of work on behalf of the province's workers, and two more names are added to the Federation's Honour Roll. One speaker quotes the people's historian Howard Zinn, saying that history can help us rediscover the times when working people have shown the ability to resist, to join together, to make a difference, and to win changes. Even if the history of work and workers is often overlooked in public discourse, the Federation has a long tradition of taking pride in the historical significance of their organization. It was there in the 1920s and 1930s when commemorative badges and souvenir booklets were being issued. It is there again today in resolutions calling for more attention to labour history within the union movement and within the schools.

We hear that message clearly when we listen to interviews that union members have recorded for the provincial archives. "The thing I find funny about labour is they don't record their history," says John Daly, who was a waterfront worker in Saint John for thirty-six years and held many local union offices. "They just take it for granted that this is the job they're supposed to do." Barb Fairley, who started at a shoe factory in Fredericton when she was a teenager and worked there for almost thirty years, including fifteen years as president of her local, says: "They teach History every day in school. I mean, why can't they include some of the labour history of the province or even as a country?" Stella Cormier, who left school at thirteen and later worked in the fish plants, says that history can teach workers their rights: "Above all, it's knowing your rights. You must know your rights. If you go to work and don't know your rights, they can make you do anything they want." Similarly, Béatrice Boudreau, who started work at the age of eighteen in an office in Moncton, putting in 54 hours a week for $20 in pay, reminds us that history is about change: "The most important thing to know is how things have improved, no doubt slowly but at certain times very suddenly. Sometimes it takes a shock. You have to understand the improvements that are due, almost entirely, to the union movement." And Yvon Godin, a New Democratic Party MP for many years now, remembers how little he knew about unions when he went into the mines at nineteen years of age; he worries that young workers today know just as little about their history:

"Look at where we are today, but how did we get here? It's not their fault, but too often I see young people who come into the labour market and see all these things in place and think that all this is normal, that it was always there. They don't know how it came to be."[7]

This book cannot capture the full sweep of labour history in New Brunswick. There is much more to be done, and this book attempts to tell the history of only one working-class organization and its place in provincial history. Even then it is not a full chronicle but a narrative of the main stages in its development and of the events in provincial history that have been important to the Federation. There is attention to many episodes of workers in action in their own workplaces and communities, but there is also an inevitable focus on the life of the institution itself, including the tensions between leaders and members, and between moderates and militants. Social historians have studied many aspects of the working-class experience in Canada in recent years, and one of their findings has been that people experience their own history in ways that are shaped by the multiple rhythms of individual lives and social, cultural, and economic opportunity. As a result, there is never a single shared identity within the working-class population, however desirable that might seem to labour leaders. In showing us the daily lives of working-class families and their struggles for security and fulfillment, social historians have documented the complexities of household, workplace, and community and revealed the hidden sources of resilience and resistance that are often embedded in those sites of experience.[8] At the same time, there is also much to be said for a critique articulated some years ago by Howard Kimeldorf in a debate on "Why we need a new old labor history." The substance of that discussion was that the "new" labour history has not only deepened the portrayal of workers' history but has also offered opportunities to strengthen explorations of classic questions, including issues of structure and mobilization, solidarities and exclusions, and representation and negotiation that determine the conditions of working-class effectiveness.[9] As Geoff Eley and Keith Nield have noted more recently, labour organizations and other social movements have contributed enormously to public discourse and have interacted with the political system to shape public policy, understanding politics as "a space of possibility" conditioned as much by human activism as by the structural forces people encounter.[10] Historical research and writing clearly have a part to play in this process. Readers may be reassured to know that this is not a book of social or historical theory, but these questions remain underlying concerns as we explore the history of a workers' institution that is also part of a larger social movement.

This book had its origins in the requests of union organizations and activists for presentations, workshops, resources, and other assistance in introducing members to their own history. In 2004, the New Brunswick Federation of Labour, together with several other labour organizations and heritage institutions, agreed to participate in a Community-University Research Alliance organized by researchers from the two provincial universities, the Université de Moncton and the University of New Brunswick. This partnership between labour organizations and public institutions was successful in securing research funds from the Social Sciences and Humanities Research Council of Canada for a team project entitled "Re-Connecting with the History of Labour in New Brunswick: Historical Perspectives on Contemporary Issues."[11] Several major tasks were undertaken in the years that followed, and one of these has been the preparation of this history. The Federation set an excellent example for unions in the province by depositing records at the Provincial Archives of New Brunswick, and the Federation and its affiliates have offered encouragement and cooperation in other ways as well, for which the research team and the author are very grateful. The book is, however, an independent work of academic research and public history that offers a sympathetic but not uncritical account of the Federation's long history. Its purpose is to help establish a better understanding of the place of workers and their organizations in provincial society. In doing so, it also sheds light on the history of the province over the past century and the persistence of traditions of labour activism and social democracy that are too easily overlooked in New Brunswick history.[12]

LABOUR CENTRAL The first meetings of the New Brunswick Federation of Labour, in September 1913 and January 1914, took place at the old Oddfellows Hall in Saint John, at the corner of Union and Hazen Streets. Several local unions had their headquarters in this building, and the surrounding streets were used to marshal some of the early Labour Day parades. Source: New Brunswick Museum, X11314.

ONE

"*An* Accomplished Fact"

1913–1929

16 September 1913

They met at the old Oddfellows Hall on Union Street in Saint John on Tuesday, 16 September 1913. It was a small assembly, but the delegates represented a large constituency and an even larger body of expectations. They came from Sackville, Fredericton, Moncton, and Saint John, carrying credentials from local unions and labour councils, and from a range of occupations, including barbers, blacksmiths, bricklayers, carpenters, cigarmakers, electrical workers, iron moulders, longshoremen, painters, plumbers, printers, railway carmen, and stonecutters. There were, in all, only twenty delegates in attendance, all of them men and mainly from Saint John and Moncton, but the *Eastern Labor News* did not hesitate to describe the event as "a large and representative meeting."[1]

The day after that short meeting, local newspapers in Saint John underlined the significance of the event. "A movement of importance to the working men of the province was advanced a stage yesterday," reported the *Standard*. "A Provincial Federation was formed and arrangements made for closer cooperation in promoting labor legislation and all matters in the interests of the working class." The *Daily Telegraph* described the aims of the new organization in similar terms: "to bring all the unions of the different towns of the province into closer touch so that demands made by the new body may have greater weight than those of any separate existing organization." Only a few items of business were transacted, but participants were pleased with the outcome. P. D. Ayer of the Moncton Trades and Labour Council, who presided at the event, predicted that, as more unions joined, "the federation will speedily become the legislative medium and the fighting machine for organized labor within the province." And a correspondent in the *Eastern Labor News* observed with satisfaction that the New Brunswick Federation of Labour was now "an accomplished fact."[2]

Plans for a federation of labour were underway at least as early as the spring of 1912, when the Saint John Trades and Labour Council invited their counterparts in Moncton to discuss the idea. In June that year, the veteran union leader J. J. Donovan, of the Saint John cigarmakers' union, spoke at a meeting of the Moncton Trades and Labour Council. Donovan explained that the provincial government too easily turned a deaf ear to labour concerns from any one section of the province: "A Provincial Federation would accomplish the desired result and lead to united action by every union in New Brunswick which no government would care to ignore." The proposal received ready endorsement, and on Labour Day that year delegates assembled at the Longshoremen's Hall in Saint John, where they voted unanimously to form "an organization to be known as the New Brunswick Provincial Federation of Labour." Also in attendance was Warren Franklin Hatheway, the Saint John reformer and former Member of the Legislative Assembly, whose efforts to advance the cause of labour had often been frustrated by the political leadership of the province. He congratulated the meeting and again underlined the logic of a federation: "A body representative of all the labor interests of the province would have a much greater influence than the individual union or the Trades and Labor Council of a particular section." Provisional officers were elected, including Donovan as president, and it was agreed to meet as early as Thanksgiving Day or at another time "at the call of the executive."[3]

Such a call was never issued, and over the course of the winter the movement for a federation came to a standstill. This did not sit well with two Saint John labour men, who used the pages of the Moncton-based *Eastern Labor News* to breathe new life into the idea. Longshoreman Fred Hyatt was an Old Country union man who had served in the British Army in India before immigrating to Canada. He was also a vocal proponent of socialist ideas, who underlined the idea that organizing workers was part of a larger effort to reform society: "The Provincial Federation of Labor could be made an actual fact and its influence felt if it was organized along the lines followed by British Columbia and Alberta, and adopted a platform which stood for the worker to receive the full product of his labor, which would be something worth fighting for." In his view, capitalism had arrived in full force in New Brunswick, and workers would have to combine for their mutual protection: "The slogan should be 'workers unite' and wake up New Brunswick." Hyatt was ably, if more moderately, seconded by James L. Sugrue, one of the younger generation of labour leaders coming to the fore in Saint John: "I think it time the matter of forming a Provincial Federation of Labor was resurrected. It would certainly be a pity to allow this matter to fall through as the time seems opportune for the formation of such an organization." Sugrue gave a telling example of labour's inability to secure meaningful reforms. After a year and a half of agitation by the unions for a fair wage clause in government contracts, the legislature had passed a Fair Wage Schedule Act that was barely two sentences long and notably lacking in standards or provisions for enforcement. "What a splendid piece of legislation," scoffed Sugrue. "The workers should certainly be proud of the lawyers, doctors and business men who are representing them." He concluded with a call to action:

THE FOUNDER The Saint John carpenter
James L. Sugrue (1883–1930) was elected the
first president of the New Brunswick Federation
of Labour in 1913 and served until 1918: "In the
long run we hope to so improve conditions here
that the people won't leave for the west in search
of better wages and shorter hours of labour."
Source: *History of Saint John Labor Unions*
(1929).

"Let's quit acting comedy, brothers, and get down to business. We need a Federation of Labor in this Province and the time is ripe for its formation."[4]

A portrait of Sugrue shows a youthful, energetic face, hair brushed high, steady eyes, and the hint of a smile. Although Saint John had a long labour history and there were plenty of local labour veterans, Sugrue was still in his twenties when he came to prominence. Born in 1883, he had grown up in west-end Saint John, the son of an Irish immigrant who was an influential teacher in the city's Catholic schools. His older brother John Sugrue became an officer of the bricklayers and masons union, and "Jimmie" Sugrue became a leader of Local 919, United Brotherhood of Carpenters and Joiners, named as their financial secretary in 1910 and in 1913 as business agent. In 1912 Sugrue was elected president of the Saint John Trades and Labour Council. The emergence of Sugrue as a local leader coincided with an upsurge of labour activism. The Saint John carpenters, for instance, had won a $3 daily wage and an eight-hour day in their trade, and in the summer of 1913 more than 1,000 men at the local lumber mills were off work seeking wage increases and union recognition. On Labour Day that year, Saint John workers came out in large numbers, estimated at 2,000, to march in the biggest

Labour Day parade in years. The unions were demonstrating their presence in the community, and leaders such as Sugrue were setting optimistic goals. As he explained in 1912, "In the long run we hope to so improve conditions here that the people won't leave for the west in search of better wages and shorter hours of labor."[5]

Sugrue's part in the renewed effort was recognized when he was elected as the first president of the Federation of Labour in September 1913 and again at the first regular convention in Saint John in January 1914. On this occasion the thirty-five delegates represented fifteen union locals as well as the labour councils in Fredericton, Moncton, and Saint John. The largest group consisted of eight men from the Saint John longshoremen, the oldest union in the province. Sugrue must have been chagrined that fully twenty-eight of the official delegates were from Saint John. When they voted on a constitution and bylaws, one of the first amendments was to elect vice-presidents in order to strengthen support in other places. Vice-presidents were chosen for Moncton, Fredericton, Sackville, and Saint John, including three men who were not present at the meeting. In addition, P. D. Ayer of Moncton was elected as secretary-treasurer and Frank Lister of Fredericton as vice-president.

In setting their course, the Federation adopted resolutions on several matters to be presented to the government. Although the texts were not reported in the handwritten minutes, the list shows the scope of their agenda: scaffolding at construction sites, payments for jurors and witnesses, free school books and supplies for children, a Fair Wage Clause, a Bureau of Labour, Workmen's Compensation, and an item headed simply "women workers." Beyond this, the officers were instructed to procure a charter from the Trades and Labour Congress of Canada, and the next meeting was set for July 1914 in Fredericton.[6] It was a modest beginning, but the Federation of Labour was now visible on the province's political landscape. When they met six months later at the Pythias Hall in Fredericton, the delegates were welcomed by the city's mayor, and there was the same formal recognition when they met at the Woman's Christian Temperance Union Hall in Moncton the following year.

Before the War

Meanwhile, two notable events in 1914 kept the larger labour question in the public eye and did so in contrasting ways. The first of these, in Saint John in late July, was a large and violent strike that reminded workers of the weak position of unions seeking recognition, even in a city with a long history of unionism. In this case, the hundred or more men who worked on the city's street railway line had organized themselves into a union. Like other workers, they were hoping to win improvements in wages and working conditions, but only three weeks after the local was formed, their president was fired for an alleged violation of company rules; it was claimed that Fred Ramsay had stopped his streetcar and gone into a saloon, a charge the union president vigorously denied. Meanwhile, the company also refused to negotiate with the union. Because they worked in the transportation sector, the street railway workers were in a position to make their case to a conciliation board appointed by the Dominion Minister of Labour. The board, to which they appointed Sugrue as the union representative, recommended a settlement. However, the company had no obligation to accept the recommendation — or even to negotiate with workers or recognize their union at all.

This was the kind of impasse that workers faced all across the country in this era, and in this situation it led directly to a test of strength on the streets. On 22 July, the workers marched through the streets in their uniforms carrying banners and calling on fellow citizens to support their strike. On every streetcorner, crowds cheered and shouted support for the strike slogan "Let Everybody Walk." The company was already unpopular in the city for its overcrowded cars and its failure to build new lines, and public opinion was lining up on the side of the workers. When the company attempted to operate cars the next morning, with strikebreakers brought in by train from Montréal, there was trouble. The assembled crowds jeered the scabs, threw stones, broke windows, and stalled the cars on the tracks. From the point of view of municipal authorities, this was a deplorable breakdown in civil order. Standing on the curb of a fountain, the mayor read the Riot Act and called out a detachment of the Royal Canadian Dragoons, who charged down King

IN THE STREETS In the early twentieth century there were no laws protecting the right to collective bargaining, and the Labour Question was often decided in the streets. When Saint John street railway workers went on strike for union recognition in the summer of 1914, large crowds came out to support the workers and stop the use of strikebreakers. This was the scene at Market Square, Saint John, on the morning of 24 July 1914. Source: New Brunswick Museum, x12493 (2).

Street into the crowds at the bottom of the hill at Market Square. The men on horseback wielded their flat-edged ceremonial swords, and the crowd fought back with sticks and stones. Two streetcars were overturned in the street. When crowds went on to attack the company's barns, there were gunshots from a force of company detectives bunked inside. An attack on the company's power plant plunged the city into darkness.

Order was eventually restored that night, but not before the mayor had called out the militia as well. Municipal leaders also intervened, and helped to broker a settlement. The union would be recognized, there would be gains for the workers — and union president Ramsay would take a job with the city. As in similar street railway strikes across North America, this one succeeded because there was animosity towards the company and support for the workers in the community. As historian Robert Babcock has written, "a deep-seated local tradition of crowd action reinforced the developing class-consciousness of Saint John workers." The settlement was nonetheless an improvised solution, a form of "collective bargaining by riot." It demonstrated the obstacles that workers faced in seeking the right to union recognition and pointed to the need for better recognition of the place of labour in provincial society.[7]

A few weeks after the strike, there appeared to be a higher level of acceptance for unions when delegates from across Canada arrived in Saint John for the annual convention of the Trades and Labour Congress of Canada. The TLC had met annually since the 1880s, but only once in the Maritimes, in Halifax in 1908. When Sugrue attended the 1912 convention in Guelph, Ontario, he proposed that the next meeting be held in Saint John. Sugrue was determined to bring the TLC to New Brunswick, once arguing, for instance, that "Montreal is not the eastern extremity of Canada, despite the fact that some of our international executive officers seem to think so."[8] Once Saint John was chosen for the 1914 meetings, Sugrue served as chair of the Reception Committee, which published 2,000 copies of a souvenir booklet whose publication was supported by a grant of $500 from the provincial government.[9] In welcoming the delegates, he hoped that the event "would tend to give an uplift to the organized workers of the Province of New Brunswick."[10] Certainly the New Brunswickers turned out in force, with a total of 36 delegates from Fredericton, Moncton, and Saint John among the 147 delegates from across the country. For a full week, the meetings at the St. Andrews Rink featured numerous speakers capable of debating labour issues with much expertise. President James C. Watters, a Vancouver Island coal miner and socialist, who often wore a stetson, presented a wide-ranging report on labour conditions, and there were well-informed speeches by delegates such as George Armstrong of the Winnipeg carpenters, who discussed the problem of counterfeit union labels, and James Simpson of the Toronto printers, who called for the payment of wages to apprentices attending technical school. James Sugrue was on the platform throughout the congress, and other New Brunswick delegates also joined the discussions.[11]

One of the highlights of the meetings was a speech by Leonora O'Reilly of New York. O'Reilly had started work in the New York garment industry at the age of eleven and joined the Knights of Labor at sixteen. As a leader of the Women's Trade Union League, she was at the peak of her influence, having won wide attention for exposing conditions at the Triangle Shirtwaist factory, where 146 women workers lost their lives three years earlier when they were unable to escape from the burning building. "Fighting O'Reilly," as she introduced herself, gave the delegates a "striking description" of organizing efforts in the United States and made "a strong plea for the organization of women." When O'Reilly declared that "we want an eight hour day, a living wage and full citizenship for women," she was interrupted by applause and went on to add: "All we have accomplished through fights, we should have written into the laws of the land so that the next generation can avoid the struggles which we have been compelled to make."[12]

The presence of O'Reilly and others drew an optimistic picture of opportunities for solidarity among workers across lines of gender, region, and country. But by September 1914 the union movement was already divided by the arrival of the Great War. For the past three years the TLC had passed resolutions denouncing capitalist wars, and on the first day of the Saint John convention one resolution condemned the war as the "organized murder of the workers of the various countries" and called on Canadian workers to bring about "a speedy termination of the war." This resolution did not come to a vote, and before the meetings ended the TLC had affirmed its support for the war effort. Still, delegates were concerned about maintaining union rights under wartime conditions. Tom Moore of the carpenters called for union rates and hours on all government contracts. When Dominion Minister of Labour T. W. Crothers arrived at the convention, he was treated to a long round of criticism for the government's failures to follow its own fair wage policy in letting contracts for public works. Sugrue and others joined in presenting resolutions for the appointment of fair wage officers for each of the provinces.[13]

Workers' Compensation

During the war years the labour cause in New Brunswick was far from dormant. Like other social reformers of the time, union leaders continued to advance a progressive agenda. At the January 1915 meetings, the Federation called for protection of the interests of New Brunswick workers in the distribution of wartime contracts. But the war effort did not loom large in their proceedings. Other resolutions in 1915 called for municipal and provincial governments to use union label supplies. There was talk of establishing a new labour newspaper, to carry on the work of the *Eastern Labor News*. Other resolutions called for free textbooks for schoolchildren as well as the provision of free medical, dental, and eye examinations in the schools.[14] In the later stages of the war, the Federation took no position on issues such as conscription but opposed the employment of interned prisoners or the importation of "Orientals" to deal with labour shortages. In 1918, they were also calling for the protection of women and girls working in factories, agricultural training for returning soldiers, representation of labour on public boards, government ownership of railways and utilities, proportional representation in politics, and extension of the franchise to women.[15]

Most of all, the Federation continued to press for improved laws for the compensation of workplace death and injury, regularly passing resolutions and sending delegations to Fredericton. This was an issue with a long history. A Workmen's Compensation for Injuries Act had been adopted by a Liberal government in 1903, but it was more accurately considered an act to limit the liability of employers for accidents. The act was based on the premise that injuries at work were a risk assumed by the individual worker, unless the employer could be proved negligent in some respect; even if the employer was held responsible, awards could not exceed a total of $1,500. At the time of the 1908 election, the Conservatives called for an improved law and increased benefits, and the election of Hatheway as a government member was a promising sign. But the revisions that followed were a disappointment: they raised the limit on benefits and closed a loophole by including accidents caused by "any person in the service of the employer," but the law still excluded many workers; moreover, claims would still have to be pursued in court, a costly and uncertain undertaking for a working-class family.[16]

With the emergence of the Federation, the compensation laws had a high priority on the labour agenda. Sugrue pressed the case at an interview with the cabinet in March 1916, where union leaders were told that a commission of inquiry would be appointed shortly. When this did not happen, Sugrue renewed pressure, writing repeatedly that summer.[17] The turning point came in early 1917, when the government named a commission of inquiry. In addition to a chairman and two employers' representatives, there were two labour members. One of them was Sugrue, due recognition of the part of the Federation in the agitation, and the choice of Fred Daley of the Saint John longshoremen acknowledged the importance of the issue on the docks, where Daley's brother, president of Local 273, ILA, had lost his life in an accident four years earlier. Although the Conservative government was not re-elected in the February 1917 provincial election, the new Liberal government continued to support the work of the commission.

One of their first tasks was to examine the new compensation laws enacted in Ontario in 1914 and Nova Scotia in 1915. These were laws of a new type, for instead of assuming individual responsibility for workplace danger they introduced a system of public insurance.[18] At the time of the Federation's annual meeting in Fredericton in May 1917, a committee of delegates was named to meet with the provincial government. This included several key union leaders: James Tighe and John Kemp from Saint John, F.C. Wilson from Moncton, and J.C. Legere and George Crawford from Fredericton. Their timing was right, as the commission had prepared an interim report. With that in place, the delegates met with the provincial cabinet and, according to their own report, "in able manner presented the claims of labour for about 2 hours."[19] Returning to the convention hall on Regent Street, they reported that the government was prepared to amend the existing legislation in accordance with union recommendations. That afternoon the convention was also addressed by the veteran Hatheway, who was undoubtedly pleased that his long struggle for better compensation laws had now been taken up vigorously by the province's unions.[20]

The promise of social reform was often invoked in the course of the Great War. At a time when the war was taking a bloody toll at the front, provincial politicians could do little about those casualties, but there seemed to be steady progress in addressing the costs of injuries and fatalities in the workplaces of the home economy. The commission's report was tabled on 15 March 1918, and a bill was introduced the same day by Attorney-General J.P. Byrne, who stated that "the principles of the bill had been approved by the Federation of Labor and also by a number of employers of labor in the province." The new law accepted the premise that workers and their families were entitled to compensation for death and injuries arising out of their employment and that the costs of accidents should be a charge upon the employers. The change was "revolutionary in its character," noted one of the opposition leaders — with approval. Sugrue watched the progress of the bill closely, and at one stage he appealed to the Saint John longshoremen to send a representative to Fredericton to help him lobby the members.[21] There were definite limitations in the bill: important categories of workers were excluded — farm labourers, domestic servants, clerical workers, police and firemen, and a variety of "casual" workers — and there was no debate on an amendment that added fishermen to the list of excluded occupations, even though at least nine men had been lost in a disaster on the water at Caraquet as recently as 1914. There was controversy about including workers in the lumber industry, as recommended by the report; but in the course of the debate, the government amended its own bill to exclude from coverage both logging in the woods and working on the river drives, two of the most hazardous occupations in the province. Opposition members charged that the government was giving in to powerful lumber interests: "The proposed amendment would destroy the effectiveness of the Compensation Act and would not be satisfactory to the province as a whole or to the labor interests."[22] With this amendment, the bill was adopted on 26 April, imperfect legislation but a sign that the province was prepared to introduce reforms in response to the expressed needs of organized workers. Much would depend on the administration of the act, and union leaders were pleased with the appointment of Sugrue as one of the three full-time members of the new Workmen's Compensation Board. He was associated above all with the Federation, and the campaign for compensation had demonstrated the effectiveness of an organization that could claim to represent the interests of provincial workers at large.[23]

It was hardly an age of harmony, however. Union membership continued to grow again after 1917, but there were no guarantees for unions. A sensational case erupted in Saint John in 1917, when a standoff between the master plumbers and the plumbers' union culminated in charges of intimidation, arson, and murder. Local 531 of the United Association of Journeymen Plumbers had been organized in 1911, and in early 1917 they were seeking a new agreement with higher rates and the eight-hour day. When employers refused to settle, the plumbers went on strike, and the union's general organizer for Canada, the spunky Australian-born John Bruce, remained on the scene almost continuously that spring and summer. The situation worsened as replacement workers were hired. A chalkboard at the union hall listed names for the "roll of dishonour," and Bruce urged the strikers to take a strong stand: "Hound the scabs, keep after them and hound them out, call them rats, but use no violence and stay away from booze." In his diary, Bruce reported "spirit good" among the strikers, but he also noted that there was "nothing doing" with the employers.

Suddenly, at the middle of June, the union was in trouble. A magistrate fined four members for liquor offences and warned against intimidation of strikebreakers. Bruce suspended strike benefits in order to pay the fines. The situation worsened when a Loch Lomond cottage belonging to one of the master plumbers burned to the ground, and two union men, John Hughes and Joseph O'Brien, were charged with arson several nights later. In addition, the local union president John O'Brien and secretary Everett Carland were arrested, initially charged with intimidation and then, more sensationally, with murder. It was alleged that the union officers were responsible for the death of a young man who was hit from behind late at night after coming off work.

Throughout these events, organizer Bruce worried about the use of trumped-up charges to discredit unions. It was only two years since the execution of the radical organizer Joe Hill in Salt Lake City, and now unions across the continent were trying to save the life of another union man, Tom Mooney, who was on death row in San Francisco. Was the situation in Saint John another frame-up to destroy a local union? After consulting with Sugrue and other leaders, Bruce moved quickly to defend the Saint John men. The local unions had already shown good support for the strike, and Bruce went on to hire lawyers, organize a defence committee, raise funds, and pay benefits to the families. The case was discussed in union newspapers across the country as well as at meetings of the TLC in Ottawa and of the international union in Toledo, Ohio. The arson charges were tried twice in court, but the juries were unable to reach a verdict, and the charges were dismissed. The murder case was heard for several days at the end of August; there was no direct evidence against the accused, and it took less than an hour for the jury to acquit them. If the outcome was a kind of vindication for the workers, none of this was reassuring for the union movement. The charges of arson and murder seemed to put unions on the wrong side of the law. Moreover, the strike itself was lost, and the issues of hours, wages, and union security had been swept aside. Within a few years, the local was dissolved, and the union was not reorganized in Saint John until 1929.[24]

Reconstruction

When the war ended, the unions hoped to leave such desultory situations behind. After the 1918 Armistice, there was renewed energy in the ranks of labour, much of it directed at building a world in which the rights of workers occupied a central place in society. This was the main theme in the Reconstruction Programme adopted by the Federation of Labour in March 1919:

> The world war has forced all people to a fuller and deeper realization of the menace to civilization contained in autocratic control of the activities and destinies of mankind. It has opened the doors of opportunity, through which more sound and progressive policies may enter. New conceptions of human liberty, justice and opportunity are to be applied.[25]

This extensive document, prepared by three of the Saint John delegates, outlined a prescription for postwar reconstruction that recognized the rights of workers and their place as citizens of the province.

The programme insisted on the right to union organization as a fundamental requirement for cooperation between workers and employers and argued that the same right should be extended to workers in the public sector. The importance of the eight-hour day was underlined as essential to health, citizenship, productivity, and moral, economic, and social well-being; to this end, the working week should be no more than five and a half days, and overtime hours should be prohibited except in emergencies. The employment of children under the age of sixteen should be prohibited as well, and women workers were to be entitled to "the same pay for equal work"— although they were also to be protected against performing jobs that "tend to impair their potential motherhood." Concerns about the labour market were also addressed: immigration was to be suspended for three years while society adjusted to postwar conditions, and private employment agencies were to be abolished in favour of public employment services jointly operated by workers and employers. There was a strongly worded statement on freedom of speech and public assembly, an echo of concerns about the use of the War

Measures Act and other restrictions in wartime. Public ownership of utilities and resources, particularly the province's waters, was seen as necessary to protect the public interest, and cooperatives were encouraged because they protected the worker from the profiteer. Educational opportunities were to be improved, especially in technical subjects (and teachers were encouraged to affiliate with the union movement). Home ownership was to be promoted by offering low-interest loans and by constructing new housing through public works in times of under-employment.

This was not a radical programme by the standards of early 1919. Indeed, the section on political policy warned that independent action by labour could divide their political influence and that improved legislation could be achieved through "the education of the public mind and the appeal to its conscience." Nonetheless, the Reconstruction Programme embraced a broader distribution of social rights and economic rewards as the basis for a democratic society. It was a call for recognition of the needs of workers and their place as full citizens in provincial society: "No element in this province is more vitally concerned in the future of this province than the working class." [26]

When the Federation met in March 1919 to discuss and adopt this document, the organization was without a president. Sugrue had taken his place at the Compensation Board as a member of the provincial labour bureaucracy in late 1918. Attention turned to the first vice-president, a young railway machinist from Moncton. Célime Antoine Melanson was born in rural Kent County in 1885, the descendant of a long-established Acadian family. As a young man he had come to work in Moncton, where the Intercolonial Railway was the city's largest employer. He started as a labourer and was soon promoted to more skilled work as a machinist. As a member of the International Association of Machinists, Melanson acquired a good knowledge of labour matters; he also improved his skills and his English by taking correspondence courses. In 1914, members of IAM Local 594 chose him as a delegate to the TLC convention in Saint John. They also named him as a delegate to Federation meetings, where he was elected a vice-president in 1915 as well as in 1916 and 1918. In January 1919, he was one of four labour candidates elected to the

Moncton city council and the first Acadian to win election as alderman-at-large. The choice of Melanson as the Federation's new president in March 1919 was recognition — even encouragement — for the participation of Acadians in the labour movement.[27]

The election of Melanson also drew attention to the importance of organized labour in Moncton, second only to Saint John as a site of labour activism. Indeed, Moncton was very much on the march in 1919. The working-class presence was visible in the streets when the Moncton Amalgamated Central Labour Union sponsored local Labour Day celebrations on 1 September. The parade was headed by the Chief of Police, the City Fathers, and the Great War Veterans' Association. There were six bands, several fire brigades, and a variety of automobiles, bicycles, and merchants' floats. Among the unions in the line of march, the railway workers were out in force, from the international unions such as the conductors, trainmen, engineers, firemen, and enginemen and telegraphers in the running trades to the

THE ACADIAN Célime Antoine Melanson (1885–1957) was the second president of the Federation (1919–21). Originally from Kent County, he came to Moncton to work in the railway shops. He was the first Acadian to serve as president and took office at a time when the Federation endorsed a far-reaching Reconstruction Programme. Source: *L'Évangéline,* 28 février 1952.

machinists, carmen, and electricians in the shops. Their ranks also included the Canadian Brotherhood of Railroad Employees, the new union that was founded among Intercolonial Railway workers at Moncton in 1908 and was now expanding across the country. One of the highlights in the parade was a float from Melanson's own machinists local, which was described years later by a leader of Unity Lodge No. 10, the IAM Ladies Auxiliary, in terms that convey this historical moment's hopeful investment in democracy and progress:

"Four symbolic figures draped in white and standing under a double archway. There was Liberty with her flaming torch, Blindfolded Justice with her balance scales, Education with her open book and Progress carrying machine gears."[28] A souvenir booklet published by the labour council promoted the city's prospects, identified the unions as partners in the march of civic progress and stated that labour relations in Moncton were on a sound footing: "Very cordial relations exist between employers and workers, with the result that when labor difficulties arise they are usually quickly adjusted."[29]

There was also evidence that union ideas were spreading into parts of the province where organized labour had a weaker presence and employers were less accustomed to unions. At the end of the summer in 1919, a spontaneous rebellion broke out among workers along the Miramichi River in the heart of the lumber country in Northumberland County. It started on the morning of 20 August at Robinson's Mill in Newcastle, and workers then proceeded to call out men at other workplaces up and down the river. They marched in turn to Chatham Head, Nelson, and Douglastown, calling on men to quit work and join the protest. By the middle of the day a dozen different operations were shut down, and some 2,000 men were on strike. They gathered on the town square in Newcastle to form a negotiating committee and present their demands to local employers. The strike was settled swiftly, and the next night the men crowded into the Opera House to approve a settlement that reduced the working day from ten to nine hours. Joseph P. Anderson, a returned soldier who worked at one of the mills and led the negotiating committee, proclaimed that times were changing: "The niggers had been freed, the Belgians had been freed, and now it was time for us to be freed from the lumber lords." Other speakers included the social reformer Henry Harvey Stuart, who urged the advantages of establishing a permanent organization. The longshoremen's organizer from Saint John, James Tighe, who was also vice-president of the Federation of Labour, arrived by train and undertook to secure a union charter from the International Longshoremen's Association. A new union local was formed on the spot, and a popular local storekeeper, J.S. Martin, was elected as secretary-treasurer. The Miramichi Waterfront

Union was chartered as Local 825 of the ILA. By the end of September they reported 1,600 members.[30] Early the next year they sent five delegates to the Federation meetings, where they made a strong impression. Martin was elected second vice-president, and Stuart as district vice-president for the Miramichi.[31]

Broader Horizons

Melanson was leading the Federation in a time of expansion and expectation. In March 1919 there were only 29 delegates at the annual meeting, but in the convention call for the 1920 meeting, he and the new secretary-treasurer George Melvin of Saint John appealed for all New Brunswick unions to send delegates: "We need the support of every Union in the Province — let this Convention be the greatest one in the history of the Federation."[32] At the 1920 convention there were almost twice as many delegates as in 1919. The following year the 1921 convention in Saint John was the most representative provincial assembly of labour to date, with 86 delegates from nine centres in attendance, representing 7,000 workers. Although more than half the delegates were from Saint John, there were also delegates from places such as Campbellton, Chatham, McAdam, Milltown, Minto, and Woodstock as well as Moncton and Fredericton, and they came from at least twenty different unions. One of the two delegates from the Hotel and Restaurant Employees in Saint John was Nellie Thorne, the first woman delegate to appear in the records of the Federation.[33] With as few as five delegates among the total, however, Acadian workers were under-represented in a province where Acadians accounted for 31 percent of the population.[34]

During this time the Federation also sought to marshal the political influence of workers. In 1918, delegates had adopted a report calling for labour candidates and a Labour Party, stating that "both political parties are so wedded to the capitalistic interests that it is practically impossible to impress upon them the necessity of working for the interests of the masses." However, a report on lobbying efforts after the convention also drew attention to the enactment of workmen's compensation, stating that the spring session had produced "some first class legislation in the interest and for the benefit of the working class and it only requires renewed interest and activity on the part of the working people of the province to assure further success."[35] The spring session of the legislature in 1919 again produced reforms, including the extension of votes to women and the application of the Workmen's Compensation Act to workers in the woods. In 1920 there were upward revisions in compensation rates (monthly payments to widows were raised from $20 to $30, for instance, and a clause limiting total compensation to $3,500 was repealed); there were also amendments to provide free hospital and medical care to injured workers; in addition the board adopted regulations listing industrial diseases covered by the act. These were the result of intensive lobbying, what Melanson called "keeping at them."[36]

While acknowledging the cooperation of sitting members, Melanson told delegates that "the workers now realize that it is necessary for them to have representatives on the floors of the House, if they ever expect to accomplish anything." Following the convention, he did not hesitate to predict changes in the next provincial election: "We will have some of our own men in the house to look after our interests there for us." The same theme was echoed in the pages of the *Union Worker*, a monthly newspaper launched in February 1920 and "Devoted to the Interests of Organized Labour in the Province."[37] The *Union Worker* made the case for the direct representation of workers in politics in these terms: "The time has gone by when a few labor men will get on their knees in a committee room of the house of assembly and be satisfied with that stereotyped phrase, 'the government will give the matters their serious consideration'. In most cases that was as far as the matter went. The delegates went away pleased that they had basked in the sunshine of the premier and a few of his henchmen for a few minutes instead of being actually thrown out the sacred precincts of the house."[38]

The announcement of a provincial election for 9 October 1920 caught the labour forces unprepared. The Liberals advertised their record of labour legislation, but they did not return to power without a challenge. In an important breakthrough in provincial politics, the well-organized agrarian reformers in the United Farmers of New Brunswick elected nine members. The new assembly also included, for the first time, two labour members. Both were from Northumberland County, where John W. Vanderbeck and John S. Martin benefited from the militancy of the local workers and an electoral alliance with the farmers in the four-member constituency; Vanderbeck led the polls with 5,663 votes and Martin was elected with 5,111 votes. Vanderbeck had suffered a bad leg injury in 1920 and died shortly after taking his seat in the legislature in 1921; his son Abram Vanderbeck won the subsequent by-election by a large margin and served with Martin as a labour member until 1925.[39] There was also cooperation between farmer and labour interests in Westmorland County, where Stuart (who had taken a position as a school principal at Sunny Brae, near Moncton) was nominated as the labour candidate; however, the school board forced him to withdraw before the election, and James A. Robinson stood in his place and, with 4,513 votes, came close to winning. In Moncton, labour candidate Clifford Ayer received 1,132 votes, about 25 percent of the total. To Stuart's dismay, there had been no labour candidates at all in Saint John, and no general alliance between farmer and labour forces across the province. Yet the traditional party system had shown its vulnerability, and the Federation meetings in January 1921 again passed resolutions calling for the formation of an Independent Labour Party.[40]

Even at this relatively high point in the early history of the Federation, in 1921 the scope of representation was far from complete. In January 1914, delegates had represented 18 of the 101 existing union locals in the province; in January 1921 they represented 34 of the 128 locals in the province listed by the Department of Labour — a larger proportion but still little more than one in four union locals in the province. In 1922, the cotton mill workers at Milltown, members of Local 1394, United Textile Workers of America, were represented by two women delegates, Lettie Glover and Sara Shannon. They were welcomed and both were elected to executive positions (Glover as third vice-president, and Shannon as vice-president for Charlotte County); but a year later there were no delegates at all from their local, and it would be another twenty-two years before women delegates appeared again at

THE LONGSHOREMAN James Edmund Tighe (1878–1937) was one of the founders of the Federation in 1913. He rose to high office in the International Longshoremen's Association but also remained a Federation strongman for many years, including terms as president from 1921 to 1929 and 1934 to 1936. Source: *History of Saint John Labor Unions* (1929).

Federation meetings. Similarly, the coal miners, who attended the 1920 and 1921 meetings and submitted resolutions for the inspection and regulation of coal mines, also disappeared from future meetings after their United Mine Workers of America local was broken by employer resistance. After 1921, the total number of delegates at Federation meetings dropped to smaller numbers for the remainder of the decade, reaching a low of 25 delegates in 1925 and rising only to 33 by 1929.[41]

Meanwhile, there was also a change in the leadership of the Federation. Melanson stepped down as president at the 1921 convention and later that year took a post as an assistant city clerk at Moncton City Hall.[42] In making adjustments to a more defensive position after 1921, the Federation had an experienced union leader at the helm. James Edmund Tighe was already a power on the Saint John labour scene before the formation of the Federation in 1913, and in the 1920s he was rising rapidly in the ranks of his international union. Born in Saint John in 1878, Tighe as a young man had worked on railway lines in Canada and the United States. Those experiences had introduced him to the international labour movement, and when he returned to Saint John and went to work on the docks, he helped bring the local longshoremen into affiliation with the International Longshoremen's Association in 1911. By 1912 he was the business agent for ILA 273 and also a vice-president of the international and a leading force in the ILA's Atlantic Coast District. He was considered a pioneer of the Federation, as he was present at the original meeting in September 1913 and played an active part in the successful campaign for the new compensation laws. On several occasions he had been elected a vice-president, most recently at the 1919 and 1920 meetings.[43]

In Tighe's first report as president in 1922, he drew attention to the troubled economic conditions spreading throughout the province. Workers faced shutdowns, wage cuts, and unemployment. A growing number of strikes and lockouts were provoked by employers who were no longer prepared to accept collective bargaining: "When the employers are approached they refuse to recognize the organizations and wish to adopt 'individual bargaining.'" The situation at the street railway in Saint John was particularly alarming in light of their dramatic battle for union recognition in 1914. The New Brunswick Power Company announced wage reductions in May 1921 and stated that the union contract would not be renewed; a conciliation board on which Hatheway represented the men failed to convince the company to renew the agreement, even with reduced wages. Instead there was a lockout, and strikebreakers were brought in from Montréal and other locations. As before, crowds attacked the cars, and there were parades of support for the strikers, but this time there was no settlement. The union operated a Union Bus Company providing an alternative jitney service on many routes in the summer and fall, with union leader Fred A. Campbell as president. The bus company was harassed by fines and bylaws and eventually collapsed, as did the strike. The conflict ended when officers of the Trades and Labour Council were arrested for unlawful assembly for parading in support of the strike.[44] The deteriorating conditions were documented in the pages of the *Union Worker*: "Unemployment is rampant and the 'big interests' are taking every advantage of the situation to crush the worker under the iron heel of the golden god." Nonetheless, the newspaper had little to suggest in addressing the crisis: "It will be well to give a little for the time being and when matters assume a more nearly normal state improvement in working conditions can be advocated and insisted upon."[45] Meanwhile, the *Union Worker* itself ceased publication in April 1922.

"No Short Cut"

The turn to a more cautious approach was already evident at the 1921 meetings. In part this took the form of adherence to the increasingly conservative and exclusionist policies of the TLC, especially under the presidency of Tom Moore, who had replaced the socialist Watters in 1918. Melanson had encouraged all unions in the province to join the Federation, regardless of their history or affiliations, but this was no longer an acceptable policy. The test case in 1921 was the status of the Canadian Brotherhood of Railroad Employees, who were expelled from the TLC in 1920 for failing to resolve jurisdictional conflicts with the Brotherhood of Railway and Steamship Clerks. At the Federation meetings a special motion was presented to enable CBRE members to participate as fraternal delegates, a position supported by delegates such as Stuart who argued that "everything possible should be done to keep all branches of labor in agreement and to heal all existing differences."[46] However, the expulsion was confirmed by the TLC convention later in 1921, and the 1922 Federation meetings even included an evening dance and social sponsored by the rival brotherhood. Meanwhile, TLC loyalists in New Brunswick were also directing similar attacks at other labour organizations that challenged the place of the TLC as the principal house of labour: the One Big Union movement was early on identified as "One Big Failure" contrary to the spirit of true trade unionism (and was more fully denounced after Minto miners started to join the OBU in 1925); and the formation of a Catholic trade union centre in Québec was also deplored: "The formation of Unions on a Provincial Religious basis cuts deeply into national unions; employers are not so organized."[47]

Even in a time of contraction, Tighe was reluctant to abandon the Federation's reform agenda.[48] The most important new initiative was the call for protective legislation for women workers and lone mothers, a characteristic early maternal and labour feminist campaign in which the Federation collaborated with groups such as the Local Councils of Women to assist those whom they regarded as the most vulnerable workers in the labour market. Progress was notably slow. In 1921 the Federation called for a Minimum Wage Act, with a board empowered to investigate the wages, hours, and conditions of female workers and to issue binding orders. A related proposal called for a Mothers' Pensions Board to support impoverished mothers and their children. A year later, Tighe reported that the province had agreed to set up a commission to investigate the matter and that the Federation had nominated a Saint John union man, F.S.A. McMullin, and Estella Sugrue, the spouse of the former Federation president.[49] At the time of the 1923 meetings, however, they were still waiting. The commission was finally appointed in September 1923 and included the two Federation nominees; a report was tabled in March 1925.[50] Soon afterwards, the Conservatives returned to power, and there did not seem to be any likelihood of action. After 1925 there were no labour members in the assembly to provide assistance, and Premier J.B.M. Baxter was less sympathetic to labour reform than his predecessors had been. Again in 1926 the Federation passed resolutions urging the introduction of Minimum Wage and Mothers' Allowance Acts, to which they also added a call for legislation to enable the province to participate in the new Dominion plan for old age pensions. In 1927 the Federation demanded to know whether any of the additional revenues secured for the province by the Maritime Rights campaign of the time could be applied to implementing "at least some of this most urgent social legislation." Baxter's response was unequivocal: "Insofar as the increased subsidy from the Federal Government was concerned there would be none of it available for such legislation."[51]

The Federation was more successful in protecting its major legislative achievement. In the years after 1918, Sugrue himself attended regularly at the Federation meetings to report on the administration and progress of workmen's compensation. At the 1923 meetings, however, Tighe drew attention to "the various attempts by the employers to destroy legislation by amendment" and recommended that efforts be focused on resisting employers' attacks on the Workmen's Compensation Act. Resolutions from Moncton, Fredericton, and Saint John also urged action, and the convention endorsed a plan to collaborate with the railway unions, who were equally alarmed about the situation. The labour concerns could not be ignored, and Premier P.J. Veniot appeared at the convention to announce that he would call a conference of employers and unions to discuss any possible changes to the Compensation Act.[52] Veniot delayed the joint conference until January 1924, when it met for three days in Saint John under his chairmanship. The employers, led by Angus McLean of the New Brunswick Lumbermen's Association, were proposing to lower the scale of benefits to the 1918 level, reduce two of the three commissioners to part-time status and permit employers to carry their own insurance in place of the government plan. Labour spokesmen, including representatives from the Brotherhood of Locomotive Firemen and Enginemen and the Brotherhood of Railway Trainmen, defended the existing system and advanced a list of amendments to improve benefits and increase the powers of the board.[53] By the end of the meeting, it was clear that the provincial government was not prepared to accept the changes demanded by the employers.[54] The issue did not entirely disappear after the 1925 election. Tighe warned in 1926 that employers were again mustering their influence to have sections of the Compensation Act repealed. However, when Premier Baxter appeared before the convention that year, he assured the delegates that he was strongly in favour of the act and that the legislation "would not be interfered with by the Government."[55] For the time being, this appeared to be the end of sustained attacks on the underlying principles of the Compensation Act.[56]

Unemployment and underemployment remained concerns throughout the 1920s, as large numbers of workers continued to leave the province for work. In 1925, Tighe lamented the poor conditions of employment and the number of industries that had closed down, "which were forcing many of our best tradesmen to move either to the United States or Western Canada." In the context of the regional crisis, Tighe allied himself with the employer-dominated Maritime Rights movement and in 1925 was one of the few labour leaders to participate in the Great Delegation to Ottawa, where the interests of the port of Saint John were vigorously promoted. Yet with new developments underway in the north of the province, Tighe noted that employers failed to give preference to New Brunswick workers. In 1928, his frustration was evident when he objected that the employment of workers with "unpronounceable names" was "forcing our own men to continue leaving the Province." His concerns were also shared by delegates who objected to the recruitment of Welsh miners for work in the coalfields, another area of expanding economic activity, and the convention adopted a resolution in favour of excluding immigrants to the province's mining district.[57]

Tighe had already expressed a wish to retire from office in 1925, and perhaps came to believe in the following years that his own association with the Liberal Party put the Federation at a disadvantage in dealing with the new Conservative government. He was also rising in influence within the international union; in 1927 Tighe was elected first vice-president of the ILA, placing him second only to "King" Joe Ryan of New York, who dominated the affairs of the ILA for several decades.[58] Before stepping down in 1929, Tighe had the satisfaction of reporting that the TLC would once again meet in Saint John, as it had in 1914. Though no longer president by the time of the meetings in August 1929, Tighe was headlined in the local press as "The Man Who Brought Labor Congress to Saint John."[59]

As in 1914, there was a large attendance of New Brunswick delegates, indeed somewhat larger than at the Federation meetings earlier in the year: twenty-two delegates from Saint John, as well as nine Moncton delegates (including the new Federation president E. R. Steeves), four from McAdam, and one each from Fredericton and Campbellton. Premier Baxter and former premier Veniot, now a member of the Dominion cabinet, both addressed the convention, and TLC President Moore pointedly expressed the hope that the province would make advances in enacting labour legislation. In welcoming the delegates, Saint John labour council president James Whitebone pointed out the significance of Saint John in Canadian labour history, noting that the delegates' badges included a replica of the waterfront bell erected in 1849 by the original longshoremen's union in the city, the Labourers' Benevolent Association. This historic bell, said Whitebone, was "the bell which had first rung out the message of hope for the workers and marked the beginning of the struggle for the shorter work day."[60]

Whitebone also introduced J. H. "Jimmy" Thomas, a longtime leader of the National Union of Railwaymen in Britain. The presence of a well-known international figure served to underline the transnational context of the labour movement, much as the visit by Leonora O'Reilly had done in 1914. Thomas himself had started work at twelve years of age and come to prominence as a union leader and then as a minister in the 1924 Labour government; in 1929 he was a member of Ramsay MacDonald's second Labour administration, with special responsibility for unemployment. Even before he spoke, the delegates gave Thomas a standing ovation and three loud cheers, and he went on to deliver an entertaining address that, according to one reporter, "convulsed the gathering with merriment." On a more serious note, Thomas stated that he would never forget his humble origins and his main goals in public life: "To bring comfort, happiness and hope to homes that are downtrodden is the greatest source of satisfaction to any man." In the context of British labour history, Thomas was a moderate who had opposed the British General Strike in 1926, and his message in Saint John conveyed a narrower version of trade union consciousness than that articulated by O'Reilly fifteen years earlier. Thomas warned Canadian unionists to follow a cautious path: "Speaking of the progress the labour movement had made in the past he said that this had been accomplished by the process of evolution rather than revolution. Revolution and bloodshed never did anything for the workers, he said and warned the delegates to beware of those who advocated the 'short cut' to Labor's aims." [61]

At the end of this first chapter in the history of the Federation, organized labour had emerged as a new force in provincial society. The house of labour had succeeded in attracting the attention of governments and in achieving legislative reforms that were important to many workers, including those who did not belong to unions. The Federation had helped win the establishment of vocational schools in several locations and worked with women's organizations to obtain free textbooks for students up to Grade 8. They had assisted women in gaining the vote and had helped elect the first labour members to the Legislative Assembly. The Federation's major achievement was a Workmen's Compensation Act that provided modest but relatively certain benefits to injured workers and their families. By the 1920s, the annual conventions of the Federation were considered notable public events, and Premiers Veniot and Baxter had accepted an obligation to address the meetings, even when they were sure to face criticism from the delegates. Yet the solidarities represented by the Federation remained incomplete. The unions were strongest in Saint John and Moncton, and even at the high tide of expectations at the end of the Great War, most union locals in the province did not send delegates to the meetings of the Federation. In the house of labour, international unions representing skilled male workers were dominant, and the Federation attracted few women workers and relatively few workers from the regions and industries beyond the biggest cities. Large ambitions for social and economic democracy had been spelled out in the Reconstruction Programme of 1919, but the rhetoric calling for "new conceptions of human liberty, justice and opportunity" was little heard at Federation meetings by the end of the decade. Provincial labour solidarity was evolving slowly. It was threatened by the regional economic crisis that took hold in the Maritimes during the 1920s, and the Great Depression soon presented new challenges.

In Sugrue, Melanson, and Tighe, the Federation had produced leaders who were pragmatists rather than radicals, but each in his own way had sought to win recognition of the Federation as the voice of labour in the province. They pursued their aims with a brave face, optimistic about the prospects for a progressive consensus within provincial society. For union stalwarts such as Fredericton Labour Council President George Crawford, a bricklayer who had been in attendance at almost every meeting since 1914, the Federation of Labour was "an unselfish organization working in the interests of both organized and unorganized labour in the province." When he addressed the convention in 1927, his sense of satisfaction was marked by a warning that "every effort must be made by the Federation to maintain what had been secured for labour."[62] To recall the terms of the hopeful predictions in 1913, the Federation had constructed itself more as a "legislative medium" than a "fighting machine." Provincial solidarities remained far from complete, but the Federation of Labour had nonetheless become "an accomplished fact" within provincial society.

STANDING FAST The Great Depression of the 1930s brought new challenges for the Federation of Labour. President E. R. Steeves (centre) stands among a large group of delegates at the 1931 convention, including (at left) James Johnston, McAdam; Norman Van Horne, Durham Bridge; Secretary-Treasurer George Melvin; John Mack, McAdam; John H. Wallace, Nelson; Steeves; and (at right) James A. Whitebone, Saint John; John S. Martin, Chatham; Thomas McDonald, Saint John; and J. A. LeBlanc, Moncton. Source: Provincial Archives of New Brunswick, New Brunswick Federation of Labour fonds, MC1819, box 247.

TWO

"What We *Were* Promised"

"The Prevention of Unemployment"

After two days of rough weather, there was a break in the snow, rain, sleet, and hail of a winter storm in Saint John. In early January 1931, a large group of men posed for an outdoor photograph on the steps of a public building. They were dressed in long coats, collars, and ties, everyone wearing a dress hat or a workingman's cap. The ribbons on their lapels indicated that these men were attending the eighteenth convention of the New Brunswick Federation of Labour. These were the early days of the Great Depression, a devastating time for workers and a discouraging time for organized labour, but in a time of hardship and difficulty, workers still continued to seek reforms and build unions. As the challenges of the Depression loomed before them, many workers looked to the Federation for leadership. In 1931 there were sixty-eight delegates in attendance at the meetings, a larger number than in most recent years, and the photograph shows them peering into the future with mixed expressions of concern and resolve.[1]

As in the past, most delegates that year were from Saint John, Fredericton, and Moncton, though there were also men from the Miramichi, McAdam, Milltown, Campbellton, and smaller centres. Near the centre, standing between vice-presidents John Wallace, the veteran woodsman from the Miramichi and James Whitebone, the motion-picture projectionist from Saint John, we see Eugene R. Steeves, the successor to Sugrue, Melanson, and Tighe as president of the Federation. Steeves had attended his first convention in 1919, when he was one of two delegates (the other was Melanson) from Local 594 of the IAM. Born in rural Albert County in 1887, Steeves had worked for the Maine Central and Canadian Pacific Railways before starting work as a machinist at the Intercolonial shops and settling down in Moncton. Always interested in civic matters, he served for ten years on the Moncton school board and later on city council. Steeves was elected first vice-president of the Federation in 1925 and replaced James Tighe as president in 1929.[2]

At the time of his first report to the members in Moncton in January 1930, Steeves had remarked on the great progress of labour organizations since their early days: "Labour now had achieved a position of prominence in the state and in the community."[3] A year later in Saint John, he could point to at least one success, the enactment of long-awaited legislation, including a Mothers' Allowance Act, a Minimum Wage Act for Women and Girls, and an Old Age Pensions Act, and he urged the government to put these into effect without delay. The delegates went on to pass resolutions in favour of new legislation, including an eight-hour day and a minimum wage of 40 cents an hour on all provincial contracts.[4] Even at the convention, statements from government spokesmen were disappointing, and by October 1931, the Federation's legislative representative reported that the government was taking no interest in their proposals; indeed, the 1930 laws had still not been proclaimed and as such were "just so much printed matter and of no benefit to anybody."[5]

But the biggest question of the day, Steeves told delegates at the convention banquet at the new Admiral Beatty hotel in 1931, was unemployment. What had started as a downturn in 1930 was rapidly turning into a deep depression with dangerous consequences for workers and society at large: "This condition would have to be remedied, as unemployment bred evil, which would result in an increase in crime, if something was not done." Steeves argued that shorter hours and higher wages would "ease the situation considerably as working men had to have money to buy products before production could be greatly increased by demand."[6] Steeves and other labour leaders welcomed the emergency funding provided for public works in the early years of the Depression, but they also reported that unscrupulous contractors were demanding long hours and paying the lowest wages. At Chatham, stated J. S. Martin at the 1931 convention, until the unions intervened contractors had been paying 27.5 cents an hour and charging workers 75 cents a day for board, including Sundays and other days when there was no work.[7]

THE MACHINIST E. R. Steeves (1887–1952) was a Moncton machinist, originally from Albert County, who became president of the Federation in 1929. Three years later, he was named to replace James Sugrue as the labour member of the Workmen's Compensation Board and continued to represent workers on the board until his death. Source: *History of New Brunswick Federation of Labor* (1934).

Delegates such as Martin had more to say the next year, when the meetings took place in Chatham, the first time the Federation had met outside the province's three major cities. On the Miramichi that winter, Martin informed the delegates, not a wheel was turning in the mills and there were ten men for every job available. The unemployment crisis was the constant theme in the sessions, and Steeves again denounced employers who took advantage of conditions to reduce wages and lengthen hours. The report from the executive officers stated that "cases of under pay and unfair conditions" on public contracts in Saint John, Devon, Woodstock, McAdam, and Tracadie had been brought to the attention of government and "at least some of them have been corrected to the workers' advantage." Relief work would continue to be needed —"to the very limit of the country's resources"— but this would not be enough:

> The time has come when the prevention of unemployment must be taken up and given serious consideration by our governing bodies, and some scheme or plan devised, such as unemployment insurance, which will assure each and every worker of an opportunity to either earn a living for his family, as he desires, or a decent living will be obtainable by him out of the country's surplus production, which he has assisted in creating, and which inevitably occurs with such periods of unemployment.

A Special Committee on Unemployment was named, chaired by former president James Tighe, and in the discussion delegates reported "similar bad conditions" throughout the province. The committee brought in a resolution stating that "immediate relief must be extended to many families" and calling on the federal government to hold an interprovincial conference on unemployment, with labour representation from all provinces.[8]

One of the few areas of the province experiencing some growth in employment in the early 1930s was the Grand Lake coalfield, where a new power plant opened in 1931. More than a thousand men worked in the shallow underground coal mines and were often exposed to dangerous conditions. In the space of six months in 1932, there were eight deaths in the mines. Three of the victims were children who were overcome by the lack of air in an abandoned pit where they were playing, and two of the miners who died were among the dozen men who attempted to rescue them. Although they no longer had a union to represent them, the miners made their views on this tragedy well known, in part through the findings of local coroners' juries. The Federation of Labour had been calling for mine safety legislation for more than ten years, and they repeated the appeal again at the 1933 convention. In the spring of 1933, the province finally introduced the province's first mine safety legislation, which provided for the protection of abandoned mines and the inspection of machinery; it also prohibited boys under the age of sixteen from employment in the mines and limited the working day to eight hours.[9]

This was a small and isolated success, and in the early 1930s the Federation of Labour continued to worry about their declining influence. This was visible in a long campaign to maintain labour representation on the Workmen's Compensation Board. After the death of James Sugrue in 1930, the government named a commission to review the board's operations and failed to appoint even a temporary replacement. When the premier requested the names of potential members in 1931, the officers agreed to submit suggestions, although the Federation preferred to provide only one nominee for such appointments. Eight different names were proposed by the affiliated locals, and the Federation submitted the two leading names, Secretary-Treasurer George Melvin and President Steeves. Several months later, they were still protesting the "undue and unwarranted delay" in appointing Sugrue's successor. At the 1932 convention, delegates reaffirmed the policy of submitting only one nominee, and on a vote of the delegates Steeves was chosen. By this time, the inquiry into the board was completed, and in July 1932 Steeves was appointed. It had taken two years, but the Federation preserved the principle of labour representation on the board they had helped to create. In August 1932, Steeves submitted his resignation as Federation president and went on to serve as vice-chairman of the compensation board for the next twenty years.[10]

On Steeves's departure, the first vice-president, James Whitebone, became acting president and was then elected president at the convention in March 1933. With the exception of two years in the 1930s, Whitebone would occupy

THE PROJECTIONIST James A. Whitebone (1894–1970) joined his first union as a young man in 1912, a year before the Federation was established. A motion-picture projectionist in Saint John, he became president of the Federation in 1932 and went on to serve a record number of terms until his final retirement in 1964. Source: *History of New Brunswick Federation of Labor* (1934).

the office of president continuously until 1959 (and again from 1960 to 1964). Like Sugrue and Tighe before him, Whitebone was the son of an immigrant. His father Jacob had come to Saint John from Amsterdam as a boy and spent most of his working life as a cigarmaker and tobacconist; he was buried in the Jewish cemetery after his death in 1917. James Alexander Whitebone was born in 1894 and was raised in the Anglican church of his mother. His generation of Whitebones were assimilated into the dominant culture; Whitebone was listed as a Church of England adherent at the time of his marriage to Lillian Gertrude Lynch, a Catholic, in 1918. Whitebone started work as an assistant projectionist in one of the city's moviehouses at the age of thirteen. In 1920 he was a founder of Local 440, International Alliance of Theatrical Stage Employees and Moving Picture Machine Operators, for which he became the longtime secretary and business agent. Whitebone was elected president of the Saint John Trades and Labour Council in 1926 and continued in that office until 1942. He began attending meetings of the Federation of Labour in 1920 and was elected first vice-president for several years prior to becoming president. Whitebone proved to be a pragmatic, often cautious, leader of the Federation, and its history for several decades often reflected his personality. As one account of his career later noted, "He could be forceful but preferred to be quiet and deal in reason and good sense rather than emotion. He was a doer, not a shouter, although he could shout with the best of them if the circumstances demanded it."[11] Whitebone dominated the provincial labour scene for so long that he came to be described as New Brunswick's "Mr. Labour."[12]

A New Politics?

The beginning of the Whitebone era was not auspicious. There were only thirty-two delegates in attendance at the Federation's 1933 meetings, and Premier C.D. Richards asked them to cooperate with the government by not requesting any new legislation. Delegates nonetheless renewed calls for implementation of earlier legislation; one of their arguments was that failure to implement the Old Age Pensions Act had already cost the people of New Brunswick almost

$1 million in taxes paid to the federal government without any return to citizens of the province. It was also clear that the appointment of Steeves to the board had not satisfied concerns about Workmen's Compensation, as there were no fewer than twenty resolutions calling for improvements in the act. When board chairman John A. Sinclair appeared at the convention, former Federation president James Tighe charged that Sinclair had instigated amendments that altered the method of calculating eligible earnings, to the detriment of most claimants. The debate lasted most of an afternoon and became so heated that Whitebone, as chairman, was forced to call the meeting to order.[13]

Meanwhile, several resolutions that year asked the province to do much more to address the worsening economic crisis. Delegates called on the province to prohibit foreclosures on farms and homes, to prevent the disenfranchisement of workers on relief, and to support plans for a system of unemployment insurance. They also called for enactment of a six-hour day and a five-day week, without reductions in weekly wages, in order to distribute existing work more fairly. The banking system in particular came under attack on the grounds that it was "holding in its hands the economic destiny of practically the entire community." There was also support among delegates for the formation of a branch of the new Co-operative Commonwealth Federation, the party of social reform organized by labour Member of Parliament J. S. Woodsworth at Calgary the previous summer. At the 1933 convention, Moncton delegates submitted a resolution stating that "large numbers of our people are unemployed and without the means of earning a livelihood for themselves and their dependents" and that "the prevalence of the present depression throughout the world indicates fundamental defects in the existing economic system." They called on the Federation to "sponsor and use its machinery to bring into being a branch of the Co-operative Commonwealth Federation."[14]

To the surprise of those who knew him as a longtime supporter of the Liberal Party, the CCF resolution was introduced by Tighe, who was chair of the Resolutions Committee. He spoke in support, stating that there was a need for more labour representation and that the resolution proposed only to assist in calling a convention, after which the Federation could "step aside."

Secretary-Treasurer Melvin was opposed "on account of the Federation not being a political body," and former president Steeves worried that "it would undo what had already been accomplished." Delegates also heard from the original authors of the resolution, notably machinist A. W. Jamieson of the Moncton Trades and Labour Council, who stated that the CCF platform was "fundamentally sound" and that "this is the body to push it and this is the opportunity to get it going because farmers and labourers are down and out." After a lengthy debate the resolution was approved on a standing vote of 21 to 9.[15]

Within months the CCF was underway in the province. On 23 June, Whitebone, as president of the Federation, chaired a founding meeting of the New Brunswick Section of the CCF. The call had gone out to labour and farmer organizations and social reform groups across the province, and ninety-eight delegates arrived in Moncton for the occasion. Whitebone stated that the Federation did not intend to dominate the new organization, and he warned that for it to succeed, "some very deep rooted convictions" would have to be overcome. Delegates then proceeded to adopt a constitution calling for "the establishment of a planned system of social economy for the production, distribution and exchange of all goods and services." The spirit of the meeting was also captured by lively resolutions on "Youth," "Unemployment," and "Lying Propaganda"; one resolution stated that "we appeal to the peoples' reason rather than their passion and selfishness and will endeavor to prove to them that we can be more truly loyal to our country and our fellow citizens than the Conservative Party which calls itself Liberal and the Liberal Party which has proven itself Conservative." Harry Girvan of Coal Creek, in the Grand Lake area, was elected president of the CCF New Brunswick Section.[16]

The guest of honour was J. S. Woodsworth himself, the Methodist minister and union supporter who had been arrested at the time of the Winnipeg General Strike in 1919 and had served as a Labour MP since 1921. That evening he delivered the CCF message at a public meeting at the Moncton Stadium. Some one thousand people turned out to hear Woodsworth denounce the failure of the capitalist system and argue the need for a new economic and social order that placed people before profits. "Capitalism is failing," he told them, "and nothing short of a new system could bring any permanent relief. We will have to change the way things are done." There would be government control of the banking system, and the CCF would bring new priorities to economic policy: "Where there is conflict between property rights on one hand and the needs of men, women and children on the other hand, the men, women and children ought to have priority over anything else."[17]

Later that year, Moncton delegates took the CCF cause to the annual meetings of the Trades and Labour Congress in Windsor, Ontario, with a proposal to endorse the new party. The resolution, proposed by IAM Local 594 President Vance Dalzell, denounced the old political parties and their leaders as "complete failures" and pointed to the New Deal of President Franklin D. Roosevelt in the United States as an example of "what real political and statesmanlike leadership will do to lift a nation out of complete chaos and back to prosperity and happiness." The TLC establishment was not pleased with this resolution, and President Tom Moore objected that endorsement of any political party was contrary to congress policy. After several hours of strenuous debate, the so-called "Moncton resolution" was withdrawn.[18]

Meanwhile, back in New Brunswick, the CCF message was being distributed by a monthly newspaper sponsored by the Moncton branch, *The Pilot*, which published the full text of the new party's Regina Manifesto in August 1933. In September, a public meeting at City Hall in Moncton, presided over by machinist W. R. Rogers, attracted several hundred people. The branch president led the audience in singing from CCF song sheets. Then they heard a lecture on the history of socialist thought by a local young man who had recently graduated from the University of Toronto; in his "lengthy and interesting address," H. Northrop Frye stated that "we are now living in a Socialistic world and have to grow up far enough and learn to become Socialist." However, the progress of the CCF was slow. An old-time socialist from Saint John who had attended the founding meeting complained that the new provincial executive was inactive, and another supporter claimed that one of the key officers was "put in by opponents to block the work and he had to do as he was told to by the Trades + Labor Council." A more vigorous secretary-treasurer was in place by early 1934, but Woodsworth's hope to have CCF candidates in the province in the 1935 elections was not fulfilled.[19]

The progress of the Federation itself also remained stalled, and only thirty-two delegates attended the February 1934 convention. "Unemployment," Whitebone stated, "is still the major problem confronting the Federation in common with every Labour organization in the land." Under these conditions, membership was falling, and the Federation reported 2,911 members among the affiliates, a substantial drop from the 3,700 workers of 1931 or the much larger numbers at the end of the Great War. Whitebone noted the recent organization of workers in the pulp and paper mills on the North Shore and hoped that they would soon join the Federation. But in the woods, workers were labouring under "disgraceful conditions," he said. "Men are compelled to work 12 to 14 hours a day for starvation wages, at the same time being housed and fed under primitive conditions." Whitebone stated that the province had started an investigation into wages and hours in the woods, and he congratulated Premier Leonard Tilley for doing so. He even saw indications that the economic situation was improving: "Let us be fully prepared to take advantage of the return to normal conditions by strengthening our organizations and maintaining a united Federation."[20]

In like optimistic fashion, Whitebone also presented delegates with copies of a new publication entitled *History of Federation of Labor of New Brunswick*. The 100-page booklet was not so much a history as a statement of past achievements —"an outline of the great work which has been carried on for the past twenty years by the New Brunswick Federation of Labor in its unselfish efforts in the interests of the welfare of working men and women and their families." The cover art was a modernist depiction of a giant male worker surrounded by mills and chimneys — an idealized, and highly masculinist, image to demonstrate the strength of the industrial worker. The text consisted mainly of short articles by stalwarts such as Melvin, Steeves, Whitebone, and others, as well as contributions from government officials such as the minister of health and the director of the vocational school. There were also more than two hundred commercial advertisements, an indication that the patronage of union workers was appreciated in the local business sector. In a few of the ads the sponsors described themselves as "Friends of Labour," and a full-page advertisement from the Province of New Brunswick extended best wishes to the Federation "in its efforts to maintain a strong, active and sane labor organization within this province." There was little in the book to indicate the frustrating conditions facing the Federation at the middle of the 1930s, although the articles on pensions, the minimum wage, and mothers' allowances each noted the continuing failure of the province to put its own legislation into effect.[21]

The 1934 convention brought Whitebone's first mandate as president to a close. The reports state only that former president Tighe, who had retired from the office in 1929, was elected in 1934 and again in 1935. It is unlikely Whitebone offered for re-election in 1934, as he had stated in his report to delegates that "some of my actions while serving as your president have displeased some" and called for cooperation with the incoming officers. Tighe may well have been alarmed that Whitebone had adopted a too-favourable attitude towards Premier Tilley. On his return to office, Tighe was certainly not slow to remind the province of its commitments. He attacked the

OFFICIAL PROCEEDINGS
of the
23rd Annual Convention
1936

NEW BRUNSWICK FEDERATION OF LABOR

MODERN MAN An idealized image of the industrial worker, first introduced in a promotional booklet published by the Federation in 1934, a representation of power often at odds with the Federation's fortunes in the Great Depression. This picture was used on the cover of published convention proceedings from 1936 to 1961. Source: NBFL *Proceedings*, 1936.

administration of the Workmen's Compensation Act —"only a skeleton of the former act"— and protested the curtailment of grants to the vocational schools and the repeal of provisions for free schoolbooks. He was particularly angry that the government had still failed to proclaim the legislation that the Federation had agitated for at length in the 1920s and that the Conservatives had finally enacted in 1930: "What it has taken us years of hard work and money to attain has been taken away from us in a very short time, and New Brunswick stands alone among the Provinces of this Dominion as the only Province without social legislation. . . . I would recommend to this convention that you still press with every power within your means for this legislation, to get back what we have lost and to receive what we were promised."[22]

When delegates to the 1935 meetings heard addresses from Premier Tilley and Leader of the Opposition A.C. Dysart, it was a kind of dress rehearsal for the coming provincial election that summer. Tilley congratulated the Federation "for the magnificent way they have conducted themselves in the past four years," while Dysart praised the value of labour organization as "very far reaching as the scope of duties is the uplift of humanity." Tilley pointed to the formation of a Forest Operations Commission, which had introduced a $32 monthly minimum wage in the woods; for his part Dysart objected that there were too many loopholes and that "the minimum wage is liable to become the maximum." Dysart promised to implement the federal old age pension in New Brunswick, while Tilley cautioned that "it was a mistake for any public man to make promises before election that could not be redeemed afterward."[23] In the election, the Liberals scored a sweeping victory, winning 43 of the 48 seats. The following year Tighe reported favourably on the new government's first Speech from the Throne and commended the Liberals for finally proclaiming the 1930 Old Age Pensions Act; although it was a limited, means-tested programme, some of the most impoverished New Brunswickers would now be eligible for the support available to citizens in most other provinces, and the Federation could claim another small victory. When Tighe also announced that he was retiring from office "to make way for younger men," the door was open for the return of Whitebone, in whom Tighe now expressed his "absolute confidence."[24]

The Right to a Union

By the middle years of the Great Depression, much was happening in the world of labour beyond New Brunswick. Protests against unemployment had culminated in the famous On-to-Ottawa Trek of 1935, and workers who had jobs increasingly recognized the need for strong unions to protect them against economic insecurity. In the early 1930s, the Communist-led Workers' Unity League had fought several big battles, and by 1937 workers in Canada and the United States were joining new unions started by the Committee for Industrial Organization, led by John L. Lewis of the United Mine Workers. In New Brunswick, the affiliation of pulp and paper workers at Edmundston and Dalhousie was an important addition to the ranks of the Federation, but there were still only thirty-six delegates at the annual meetings in March 1937. When Minister of Health and Labour Dr. W. F. Roberts addressed the Federation meetings in Fredericton, he stated that "he was glad there was little or no labor trouble in the Province when there was so much in other places."[25] Before the year was out this observation proved misleading, as two large labour upheavals shook the province and raised challenges for the Federation.

There was a stronger note of militancy than usual in Whitebone's report as president in 1937. While he commended the government on the first payments under the Old Age Pensions Act, he stated that many pensioners were receiving less than the full amount of $20 per month. He also objected to the "alleged enforcement" of the Fair Wage Act brought in by the new government: "Not one instance has been reported wherein any worker has been benefitted"; one of the weaknesses of the Act was that, despite the Federation's suggestions, no labour representatives were appointed to help administer the legislation. Whitebone also reported that the Liberals had attempted to remove former president Steeves from the Compensation Board, and he warned of "disastrous consequences should the Act be permitted to become a creature of political vagaries." Whitebone was also critical of the Federation's own weak record in winning concessions and suggested that "we have, perhaps, been prone to depend too much upon the willingness of the government of the day for alleviation of conditions." More influence could be achieved by strengthening the ranks of organized labour: "Let every worker in this province take up membership in the legitimate organization of his or her trade or employment and then, by sheer force of our economic strength [we] will be enabled to abandon the hat-in-hand, begging policy into which we seem to be drifting."[26]

The most important change sought by the Federation during the 1930s was the enactment of legislation to protect the right to union membership. Although the Trade Union Act (1872) had established that unions were not illegal in Canada, there was nothing to prevent employers from firing or otherwise punishing anyone who joined a union — or even talked about joining a union. The need for unions was one of the conclusions workers were drawing from their experience of powerlessness during the Great Depression, and at the 1937 meetings the Federation approved four separate resolutions calling for union rights. One of the new affiliates, Local 146, International Brotherhood of Pulp, Sulphite and Paper Mill Workers, representing workers at the Dalhousie paper mill, introduced a resolution stating that the need was becoming urgent:

> Whereas: Most industries in the Province of New Brunswick still refuse to bargain collectively with their employees; and,
>
> Whereas: Such refusal is all the more insistent when the workmen are organized into unions; and,
>
> Whereas: Such a situation has placed New Brunswick as the most backward Province in social and economic progress; and finds the New Brunswick workers ranked amongst the lowest paid in their respective industries, particularly in the pulp and paper industry; be it, therefore,
>
> Resolved: That this federation endorse the principle of "collective bargaining," through the Labor Unions, wherever they are in existence, and their accredited representatives; and that our Provincial Government be urged to pass the necessary legislation giving such rights to all New Brunswick workers.[27]

In passing such resolutions, New Brunswick workers were joining a larger movement for union rights. The Wagner Act adopted in the United States in 1935 was a model of the kind of positive union law unions were seeking, and in 1936 the Trades and Labour Congress launched a campaign to secure new provincial laws. As drafted, the TLC's Freedom of Trade Union Association Act provided that workers were entitled to organize and join unions free from employer domination and to engage in collective bargaining through their chosen officers; employers were prohibited from limiting these rights by threats, dismissals, or contracts such as the notorious "yellow dog" agreements that required workers to abstain from union membership as a condition of employment.[28]

While the province failed to respond to this agitation, the spring session in 1937 established a Fair Wage Board to direct the work of the fair wage officer appointed a year earlier.[29] This board provided for two employer and two worker representatives. On behalf of the Federation, Melvin made a strong case for the appointment of John S. MacKinnon, a Saint John labour council and Federation leader who was president of the longshoremen's union. The second name, Raymond Roy, came from the opposite end of the province; Roy was a native of Restigouche County who had worked in paper mills outside the province before returning to work at the new mill at Dalhousie, where he was an officer of the local of the International Brotherhood of Papermakers; moreover, Melvin pointed out, Roy was "a French-Canadian, having a thorough knowledge of both the English and French languages as spoken in this province"— a matter of much relevance, as the board would likely "find it necessary to hold hearings in districts where very little English is spoken." The Federation's efforts were successful, and both MacKinnon and Roy were appointed to the board. Their satisfaction was qualified by the additional appointment of Moncton's Frank Gillespie, a longtime officer of the Canadian Brotherhood of Railway Employees who had been endorsed by the provincial council of the All-Canadian Congress of Labour, an organization that was beginning to challenge the Federation's claim to be the main voice of labour in the province.[30]

Miramichi and Minto

The fight for union rights extended well beyond the Federation's meeting rooms. Shortly after the 1937 convention, officers were pondering their response to a new organization that had appeared on the Miramichi, only loosely connected to any of the Federation's affiliates. Established at a public meeting at the Labour Hall in Nelson on 13 January, the Northumberland County Farmer-Labour Union announced itself as the defender of the labouring classes of the Miramichi. Their populist rhetoric was directed not just at employers but at members of the public and business community who shared the workers' concerns. It was time, they said, for "government of the people and for the people, rather than government of the Privileged Few for the Privileged Few."[31] Speakers at the first Farmer-Labour Union meeting in January included two local leaders long associated with the Federation, John Wallace and J.S. Martin, who supported the agitation for better wages and conditions.[32] The campaign featured strong rhetoric — "We, the labor people of the Miramichi here assembled" was the beginning of one resolution that went on to state that "the laboring Class feel that their wages are insufficient to sustain themselves and their families in a decent manner." They called for higher wages for the longshoremen, mill workers, river drivers, and boommen who worked on the river.[33]

During the spring and summer months, new branches of the Farmer-Labour Union were organized, and union demands were presented to the Fair Wage Board. At the middle of August, workers at one sawmill walked out — it was one of the worst operations, where workers put in ten-hour days for as little as 17.5 cents an hour and the employer refused to discuss any changes. This was the spark, and a week later the new union was leading a general strike along the Miramichi. In a remarkable display of the union's appeal, on 20 August 1937 President Gregory McEachreon carried a Union Jack from mill to mill, rallying hundreds of workers to join the strike, much as had happened in the summer of 1919. After a similar parade the next day, more than a thousand workers were off work at twelve different operations along a 40-mile stretch of the river. Premier Dysart responded by expressing his regrets that the workers did not wait for the Fair Wage Board to complete its investigations. From Saint John, however, James Tighe sent a telegram to congratulate the union "on the great fight you are waging for the working man's rights" and added: "All labour men in province solidly behind you and trust you will win out."[34]

The strike ended within ten days. There were no direct negotiations, but a citizens' committee arranged for a settlement that included a minimum wage of 28 cents an hour and a nine-hour day. There was no formal recognition for the union, but the success of the strike was instructive for the Federation of Labour, which had played no part in organizing the union or leading the protest. In this situation a large number of workers ignored existing unions and improvised their own forms of organization and action. The New Brunswick Farmer-Labour Union, as it came to be known, was a multi-occupational, community-based union that did not fall within the jurisdiction of any existing "legitimate" union. Although it had been Federation practice for years to disparage "outlaw" unions that did not conform to the policies of the Trades and Labour Congress, Whitebone welcomed representatives of the new organization at the 1938 meetings of the Federation and stated that "their objects coincide with those of the International Trade Union Movement." In their own way, the workers of the Miramichi were reminding the Federation of the continuing need among New Brunswick workers for union organization and leadership.[35]

They were not alone. During that same year, in 1937, workers in central New Brunswick were also looking for union recognition, and their struggle precipitated a long battle over the future of labour relations in the province. The coal miners of the Grand Lake district had formed a local of the United Mine Workers of America in 1919 and then a unit of the One Big Union in 1925, but each effort had ended in failure. In 1931, one local worker wrote to the Workers' Unity League requesting that the legendary Cape Breton union leader J.B. McLachlan be sent to the district: "He knows how to organize the men . . . . we want him here in the worst condition."[36] But even without an organization to join, the coal miners continued to form committees, sign petitions, and send delegations to visit the provincial government. In 1934 they formed a short-lived union with a deliberately parochial name — the Northfield Central Provincial Miners' Union — in the belief that the operators would be less hostile to an entirely local union. All this was to no avail in gaining recognition, and the coal miners turned again to the United Mine Workers of America. In February 1937 they received a charter as Local 7409 of the UMWA, signed by international president John L. Lewis, whose name was becoming synonymous with the "CIO idea" and the cause of industrial unionism in North America. In Minto the local president was Mathias Wuhr, one of the heroes of the 1932 mine rescue efforts who had received a Carnegie Medal for his bravery.

In October the new union was confident enough of its support to call for negotiations, and when none of the coal operators agreed to meet, they voted almost unanimously to go on strike.[37] By 15 October some one thousand men were off work at eleven companies in the coalfield, and additional RCMP officers were called in to patrol the district. Every morning at 5 a.m. hundreds of men marched in parades, traveling from mine to mine to discourage strikebreakers. They also crowded into public meetings to hear visiting union speakers from District 26 headquarters in Nova Scotia and the occasional sympathetic clergyman such as the Reverend John Linton of Fredericton. Students from the University of New Brunswick raised funds and delivered supplies, and women students from the Student Christian Movement encouraged the miners' wives to take part in strike demonstrations and join a women's auxiliary to distribute food and clothing. As Allen Seager has written, the "big strike" was "a remarkable demonstration of the power of the union ideal in Minto in the late 1930s."[38] The *Minto Strike News* was articulate in defending the miners' right to a union and arguing against "Stone Age Conditions" in the local mines: "An individual miner airing a just grievance stands a chance of being fired. Only a union can protect him. . . . The miners want recognition as an absolutely necessary first step in their fight for better wages and working conditions."[39]

COAL MINERS The Minto coal miners fought long and hard for union recognition, and their strike in 1937–38 led to the province's Labour and Industrial Relations Act. Seated in the front, fifth from the left, in this 1934 group of miners employed by the Miramichi Lumber Company is Mathias Wuhr, who in 1937 became the first president of Local 7409, United Mine Workers of America. He was also a working-class hero who was decorated for his courage in a dramatic mine rescue in 1932. Source: New Brunswick Museum, 1978.110.2.

The strike dragged on for almost two months. In November the province attempted to have the Fair Wage Board investigate the situation, but the coal miners considered this a poor substitute for negotiations. This provoked Attorney-General J. B. McNair to announce that the strike was turning into a question of "whether the CIO or the government is going to run New Brunswick." For their part, the coal operators prepared to issue eviction notices on 1 December, to take effect within thirty days and threatening to turn four hundred families out of company houses into the snow in winter conditions. At this stage the union announced a change in tactics, ending the strike and applying to the federal Department of Labour for a conciliation board. As a result, many strikers returned to work — at first on the condition of signed individual "understandings" with the operators — while militant local leaders such as Wuhr remained on the blacklist.

The Labour and Industrial Relations Act

The strike failed, but it had a large impact in the province. The miners had aroused public concern about the powerlessness of workers and the inadequacy of provincial labour laws. The Fair Wage Officer recommended better housing, better working conditions, and standard wage rates; and by the summer of 1938 the federal conciliation board produced a catalogue of deplorable living and working conditions. These findings helped explain why there was discontent in the mining communities, but both reports failed to acknowledge that union recognition and collective bargaining were the central issues in the dispute.[40]

As Whitebone pointed out at the Federation convention in January 1938, the Fair Wage Board might be useful in improving conditions for unorganized workers, but it was not suited to meeting the needs of workers who were already organized and wanted to negotiate with their employers. The Minto situation, he said, was important for all workers in the province: "The whole question now simmers down to whether or not the mine workers of this province shall have the right to belong to the recognized union of their craft or whether they must continue to be dominated by local representatives of big business and autocratic government officials." This was a strong statement, and for making these remarks Whitebone was forced to resign from the conciliation board, which at the time was still considering the Minto situation.[41] In his address to the convention two days later, Premier Dysart announced that the province was considering new labour legislation: "I think men should be allowed to stand in a body and organize and bargain collectively"— but almost immediately he added a qualification: "It is wrong, however, for workers to band together to compel acceptance of their solution to a problem."[42] However, a day earlier the Federation had already adopted a resolution, sponsored by Local 7409, UMWA, for an Act Respecting the Right of Employees to Organize, with key provisions copied from the Nova Scotia Trade Union Act of 1937.[43]

The highlight of the spring session of the legislature in 1938 was a bill for a Labour and Industrial Relations Act, announced in the Speech from the Throne as a measure to "promote the security and well-being of labour and industry." Bill 64 was introduced by Attorney-General McNair, who stated that the new legislation "declares as positive law of this Province that employers and employees have the right to organize and bargain together collectively. No longer will there be any question raised in this Province on that point." One section of the bill incorporated the existing Fair Wage Act, which would continue to be available for establishing employment standards. Another section provided for the compulsory conciliation of disputes before a legal strike could be permitted, a provision that had been a staple of federal labour legislation since 1907. In the course of the debate, McNair added a further section to provide penalties for employers who threatened dismissal or punished workers for joining a union. In the debate, there was recrimination over which political party was to blame for "fomenting" the Miramichi and Minto strikes of 1937, but the bill received unanimous approval from both Liberals and Conservatives.[44]

Although the bill was almost thirty pages in length, there was less substance to the new law than met the eye. A young lawyer in Fredericton, a McGill University graduate originally from the Miramichi who was sympathetic to the cause of labour, watched in wonder as the new legislation was "hailed in the press as a Bill of Rights for N.B. labor." At the time the bill was before the assembly, Frank Park had written a sharp critique of its deficiencies. To begin with, the definition of "employee" was too limited — it excluded agricultural workers ("Is this aimed at the Farmer-Labor Union?") and domestic servants ("in many cases . . . the worst treated class of labor in the province") as well as employees "by or under the Crown" ("There is no reason in the world why this class of Labor should be set apart and marked off from the rest of the labor movement"). As for the provision to make it lawful for employees to bargain collectively with their employer, this was hardly a breakthrough, for the simple reason that collective bargaining was already lawful and had been so for many years. The real trouble came from the fact that employers refused to recognize unions and engage in bargaining: "The Act is as flat as a pancake if there is no provision dealing with Union recognition." Specifically, the law did not contain the essential provision contained in the Nova Scotia Trade Union Act: "Every employer shall recognize and bargain collectively with the members of a trade union representing the majority choice of the employees."[45]

Reviewing the 1938 Act at the time of next Federation convention, Whitebone was very aware of its deficiencies. He pointed out that the Federation had withheld support until several amendments were added, but he was also prepared to state that McNair "evinced a sincere desire to meet our wishes" and that the government had introduced the law "in an honest endeavour to reduce to a minimum the possibility of future serious labor disturbances in this Province and to this end we lend our fullest co-operation." Like Park, he objected to the exclusion of public employees from the Act: "Surely the Government, the largest employer of labor in the Province, is exercising discriminatory powers when they practically serve notice on their own employees that it is illegal for them to belong to a union, while at the same time declaring the legality of organizations of employees in private industry." Moreover, in almost a year of operation, the procedures for solving disputes had been of little benefit: "It is doubtful if any labor organization in the Province has been successful in securing assistance under this part of the Act in adjusting a dispute with their employers."[46]

Certainly the new law did not help the Minto coal miners. They were warmly supported at the 1939 Federation convention, which adopted resolutions for revision of the act to prohibit the recognition of employer-dominated unions and to meet the standards of the Nova Scotia legislation for union recognition and collective bargaining.[47] Since the defeat of their strike, some coal miners had now joined organizations favoured by their employers, such as the Miramichi Mine Workers Union and Rothwell Mine Workers Union, but the Federation rejected applications for affiliation from employer-supported unions in the strongest terms: "The company union is the lowest most despicable weapon ever devised by unscrupulous employers to crush the worker and prevent his belonging to the legitimate union of his trade or calling."[48] Even without recognition, Local 7409 survived, stubbornly leading protests at individual mines and agitating in favour of free textbooks to Grade 12 in light of the impoverished conditions in the district.[49] As local president Joseph

Vandenbroeck informed Whitebone in early 1940, an amended law was still needed: "The past year and a half have not given us any benefit under the present wording, as the operators take the stand they are not compelled to recognize any Union."[50]

Ending the Depression

While the unions faced frustrations and obstacles in their quest for recognition, the Great Depression had also demonstrated the need for stronger social legislation to help all citizens. At the 1939 convention, delegates called for the introduction of public hospital, medicine, and health insurance. The Federation also went on record in favour of giving the Dominion government the power to legislate in areas such as pensions, health insurance, hours of work, and recognition of unions. In this they were critical of provincial governments, including New Brunswick's, who opposed the extension of federal power in these areas. The most pressing situation was in the case of unemployment insurance, a reform that was stalled by debates over the constitutional authority of the Dominion and was waiting for an amendment to the British North America Act. In words that recalled the comments of Steeves at the start of the decade, Whitebone warned that it was time for action:

> Unemployment remains the most distressing problem in New Brunswick as well as throughout the entire country and as yet the solution of this great blight on civilization is not in sight. . . . Millions have been spent in relief and in providing temporary work but these methods are admittedly only palliatives. In our own province of New Brunswick thousands of men tramp the streets and highways desperately seeking any kind of work. By all the laws of nature this condition cannot much longer exist and productive employment of a permanent nature at decent wages will soon have to be provided for all employable persons if we are to prevent the collapse of modern civilization.[51]

At the very least, it was time to introduce a contributory unemployment insurance plan for all Canadian workers and for New Brunswick to withdraw its objections. Delegates went on to adopt a resolution calling on the Dominion government not to wait for an amendment to the British North America Act but to declare a state of emergency and enact the legislation without delay.[52]

In his reports of the late 1930s, Secretary-Treasurer Melvin was able to report signs of renewal in the ranks of the Federation. There was an increase in participation at the convention in 1938, when 42 delegates attended, and by the time of the 1939 meetings, there were 75 delegates in attendance, the largest number since 1921, and they represented an affiliated membership of 5,500 workers.[53] However, there had also been warnings during the course of the decade that the Federation's claim to be the voice of labour in the province was not unchallenged. On several occasions in the early 1930s, Federation delegates debated the question of relations with "outlaw" organizations that did not fall within the jurisdictional scope of the TLC and its international unions affiliated to the American Federation of Labor. In 1931, a resolution in favour of "amalgamation" among Canadian unions was overwhelmingly rejected, and in a 1932 visit, TLC President Moore singled out threats from a list of rival groups, including "the One Big Union, the Communists, National Catholic Union and the National Union or All-Canadian Congress."[54]

WOMEN WORKERS Women workers were not a priority for most of the Federation's affiliated unions, and no women delegates attended Federation meetings between 1923 and 1943. New industrial unions showed more ambition in organizing the unorganized, and in 1937 workers at the Atlantic Underwear factory in Moncton joined a textile workers' union belonging to the rival New Brunswick Council of Labour, established in 1935. Source: Moncton Museum Collection.

Of these the most important in New Brunswick was the All-Canadian Congress of Labour, which was established in 1927 as a federation of purely Canadian unions and had a core membership drawn from the Canadian Brotherhood of Railway Employees, which continued to enjoy strength in the province's railway towns.

The conflict had deepened when ACCL unions formed their own "federation" of labour in the province. In 1935, delegates from Saint John, Moncton, Fredericton, Edmundston, Campbellton, and Newcastle met to establish a New Brunswick Council of Labour, with R.J. Harrington, a CBRE member from Saint John, as president. Following that meeting, Federation President Tighe was reported to have stated that "the newly-formed organization has no connection whatever with the New Brunswick Federation of Labour, and will have no effect on it whatever"; of this claim, one of the Council leaders observed sardonically: "That, of course, remains to be seen, and we will do our utmost to see that the new organization does have some effect on the NBF of L."[55] In short order, the new Council was operating as a rival provincial federation of labour, pressing the government for appointments to bodies such as the Fair Wage Board and for a list of legislative reforms. Most importantly, the ACCL was also organizing new groups of workers in the province. In 1937, for instance, they issued charters to textile workers at Atlantic Underwear

and J.A. Humphrey and Sons in Moncton, factories where large numbers of women workers were employed, and they also organized workers at the Atlantic Sugar refinery in Saint John. The skilled craft unions that dominated the Federation of Labour had little to offer these workers, and the ACCL's new industrial unions were filling a need.[56] By the time of their fifth annual meeting in June 1939, the New Brunswick Council of Labour boasted more than fifty delegates from seven centres in the province, including labour councils at Minto, Moncton, and Saint John. Their numbers included at least three women delegates, from beauticians in Saint John and biscuit factory workers in Moncton. In his address to the delegates, ACCL President A.R. Mosher congratulated the Council on their progress and stated that New Brunswick was "one of the most active provinces insofar as the National Labour Movement was concerned." In accordance with the conservative nationalism of the ACCL, Mosher repeated the usual criticism that "the so-called international unions" were American-dominated, but he also pointed out that they were failing to meet the needs of workers for new forms of organization: "These old Unions were now disorganizing the workers, due to the determination of the old-line Labour Leaders to stick to the outmoded craft system of organization." As one organizer for the Council stated, there was ample scope for union efforts in a province where some employees worked ten to twelve hours a day for wages as low as $3 a week.[57] The rivalry between "old" and "new" unionism was not going to go away, and the new industrial unionism had significant effects on the Federation in the years ahead.[58]

Also on the horizon in these years was the threat of a worsening international situation and the spectre of a new world war. In 1938 the Federation convention was addressed by Dr. R.H. Wright of the Fredericton Peace Council, and in 1939 Whitebone commented directly on the need to open Canada's doors for "sorely oppressed minorities who are being persecuted in certain totalitarian European countries" and stated that "our sympathies are whole-heartedly with the movements under way to alleviate their sufferings and to find homes for those of them who are being forced to leave their native lands."[59] At the 1938 meetings, delegates called for an embargo on the export of war materials to Japan, and at the 1939 meetings a resolution called for the boycott of imports from Nazi or Fascist regimes, although it was adopted in a milder form than first proposed.[60]

At the end of the 1930s, workers, employers, and governments increasingly recognized that the promise of industrial legality had arrived in New Brunswick. The Federation's agenda had expanded during the 1930s. The devastation of unemployment in the early years of the Great Depression underlined the need for more aggressive government intervention in the economy. By the time of the strikes of 1937, New Brunswick workers were on the move, and the Federation was calling for the extension of union rights under the law. Although the Fair Wage Act had a limited effect and the Labour and Industrial Relations Act was only symbolic, the expectations of New Brunswick workers were rising. In the worst years of the Depression, there was support for the CCF, but the established parties had responded by once more presenting themselves as the friends of labour. By 1939 the Liberals could even claim the election of a "labour" candidate in the person of Campbellton machinist Samuel Mooers, who would later become minister of labour. Progress was painfully slow, but social legislation was advancing. Even the enactment of unemployment insurance was imminent — although it had taken an entire decade of unprecedented unemployment for Canada to begin to address the need. The most hopeful sign for organized labour at the end of the Great Depression was the desire of large numbers of workers to join unions and achieve greater security in their work. The years of war and reconstruction that followed would create renewed expectations for union recognition and for social and economic democracy.

AT THE FRONT The Second World War was a turning point for organized labour in Canada. In February 1945, an army officer discusses conditions at the front with a delegation from the Trades and Labour Congress, including (from left) J. A. Sullivan of the Canadian Seamen's Union, C. S. Jackson of the United Electrical Workers, TLC Vice-President James Whitebone, and Nigel Morgan of the International Woodworkers of America. In 1945 they were all on the same page as supporters of the war effort and the recognition of unions. Source: United Electrical, Radio and Machine Workers of America / Library and Archives Canada, PA-094333.

THREE

"A Province Fit *for* Heroes"   1940–1956

Defending Democracy

On 7 May 1945, James Whitebone prepared a radio broadcast to celebrate the victory of the Allied forces in Europe. In his talk he recalled his tour of the battlefields and his conversations with New Brunswick soldiers there. When they told him about their hopes for life in Canada after the war, said Whitebone, "their chief desire was to get an unpleasant job finished and get back home as quickly as possible. They had confidence that the people back home would not fail them." In this moment of triumph at the end of the war, Whitebone reminded fellow citizens of the challenges ahead: "We are all thankful and happy that at long last complete victory has been achieved by our forces over a bestial and ruthless enemy and we have every right to celebrate that victory; but we must not forget there is still a tremendous job to be done."[1]

More than five years earlier, in January 1940, delegates had assembled at the Brunswick Hotel in Moncton for the first convention of the Federation of Labour since the declaration of war. There were 79 accredited delegates from nine centres in attendance, a larger number than in any year since 1921, with the exception of the 91 delegates in 1939.[2] At this meeting the Federation pledged full support for the war effort. Their resolution stated that union members had a big stake in the outcome: "This war is being waged against the tyranny of dictatorship and in defence of those democratic principles of life so dear to the members of Organized Labor." In his address to the delegates, Whitebone warned that workers must protect their interests during the war and in the peace to follow: "It is no secret that the wage-earner is the one called upon to make the greatest sacrifice and bear the heaviest burdens in any war, not only during the actual days of conflict but throughout the inevitable period of depression after hostilities have ceased."[3]

For the duration of the war, the Federation supported a policy of "economic peace" with employers and governments. As Whitebone repeatedly pointed out, labour was offering "full cooperation with our Government in the crushing of the Axis tyranny that is menacing our country." Union members were enlisting in the services in large numbers and contributing generously to Victory Loans, and Whitebone pledged that the Federation would be making no "unreasonable requests" in wartime. In Whitebone's view, the unions should be a source of stability in the wartime economy, promoting cooperation and improving efficiency, even functioning as "a medium to prevent radical and ill-advised outbreaks."[4]

At the same time, he also warned that "we must be on guard that our readiness to lend fullest cooperation is not exploited." "Undue profiteering" had to be controlled, and governments should be expected to enforce labour standards and protect the rights of workers. At Bathurst, in October 1941, Whitebone congratulated northern workers on overcoming the "active antagonism of the lumber barons" and establishing "the splendid labor organizations here represented." He also praised the province's Fair Wage Board for exposing conditions in canning factories, where, he said, "women are paid as low as eight cents an hour and grown men fifteen cents an hour by unscrupulous and greedy employers." And with many new workers taking jobs in wartime industry, Whitebone called for an Apprenticeship Act — in order to avoid flooding the labour market with "an army of half-trained mechanics constituting a menace to labour standards and bringing chaos to industrial and economic conditions." As an example of progress in the right direction, union leaders welcomed the implementation of the federal government's Unemployment Insurance Act in 1941 — even though it had been such a long time in the making and arrived too late to address the unemployment of the Great Depression.[5]

Meanwhile, the cornerstone of provincial labour law, the Labour and Industrial Relations Act, remained far from satisfactory. At their convention in Edmundston in October 1940, the Federation called for an extensive review, and a similar resolution at Bathurst a year later called for amendments to enforce union recognition and collective bargaining and to extend union rights to public employees. By 1942, in Campbellton, Whitebone was protesting the failure of governments to consult with labour leaders about wartime policy. His objections were even stronger a year later at Milltown in 1943, where he stated that the government was creating "confusion and distrust" among workers: "In spite of Labor's splendid record during the war years and the fulfillment of every pledge of all-out support in the prosecution of the war, it is regrettable that we are still being shackled and discouraged." The delegates called for the adoption of a federal labour code providing uniform rights and standards for workers across the country.[6]

Such protests were not unique to New Brunswick. Wartime labour policy in Canada amounted to a patchwork of orders-in-council regulating the labour market, imposing wage controls, and prohibiting strikes — but still failing to deliver the right to union recognition and collective bargaining. Across Canada in 1943 there was more labour unrest than in any year of the war to date, causing a loss of more than one million working days. In New Brunswick, twenty-three strikes were reported in 1943, though they were short-lived and the impact was estimated at only five thousand working days.[7] In early 1944, the federal government finally responded to the unrest by introducing PC1003, an order-in-council requiring that union recognition and collective bargaining be accepted in workplaces where a majority of workers voted for a union. It was only a temporary wartime order, but it applied to most of the Canadian economy. In New Brunswick the provisions were administered by officials in the Department of Health and Labour. At the 1944 convention, Whitebone noted that New Brunswick was the first province to adopt enabling legislation and that unions were already securing good results.[8] In the first year PC1003 was in effect, twelve certification orders were issued in the province, including one that finally secured recognition for the United Mine Workers; another 117 locals were certified between 1945 and 1947.[9]

"A Blue-Print of Peace"

Postwar reconstruction was also on the Federation agenda throughout the war. As early as 1941, delegates adopted a resolution calling for "a blue-print of peace" for New Brunswick — just as Britain in the midst of the Blitz was already preparing plans "to build a greater and better Britain in the post war period." The language underlined the new expectations that were arising from the experience of the Depression and the war: "No hit or miss method is good enough for this Province as it should be able to give its boys who are bearing the brunt of war a chance to settle down and the opportunity of making a decent living in a Province fit for heroes to live in."[10] In 1942 the Federation adopted a Reconstruction Report that called for an enormous expansion of public spending at the end of the war. The purpose was to develop the province's resources and to provide a better quality of life for citizens, especially by improving municipal services, opening parks, clearing slums, building municipal housing, and assisting workers in home ownership. Additional resolutions called for the eight-hour day, a minimum wage for all women workers, free schoolbooks for students to the end of Grade

8, and the prohibition of full-time work for children under the age of sixteen.[11] By the summer of 1943, the province had appointed a Committee on Reconstruction, and the Federation submitted a brief that asked the central question on behalf of all New Brunswick workers: "Are we going to return to prewar conditions with all its privations and want amidst plenty?" The answer, said the Federation, was that the province needed "a complete new conception of social security, wherein everybody willing to work will be guaranteed a decent living."[12]

There was some evidence that the ever-cautious Liberal premier, J.B. McNair, was listening to labour's concerns. In September 1943 he assured delegates at the Federation convention that times were changing: "The whole trend of the times is for greater control of social and economic activities by the people themselves through their representative institutions. Call the movement socialism, socialization or social planning, whatever you will, certainly the system is on the march."[13] That year the province finally proclaimed the Mothers' Allowance Act, originally enacted in 1930, and in 1944 a new Apprenticeship Act was approved and the Workmen's Compensation Act was amended in order to bring both programmes up to national standards.[14]

The changing political climate in the province was also notable in the growing interest in the Co-operative Commonwealth Federation, which the Federation of Labour had originally helped organize in the province in 1933. There had been several breakthroughs in neighbouring Nova Scotia, where coal miner Clarie Gillis was elected to Parliament in 1940 and three CCF members were returned to the provincial legislature in 1941. By the last years of the war, CCF fortunes were on the rise across the country too, and in June 1944 Saskatchewan voters elected the country's first CCF government, led by the former MP and Baptist minister Tommy Douglas. By the time of the New Brunswick provincial election a few weeks later in August 1944, there were dozens of CCF clubs across the province. Instead of the single candidate who stood for office in 1939, the CCF nominated 41 candidates, only a little short of a full slate of 48. The party platform, promoted by publications such as

Maritime Commonwealth but rarely reported in the daily press, appealed for labour support, calling for legislation giving workers the right to unions of their own choice and for the representation of labour, farmers, and fishermen on all provincial boards. The party supported higher old age pensions and a federal system of free medical, hospital, dental, and nursing services. The "People's Party," as the CCF advertised itself, also called for "full development of provincial resources under public ownership for the benefit of the people of New Brunswick."[15]

MARITIME COMMONWEALTH A cartoon in the regional newspaper of the Co-operative Commonwealth Federation at the time of the 1944 provincial election depicted labour's anxieties about the capitalist economy's lack of social responsibility. The CCF promoted a social democratic platform, including "full development of provincial resources under public ownership for the benefit of the people of New Brunswick." Source: *Maritime Commonwealth*, 5 July 1944.

Among the CCF candidates in 1944 there was a notable union presence. The most prominent was the Federation's first vice-president, Roy Myles, a machinist from Local 594 in Moncton, who was one of the CCF candidates in Westmorland. The party leader, J. A. Mugridge, was a member of Local 502 of the International Brotherhood of Electrical Workers in Saint John. The CCF candidates also included J. D. Williams of the carpenters' union in Saint John, Moncton machinist Laurie K. MacNintch, Minto coal miner Frank Vandenbore, Atholville papermaker G. W. Yorston, and Edmundston loco-motive engineer Daniel Laboissonnière. When the results were counted, the CCF had won 68,248 votes — more than 13 percent of the provincial total. In Moncton and Saint John the party received 25 percent of the vote. The biggest success was in the predominantly Acadian county of Madawaska in the northwest, where the railwayman Laboissonnière and his running mate Harry Marmen, an electrical engineer employed by the town of Edmundston, received more than 32 percent of the vote; indeed, the working-class vote in Edmundston, one of the new union strongholds in the north of the province, supported the CCF so strongly that they won majorities in five of the town's ten polls. No CCF candidates were elected, however, and the 1944 results proved to be the high tide in the party's history.[16]

In the wake of the election, the McNair government renewed its attention to labour matters. A separate Department of Labour had been approved earlier in the year, and the premier himself served as the initial minister. Soon after the election, McNair assigned the portfolio to a card-carrying union member. The Liberal MLA for Restigouche since 1939, Samuel Mooers had worked for Canadian National as a railway machinist in Campbellton and had served as a union officer. He was a member of the International Association of Machinists for more than thirty years and, he had boasted to delegates at the Campbellton convention in 1942, was "still working with the tools."[17] At the spring session of the legislature in 1945, the most important decision on labour matters was the adoption of a new Labour Relations Act. This law continued most of the wartime provisions of PC1003 and established a New Brunswick Labour Relations Board to administer the recognition of unions and the conduct of collective bargaining in the future.[18] The new law was expected to ensure an orderly transition to provincial authority when wartime controls ended, and union leaders hoped it would at last repair the omissions and inadequacies of the 1938 laws.

During the later years of the war, delegates to the Federation meetings were encouraged by reports of increases in membership and affiliation. Whitebone had correctly predicted that membership would be rising during the war: "Every worker needs the union and will need it more than ever in the critical times following the war."[19] Union membership in the province increased from 13,936 in 1939 to 18,659 in 1946, and the Federation's affiliated membership almost doubled from 5,500 members in 1939 to 10,477 in 1946. Whitebone pointed to the strong representation of workers from unions in the pulp and paper mills in Edmundston, Atholville, Dalhousie, and Bathurst and from the textile mills in Moncton and Milltown. And in Fredericton in 1944, he welcomed Merelda Bourque and Lily Boudreau, both from the United Textile Workers of Canada in Moncton, the first women delegates to attend the convention since 1922. The presence of women delegates, however, did not become permanent until 1951, when women from a local of the Laundry Workers International Union attended, joined in 1952 by women telephone operators from Saint John who belonged to a local of the IBEW.[20] In 1946 Whitebone also noted that returned veterans were joining the union movement in large numbers, and he commended the unions that had kept members on the books in good standing while they served in the war.[21]

Industrial Unionism

For the Federation, there was also a challenge in the rising support for unions. Much of the growth was due to the expansion of new industrial unions not associated with the Federation. The final break between the Trades and Labour Congress and the Congress of Industrial Organizations in 1939 left some older unions, including the United Mine Workers, no longer eligible for membership in the Federation; they now belonged to a new body, established in 1940 as the Canadian Congress of Labour. The CCL's provincial branch, the New Brunswick Council of Labour, originally created by the All-Canadian Congress of Labour in 1935, was again active, and as a result there were now two rival labour centrals seeking to speak for the workers in the province. In 1947, for instance, the Federation reported that two large textile union locals had been lost to the rival federation and its Textile Workers Union of America, which caused a small net loss in Federation membership for the first time since the 1930s.[22]

The new industrial unions were led by dedicated and aggressive organizers who wanted to expand the union movement as never before. One of the leading figures was Angus MacLeod, who would later be a president of the Federation itself. Born in 1899, and only a few years younger than Whitebone, he had grown up within sight and sound of the Sydney steel plant in industrial Cape Breton in Nova Scotia. Unlike many working-class youth of his generation, MacLeod received a relatively good formal education and graduated from Sydney Academy. He started work at the Sydney Foundry at sixteen years of age, where he learned his trade as a machinist and joined

ANGUS MACLEOD A pioneer of industrial unionism in Saint John in the 1930s and 1940s, MacLeod (1899–1980) was a founder of the Maritime Marine Workers Federation: "Organized Labor refuses to believe that after this war we are going to be faced with the same conditions which existed before the war." Source: Courtesy of Judith Glover.

the International Association of Machinists. In 1921 MacLeod came to Saint John, where he worked as a machinist and mill operator at several industrial establishments, including the Saint John dry dock. By the 1930s, MacLeod was emerging as a local leader in Saint John who was never at a loss for a few salty words to defend fellow workers, on one occasion leading a delegation of unemployed workers to City Hall even though his employer threatened him with dismissal. During the war years, when the Saint John waterfront was busy with ship repairs and plans for vessel construction, MacLeod helped to build up the Industrial Union of Marine and Shipbuilding Workers of Canada. This union, committed to the principle "One Industry — One Union," represented hundreds of workers of different skills and trades in the Saint John shipyards.[23]

As the war came to a close, MacLeod articulated workers' expectations for the future at least as well as Whitebone: "Organized Labor refuses to believe that after this war we are going to be faced with the same conditions which existed before the war. We know that if the vast energies now used to wage war is [sic] utilized in the post-war period in the building of a permanent peace and in providing everyone with a decent standard of living, nothing will be impossible."[24] In March 1945 the union helped to found the Maritime Marine Workers Federation, which represented shipyard workers in both New Brunswick and Nova Scotia. Under the leadership of individuals such as J.K. Bell, who left Saint John for Halifax to become secretary-treasurer of this regional union, the Marine Workers became known for taking strong stands on issues such as the preservation of a Canadian merchant marine at the end of the war. MacLeod himself became president of the Marine Workers Federation later in 1945, and president of the New Brunswick Council of Labour when it was reorganized in 1946. As a regional representative for the CCL for the next several years, MacLeod was an enthusiastic organizer, issuing charters throughout the province to new groups of workers neglected by existing unions.[25]

As unions turned their attention to preserving wartime gains and shaping the peace, the wave of strikes across Canada in 1946 and 1947 reached levels not seen since the end of the First World War. In New Brunswick, however, the unrest was more limited than elsewhere. The province accounted for only 11,000 of the 4.5 million strike-days in Canada in 1946 and 73,000 of the 2.4 million strike-days in 1947.[26] There were local strikes of carpenters in Saint John and St. Stephen and truck drivers and freighthandlers on the Miramichi, but the two largest disputes involved New Brunswick workers in interprovincial campaigns. From February to June 1947, the 600 mineworkers at Minto and Chipman, as members of District 26 of the United Mine Workers, took part in a strike that included coal miners in both New

Brunswick and Nova Scotia. Although the union officers originally hoped to receive the same $1 a day increase that Dominion Steel and Coal agreed to in Nova Scotia, the New Brunswick miners were satisfied to accept a 75-cent increase from the local operators.[27] Later in 1947, some 150 employees of the Swift Canadian plant in Moncton participated in a strike by the United Packinghouse Workers of America that involved more than 14,000 workers across the country. The Moncton plant was one of the first to go out at the end of August, in a conflict that lasted until late October. This proved to be a successful example of industry-wide bargaining. The settlement established union security in the industry and reduced the working week to forty-four hours; it also achieved an increase of 10 cents an hour in wages, with some plants, including Moncton, receiving an additional 3 cents an hour.[28]

Workers in smaller establishments also fought hard for their gains. The fifty-two workers at the Chestnut Canoe factory in Fredericton, for instance, had a particularly difficult round of conflicts. When they formed a union local in April 1946, their main goals were to achieve pay for public holidays and one week's vacation. Once they had followed the procedures for certification, they ran into resistance from the employer. In February 1947, conciliation officer Charles Hughes gave his opinion that "the employers have no intention of ever reaching an agreement and are unwilling to compromise on even the smallest matters." By April the workers had nonetheless won an increase of 10 cents an hour, but the following year they were out on strike from May to August to win another raise. That summer, company president Maggie Jean Chestnut repeatedly attempted to ship canoes from the strikebound factory on York Street, and police were called out to assist. Meanwhile, in a demonstration of local solidarity, union workers from the Marysville cotton mill turned out in force to help block the gate. One local resident recalled a protest march in which strikers marched through town and burned an effigy in front of the Chestnut home on Waterloo Row. By July, organizer Angus MacLeod was calling on Premier McNair to intervene personally in the dispute, and in the end, after ninety-four days on strike, the workers received 8 cents an hour — the same amount recommended by a conciliation board prior to the strike.[29]

Industrial Legality

The new labour relations system at the end of the war, sometimes referred to as the "postwar compromise" between workers and employers, had definite limits.[30] From the point of view of the provincial Department of Labour, employers and unions had to learn to work within the provisions of the Labour Relations Act, which came into effect in May 1947. It required them to "negotiate in good faith with one another and make every reasonable effort to conclude a collective agreement."[31] This was not always easy to achieve. As the conciliator in one case noted, the employer stated flatly that "he would sign no agreement" and that "while he was paying the wage bills, he would have the final say on what they were to be . . . if this was not satisfactory to his employees, they could go elsewhere."[32] For their part, unions also faced restrictions: even after they applied for certification and held government-supervised votes to achieve recognition, there were no guarantees of reaching a successful collective agreement. If they wanted to pursue strike action, unions were required to proceed through a long conciliation process before they were in a "legal" position to go on strike; otherwise, union officers faced penalties under the act. Nonetheless, the compromises embedded in the new labour laws were taking hold and gaining acceptance. A study in the 1950s noted that from 1947 to 1951, 17 of the 25 strikes that took place under provincial jurisdiction were illegal; but from 1952 to 1956 there were fewer strikes, and only 3 of the 12 strikes were considered illegal.[33]

The Federation also found the new system less comprehensive than they had hoped. When the Labour Relations Act was in preparation in February 1945, Whitebone heatedly objected to the most significant omission — the definition of "employer" excluded provincial and municipal governments as well as the agencies, boards, and commissions they appointed. As a result, public employees would not be entitled to the same rights as other workers. In 1946 Whitebone used some of his strongest language to attack the "ridiculous and stupid policy" of excluding public employees: "It is difficult to understand why the Provincial Government persists in refusing to recognize and bargain with legitimate Unions of its own employees while enacting and attempting to enforce laws which required private employers to do so."[34] In 1948 the Federation's presentation to the cabinet went so far as to point out that there was good precedent for the "Crown" to be considered an "employer," as even His Majesty the King had "signed an agreement with employees of Buckingham Palace and Windsor Castle."[35] Resolutions objecting to the inferior status of public employees were adopted repeatedly at Federation conventions.[36]

There were additional exclusions when the provincial law was amended in 1949, although at the time these were not considered alarming to organized labour: the definition of "employees" excluded workers in domestic service, agriculture, hunting, or trapping, as well as managers or superintendents and members of the medical, dental, architectural, engineering, or legal professions.[37] Meanwhile, as one student of this period has explained, the achievement of "industrial legality" in postwar labour relations was accompanied by a shift to a form of "low-intensity conflict" in which workers' rights were subject to a variety of ad hoc designations, rulings, and judgments.[38] In one case in 1947, a Saint John company argued that 30 of their 60 office employees were engaged in "confidential" duties and should be excluded from the bargaining unit represented by Local 207 of the Office Employees International Union, which 51 of the workers had already joined; in situations such as this, Federation Secretary-Treasurer George Melvin noted, "the real desire of the company" was "to reduce the unit to a non-effective organization."[39]

Soon the Supreme Court of New Brunswick was also making decisions related to the new laws. When workers at the Gorton-Pew fish plant in Caraquet joined a union, they were among the first to fall victim to such rulings. In 1951, after a long set of manoeuvres about the definition of bargaining units and an attempt by the company to establish a company union, the Labour Relations Board finally certified Local 4 of the Canadian Fish Handlers Union to represent workers who had voted by a margin of 169 to 30 in favour of the union. However, a year later the court accepted an appeal by the company and reversed the certification on a number of procedural grounds, thus depriving the workers of the right to be represented by the union of their choice.[40] Another controversial decision applied to the members of the police force in

Fredericton, who had been represented since 1953 by the Fredericton Police-men's Federal Protective Association and had signed two collective agreements with the city after their certification by the board; during the bargaining process in 1955, however, the city appealed to the Supreme Court, which came to the conclusion that members of the police force in Fredericton could not be considered "employees" within the meaning of the act. As a result, their certification was also revoked.[41]

Judges were also prepared to issue court orders to assist employers who wanted to use replacement workers and break unions during strikes. One notable example arose from a picket-line confrontation in east Saint John, where one of the new industrial unions, Local 15 of the United Oil Workers, was seeking to negotiate a first collective agreement for some forty-five workers at the Irving Oil distribution plant. The workers had voted for the union in January 1948, and the union was duly certified in February; but by April there was still no contract, and after a conciliation board had proposed a draft agreement in September without success, the workers went on strike in November. On the second day of the strike, the workers were holding the line and blocking access in and out of the plant. When one truck driver refused to drive through the picket line, the employer himself took the wheel and ploughed through the line. While the rest of the strikers scrambled for safety, he was followed by two more vehicles that hit several pickets. According to one Department of Labour official, the employer in question, K. C. Irving, received a warning from the RCMP not to engage in reckless driving in the future. Two days after the incident, company solicitors obtained a court injunction that declared the picketing illegal and prohibited workers from continuing to obstruct operations at the plant. The strike ended in defeat soon afterwards.[42]

The new system of industrial legality was put to its most dramatic test on the waterfront in Saint John. At the centre of the story was the Canadian Seamen's Union, which had been organizing sailors since 1936 and was affiliated to the Trades and Labour Congress of Canada and in due course the New Brunswick Federation of Labour. The CSU came of age during the war, when hundreds of members served in the dangerous North Atlantic waters on merchant vessels that crossed the ocean in convoys to supply the Allied effort. With more than 1,100 sailors lost at sea, they were often described as Canada's "fourth fighting force" for their contributions to the war effort. The CSU was considered to be one of the more militant unions of the day, bringing in reforms such as the eight-hour watch and the union hiring hall; they were also notable for accepting black members in their ranks, demanding better foods, and challenging the petty tyrannies of shipboard officers. At the end of the war their union continued to bargain hard for the sailors. The CSU's militancy did not sit well with the shipping companies, who invited the American-based gangster-ridden Seafarers' International Union to enter Canada and sign "sweetheart" contracts.[43]

For the Federation of Labour, as for its parent body the TLC, this was a case of an outside union "raiding" a legitimate affiliate. In 1947 the Federation endorsed a resolution against admitting the SIU, and the following year a resolution offered financial and moral support to the CSU. The situation was complicated by the claim that many of the CSU leaders were Communists, and in 1948 even the conservative Whitebone felt obliged to defend himself ("I am not a communist and never have been") and to state that "if there are communists in our Labor Movement in New Brunswick as represented by this Federation, I do not know it."[44] Another complication was the desire of many shippers to transfer ownership of the fleet to offshore registries, effectively avoiding Canadian unions and labour standards and threatening the survival of a Canadian-owned merchant marine — a strategy fiercely opposed by the CSU and allies such as the Marine Workers Federation.

All this came to a head early in 1949, when the union's attempts to negotiate a new contract were fatally stalled, and the shipowners started signing agreements with the SIU and forcibly replacing existing union crews. The CSU members retaliated by adopting a form of direct action — refusing to abandon their ships and "sitting-in" on vessels as they tied up in ports around the world. In April 1949 there were 3,000 men on strike on 90 ships around the world — one New Brunswicker has recalled that he was

ON THE WATERFRONT The photograph captures a moment of truth in Canadian labour history. Saint John longshoremen supported the Canadian Seamen's Union during their final struggle for survival in 1949. On 5 May 1949, CSU port agent Eddie Reid (front left) appeals to longshoremen to respect their picket line on the Saint John waterfront, as did ILA 273 vice-president Frank Crilley (front right). CSU President Harry Davis (with hat) is protected by bodyguards. Source: New Brunswick Museum, 1989.6.l.

in Capetown, South Africa, when the strike started — on what has been described as the world's longest picket line. The three ships that were tied up in Saint John during the strike were the Ottawa Valley, Federal Trader, and Cotterill, which had just arrived from ports such as Jamaica and South Africa with about 100 union men on board. The Saint John Trades and Labour Council pledged "all out support" for the CSU, as did Local 273 of the International Longshoremen's Association, led by Vice-President Frank Crilley and President William Carlin, who declared: "Cross a legal picket line? Never!" For more than a month the longshoremen respected the sailors' picket line and refused to unload the strikebound ships. The tide turned when large gangs of strikebreakers were delivered to the docks by train, boat, and seaplane, and it took scores of outside police to fight their way onto the ships with baseball bats and pickhandles in order to expel the union members and replace them with scabs. Meanwhile, the ILA international headquarters had ordered the longshoremen to return to work and supported the election of new officers.[45]

This was an extraordinary outcome in which, contrary to the provisions of the new labour laws, unionized workers lost their right to be represented by an established union of their own choice. Few CSU members ever worked on the boats again, and the episode is remembered as one of the most shameful betrayals of union workers in Canadian history. At the 1949 meetings, Whitebone reported that the Federation's support for the CSU had been "rescinded" since the previous convention and that the Trades and Labour Congress had suspended the union. The Federation lost some 500 members as a result. It had been a "difficult period," Whitebone explained, but he argued that the fault was with the CSU, who stood accused of unlawful and violent tactics and interfering with the obligations of other unions: "Leaders of this union created a situation most injurious to the Labour Movement."[46]

Power and Politics

There was a more promising conclusion to the test of industrial legality in the 1952 provincial election campaign. The issue arose prior to the election, when Premier McNair declared that the government-owned New Brunswick Electric Power Commission would not negotiate an agreement with some four hundred employees who had joined the International Brotherhood of Electrical Workers. McNair insisted that public servants were not entitled to union rights under the law: "If the laws of New Brunswick are to be changed to permit the public servants of this province to join with an international union, and go out on strike when ordered, it must be done under a government representing some other political party." Although the workers might join an independent association, he stated, they were not entitled to the protections of the Labour Relations Act, and if any workers went on strike, they would be considered to have given up their employment. McNair warned that he was prepared to call an election on the issue: "The election will be the first in Canada with recognition of a government employees' union as a major issue. The nearest similarity occurred in 1937 when Mitchell Hepburn opposed entry of the C.I.O. into Ontario." Meanwhile, the IBEW members voted not to pursue strike plans immediately but to wait for the election, which McNair announced almost at once. As the reference to Hepburn's 1937 showdown with the automobile workers implies, McNair's reading of "liberalism" was now at odds with his earlier support for labour legislation in 1938. McNair now argued that the claim to bargaining rights for public employees was a challenge to the democratic way of life as he understood it: "In my view, no issue of such importance has arisen since the days when our forefathers fought for and won the right to responsible and representative government. It is a cardinal feature of Liberalism that the authority and power of the State — meaning the people — should be used to promote the common welfare."[47]

On such a fundamental issue, a full-scale confrontation with the government was unavoidable. Unlike the Oil Workers (who belonged to the rival New Brunswick Council of Labour) or the Canadian Seamen's Union (who had been judged by the labour establishment to be less than respectable), the IBEW was one of the most successful and influential unions of skilled workers in North America. Although only Saskatchewan had fully accepted the unionization of public employees, unions were a fact of life at power commissions in most Canadian provinces. By the time of the Federation meetings in Fredericton in September, the election campaign was in full swing, and the government was accusing the unions of working hand in glove with the Progressive Conservatives. There was some truth in this, as one of the IBEW leaders stated in July that the threat of a strike would be postponed "at the sincere request" of Hugh John Flemming, which enabled the Opposition leader to present himself as a moderating influence in labour relations. Moreover, a leader of the bricklayers' union was one of the party's candidates in Saint John and was said to be slated to become minister of labour in a new government.[48]

In addressing delegates at the 1952 convention, Whitebone stated that the government's refusal to recognize the IBEW was "a form of dictatorship as to what organization labor may belong to." He urged members to take this issue into account in the provincial elections the following week and to remember an old principle often applied by the American Federation of Labor: "Elect your friends and defeat your enemies."[49] Meanwhile, the Trades and Labour Congress of Canada, meeting in convention in Winnipeg, had also condemned the McNair government for "its red herring tactics in having made union recognition an election issue" and for statements "to the effect that employees of his government would not be permitted to hold membership in any organization having affiliations outside the province."[50]

When the returns came in, the Liberals had elected only sixteen members, and the Progressive Conservatives, with thirty-six seats, formed the government. In this highly polarized contest, in which a labour question was one of the central issues, the twelve CCF candidates received little more than 1 percent of the vote.[51] Within months after the election there was a collective agreement covering IBEW locals with members working for the Power Commission, signed and approved by the cabinet in February 1953. At the first session of the new legislature, the Labour Relations Act was amended to allow employees of government boards or commissions to be brought under the Act by order-in-council. The Progressive Conservative government later allowed municipalities and their boards to make similar provisions but failed to introduce recognition of union rights for all public employees.[52]

The new government acknowledged its debt to the unions when they named a new minister of labour. As predicted, Premier Flemming gave the position to an experienced labour leader who was elected as an MLA from Saint John. Art Skaling was a longtime leader of Local 1, New Brunswick, of the Bricklayers, Masons and Plasterers International Union; he had also served as president of the Saint John Trades and Labour Council for many years and was a familiar figure at Federation meetings.[53] Under Skaling's administration, the new government also acted on several of the Federation's other legislative demands. A Fair Wages and Hours Act, which applied to standards on government contracts, was adopted in 1953. The next year, two new employment standards laws were enacted, again responding to concerns that the Federation had advanced. The Weekly Rest Period Act required that employees be given at least one day's rest in seven, thus giving "the weekend" statutory recognition as an employment right; in addition, the Vacation Pay Act provided that employees were entitled to one week of paid vacation time per year.[54] The province in 1956 also adopted a Fair Employment Practices Act to protect workers against discrimination on the basis of "race, national origin, colour or religion."[55] When the province's Supreme Court ruled against the recognition of police officers as "employees," the Federation secured an amendment to the Labour Relations Act in 1956 that confirmed the power of municipalities to act as "employers" with respect to the police.[56]

In the years after the 1952 election, there was a new level of satisfaction in Whitebone's speeches to the Federation. Minister Skaling's continued attendance at the annual Federation meetings, and the equally frequent presence of federal Minister of Labour Milton Gregg (the former University of New Brunswick president who was the senior cabinet minister for New Brunswick), were indications that the voice of labour was being heard in government.[57] In 1954, Whitebone reported "a very substantial increase in membership" and claimed that in proportion to population "New Brunswick is one of the most highly organized Provinces in Canada." However, there was still work for the Federation to do. The Federation boasted 140 affiliated locals, but there were another 80 local unions eligible for affiliation that had not taken the step towards greater solidarity: "Some local officers appear to believe that membership in the Federation does not offer any benefits or advantages to their members and they cannot see any advantage in recommending affiliation to their membership. This line of reasoning is directly in opposition to the fundamentals of Trade Unionism. We are banded together for the common good, not for the benefit of a few, and if as some maintain, there is no direct benefit to an individual or a single local union, surely such individual or union would not be so selfish as to withhold support to those who may not be so fortunate themselves."[58]

The Federation leaders also addressed the challenges of protecting and promoting economic development in the province. There was support for mining development in the north and for new electric power developments. One common theme was the need to build a Chignecto Canal, a project much discussed in the history of the region, that would strengthen the regional economy by allowing ships to pass between the Bay of Fundy and Northumberland Strait. The St. Lawrence Seaway was expected to benefit Central Canada handsomely, and the Chignecto Canal was considered an equivalent project for the Maritime provinces.[59] The most aggressive responses to regional underdevelopment came from the new industrial unions associated with the New Brunswick Council of Labour. From the end of the war onwards, the Marine Workers Federation called repeatedly for stabilization of the shipbuilding industry and protection of the Canadian merchant fleet, which they considered to be matters of local, regional, and national interest; they criticized employers for failing to seek new contracts for shipyard work at the end of war and called for a national policy for shipbuilding and shipping to build a new deep-sea Canadian fleet.[60]

A notable struggle to protect local employment took place in Milltown, where Local 858, Textile Workers Union of America, led community opposition to the closure of the cotton mill, which was one of the largest mills in the country and had been at the centre of the local economy since the time of the National Policy in the 1880s. As the government removed tariff protection for the industry and the Canadian market faced new competition, companies such as Canadian Cottons were closing down mills all across eastern Canada. In Milltown, however, the union helped to undertake an innovative experiment in industrial democracy. With full support from the union, the Milltown Textile Cooperative took over production in 1954. Three years later, however, the mill was still in trouble. Without support from provincial or federal governments for such efforts in community-based economic development, the mill was finally forced to close.[61]

House of Labour

Meanwhile, there were efforts to set aside rivalries in the house of labour in order to strengthen the union movement in Canada. A "no-raiding" pact was concluded between the TLC and CCL unions in 1954. This was a first step, said Whitebone, towards "one great Labor Centre" that would repair existing divisions. "It is not natural that rivalry should exist in Labor's family," he said, "and I am sure we would all be most happy to work together in complete unity in the common cause." The Federation and the council also cooperated in calling on the province to support the federal government's plan to cover hospital and diagnostic services for all citizens, an important stage in the establishment of medicare in Canada. Although the merger was approved at the TLC convention in June 1955, Whitebone still remained cautious at the time of the Federation meetings in September that year. He reported that amalgamation of the two labour centrals was well underway but that there was no need to be "stampeded into regrettable actions," and he did not recommend any further action until the merger was completed at the national level.[62]

A year later, when delegates assembled in the ballroom of the Brunswick Hotel in Moncton at the end of August 1956, it was in many ways the end of the "old" Federation of Labour originally chartered by the TLC in 1914. On the first day, the only living past president of the Federation, Célime Melanson, was briefly introduced (and mistakenly referred to as the first president of the Federation); he received "an enthusiastic welcome" from the delegates — but for all but a few he was a relatively unfamiliar figure from the past.[63]

The delegates in attendance at this forty-fourth convention in 1956 seemed to represent a new level of maturity for the Federation. There were 179 accredited delegates from 20 different locations in attendance, and there were 83 locals represented, more than double the number in 1940.[64] This was the first convention at which Moncton delegates outnumbered (by one) those from Saint John. Although 65 percent of the delegates came from the three largest cities, workers from the north were strongly represented, including 13 delegates from Dalhousie, 10 from Bathurst, and 7 from Edmundston. There were also a rising number of delegates from the public sector, who accounted for one in five delegates, an early hint of their future importance in the Federation. Most of them were from the TLC's directly chartered federal labour unions, an organizational form used to organize "new" workers in situations where there were no existing affiliates for them to join. The public sector representatives came from all three levels of government: they included 21 delegates from the province's Department of Public Works and 9 delegates from municipal employees (and 4 from the Policemen's Protective Association in Saint John) as well as 3 delegates from a storage depot operated by the Department of National Defence. There were also a larger number of Acadians, who accounted for a total of 30 delegates, most of them from northern communities. The most prominent was Rolland Blanchette, one of the leaders of the pulp and paper workers union at the Fraser mill in Edmundston.[65] Although women had been present at the meetings every year since 1951, they remained significantly under-represented. They accounted for only five of the delegates (three from the telephone operators and two from the laundry workers), less than 3 percent of the total.[66]

By the time of the August convention, changes were well underway in the world of organized labour in Canada. The TLC had entered the new Canadian Labour Congress at a founding convention in April that year (and Whitebone was elected one of the regional vice-presidents). However, Whitebone was careful to reassure delegates that the Federation was not going out of existence. There would be continuity, and the merger would simply heal a split "which never should have occurred in the first instance." Now, Whitebone told delegates, "we may plan to go forward, in full united effort, in pursuit of the purposes to which we are dedicated, promotion of the welfare and protection of the interests of the working men and women of New Brunswick, of the Province as a whole and of the communities in which we live and work."[67]

Officers of the Federation and the council had already agreed that the combined organization would retain the name of the New Brunswick Federation

MR. LABOUR James Whitebone was president of the Federation longer than any other individual. By the 1950s, he was known to many New Brunswickers as "Mr. Labour": "He was a doer, not a shouter, although he could shout with the best of them if the circumstances demanded it." Source: Provincial Archives of New Brunswick, New Brunswick Federation of Labour fonds, MC1819, box 192.

of Labour. It was also agreed that there were would be no promises of executive positions in the newly renovated NBFL; officers would be chosen by delegates to the first merged convention the next year. These considerations went some distance towards allaying any worries that the Federation was in danger of losing ground in the merger. In fact, there was little to fear from numbers. In response to a delegate's question, Secretary-Treasurer Ralph Evans of the New Brunswick Council of Labour reported that their organization had an approximate membership of 4,000 people in 28 locals. This confirmed the fact that the Federation, with a membership of more than 15,000 at this time, was much larger than its rival.[68]

When New Brunswick Council of Labour President Angus MacLeod was invited to address the convention, his remarks were reassuring. He stated that the council had agreed to the merger without any special concessions and only the hope that "past differences will be forgotten and that the working people we represent will benefit from the merger." Nonetheless, he made no apologies for the part they had played in provincial labour history: "We admit we are smaller and do not have the same history in this Province as your Federation, but I think our record stands up well with regard to efforts to better the conditions of workers. There is an old saying that it is not the size of the dog in the fight but the size of the fight in the dog that counts. I think our organization, though young in comparison to yours, has proven itself worthy."[69]

On this basis, delegate John Simonds of the Sugar Refinery Workers Union in Saint John presented a motion to approve the merger. Simonds was an interesting choice for the occasion. Delegates were aware that only a few months earlier, he had been walking a picket line in subzero temperatures along with seven hundred other workers at the huge industrial site on the south end of the harbour. His union, a direct charter local of the TLC affiliated to the Federation, had gone through several incarnations since the early days of the Atlantic Sugar refinery in the 1910s and then as an ACCL union in the 1930s. When negotiations for a contract broke down in August 1955, a conciliation board unanimously supported the union's call for a 44-hour week and a union shop, and the workers went out on strike at the start of December. Carpenters and other construction workers refused to cross the line, and retailers worried about the supply of sugar from the region's only refinery. This was an impressive demonstration of labour solidarity, but it was not enough to fully win the day. The workers went back with small raises in pay and reductions in hours, but the cause of union security (in this case a requirement that workers become union members after four months on the job) was not achieved. Clearly there were still battles to be won, but the support for the refinery workers was evidence that the "old" Federation, following the example of the Council of Labour, was prepared to take up the cause of industrial unionism.[70]

The unity motion was adopted by a unanimous vote, and Whitebone invited the President of the new Canadian Labour Congress, Claude Jodoin, to address the convention. Welcoming the Federation into the CLC, Jodoin asserted (not entirely correctly) that the New Brunswick Federation was the oldest provincial federation of labour in existence in Canada. He paid tribute to the courage and perseverance of the founders of the union movement in Canada — as well as "younger" pioneers such as Whitebone. New Brunswickers could be proud of their place in Canadian labour history, said Jodoin, including their part in achieving workmen's compensation, unemployment insurance, and other social legislation: "Not so long ago in this country of ours, Organized Labour was considered in many spheres of our society as being just a plain conspiracy. All kinds of legislation that was suggested in those days was considered preposterous." He also had a message of reconciliation for delegates, in which he appealed to the metaphor of the family: "If we have differences of opinion and differences of principal [*sic*] on certain matters, let us discuss our own problems in our own home, in one single house of Labour." With more than one million union members, Jodoin declared, the Canadian Labour Congress would continue to "organize the unorganized" and fight for "full employment, and the highest possible standard of living."[71]

Although Whitebone would remain president of the Federation for several more terms, the humorous references to his "youth" in 1956 hinted that the Whitebone era was coming to a close. As Whitebone sometimes recalled, he had joined his first union in 1912 — a year before the Federation of Labour was organized. Much had happened since then, and an older generation of leaders was withdrawing from the scene. The loss of George Melvin, who had served as secretary-treasurer of the Federation almost without interruption from 1918 until his death in 1954, weighed heavily on Whitebone. He paid tribute to Melvin with words from the Bible —"well done thou good and faithful servant"— which were later inscribed on the memorial erected by the unions at Fern Hill cemetery in Saint John. Melvin and other pioneers were given a minute's silent tribute at the 1956 convention.[72]

At this time Whitebone was still looking ahead, certain that the Federation had need of his long experience and cautious leadership. At the closing session, he announced that the 1956 convention was "the finest convention we have ever held" and expressed his belief that "decisions arrived at here would have far-reaching effect on the working people of New Brunswick whom we were here representing."[73] Meanwhile, Henry Harm, a veteran unionist from the Dalhousie paper mill who was now the CLC's director for the Atlantic Region, predicted big increases in union membership in the years ahead: "In the Atlantic Provinces we are making great progress in organizing the unorganized. . . . With continuance of the support and assistance we have had from your Federation, and the co-operation of Federations in the other Maritime Provinces, we will set an example for the people in the rest of Canada."[74]

NEW FACES There was a new level of confidence among delegates to the annual meetings in the years after the formation of the Canadian Labour Congress. The level of union membership more than doubled between the 1950s and the 1970s. The Federation represented a majority of union members in the province and was a force to deal with in provincial affairs. Source: Provincial Archives of New Brunswick, New Brunswick Federation of Labour fonds, MC1819, box 192.

FOUR

"The New Unionism"

Equal Opportunities

When Premier Louis J. Robichaud addressed delegates at the New Brunswick Federation of Labour convention in the ballroom of the Brunswick Hotel in Moncton at the end of August 1965, he presented himself as a friend and ally of the union movement. From the start, speaking in French, he declared his respect for the mission of organized labour: "Je considère très important le mouvement que vous avez entrepris et j'ai à coeur les intérêts de tous les travailleurs, de tous les ouvriers du Nouveau-Brunswick." He also paid tribute to former president James Whitebone, who had been honoured for his long service earlier in the day, briefly joking that Whitebone probably did not understand him when he spoke in French. For the rest of the hour, Robichaud followed his text in deliberate and articulate English, elaborating on the theme that the provincial government and the Federation must continue to "work together on the common ground of improving the lot of the citizens of New Brunswick."[1]

Turning to history, Robichaud quoted Thomas Carlyle, the great nineteenth-century social critic of the British Industrial Revolution: "A man willing to work and unable to find work is perhaps the saddest sight that fortune's inequality exhibits under the sun." "This sight," said Robichaud, "is no less sad today than it was in Carlyle's time. Today we do not ascribe it to fortune's inequality. We see it as a social waste and are determined to end it." This could only be achieved, he said, by recognizing that modern New Brunswick was in the middle of a social and economic revolution as dramatic as the Industrial Revolution of the previous century and as daunting as the challenge of decolonization in the modern world: "Most nations today are development minded. The less developed countries which have been poor and stagnant for centuries are in a state of revolt against poverty, disease and dominance by stronger nations. They are no longer disposed to entrust their future exclusively to the forces of the market, the whims of nature or the judgement of colonial rulers."[2]

Robichaud's cautious allusion to a rhetoric of decolonization implied that the province was on the road to a kind of liberation from the limited visions of the past. Economic growth in New Brunswick had been accelerating since 1945, he said, but the province needed major improvements in training and education. Furthermore, New Brunswick workers needed better working conditions and wages, and regional disparities would have to be addressed as never before: "We will have to recognize that the wage gap between the Atlantic Region and the rest of Canada must close. If we ignore this fact we will merely train for export." In short, future economic growth would depend not just on natural resources and industrial activity but also on investment in the people of the province. Modern development, Robichaud concluded, was not just an economic matter but the opportunity to enrich provincial society in all respects:

Human resource development is the process of increasing the knowledge, the skills, and the capacity of all of the people in a society. In economic terms, it could be described as the accumulation of human capital and its effective deployment in the development of an economy. In political terms, human resource development prepares people for adult participation in society, particularly as citizens in a modern democracy. From the social and cultural point of view the development of human resources helps people to lead fuller and richer lives, less bound by tradition.[3]

This commitment to social change was a welcome message for the labour delegates. They understood that Robichaud's social outlook had been framed by his modest origins in an Acadian family in Kent County. Like many New Brunswickers, Robichaud wanted his province to join the modern march of progress. His education by reform-minded teachers at Laval University had convinced him that enlightened public policies and an interventionist state could make a difference. In the 1960 election campaign, Robichaud had already appealed for labour support by promising to pass an Equal Pay Act to ensure better pay for women workers, and he had promised to pay for the province's new hospital insurance plan without imposing premiums. By 1965 his Programme of Equal Opportunity, sometimes described as New Brunswick's parallel to the Quiet Revolution in Québec, was hitting its stride with plans for higher standards of education, health, and services. Such reforms served the purposes of employers and governments who wanted to modernize the economy, but they were also elements of the modern welfare state with its promise of greater security and higher standards. The Federation of Labour had been pursuing these kinds of social democratic goals from its earliest years, and those in the union movement in the 1960s came to see Premier Robichaud as a partner in advancing their own agenda for social reform.[4]

The expectation that labour was coming into its own in New Brunswick had been there since the end of the Second World War, but the province still had a long way to go. When a University of New Brunswick economics student

completed a survey of wages, hours, and working conditions in 1957, he came
to the conclusion that most workers in the woods, mining, agriculture, and
manufacturing in the province did not earn the "standard wage" of $900 a
year required to support a family.[5] Government reports repeatedly indicated
that New Brunswick citizens had incomes about one-third lower than the
Canadian average, placing them behind all provinces but Newfoundland and
Prince Edward Island.[6] Yet, there were hopes at the end of the 1950s that
the tide was beginning to turn. According to a new magazine published by
the Canadian Labour Congress, there were signs of a "New Day" in New
Brunswick based on new industrial developments. The power of the St. John
River was being harnessed at Beechwood, the pulp and paper mills were
expanding in several parts of the province, and there were new lead, zinc,
and silver discoveries in the north.[7]

New Brunswick workers wanted unions to be part of this new wave of
progress in the province. During the 1950s and the 1970s, they were joining
unions in large numbers, and collective bargaining was becoming an accepted
part of the world of work. Between 1957 and 1962, a total of 182 new union
locals were certified to represent workers; between 1963 and 1968 the total
was 400, with a record of 101 locals certified in 1966 alone.[8] The number
of union members in the province more than doubled from 31,421 in 1958
to 79,161 in 1975. This indicated a substantial rise in union density, from
17.2 percent of the workforce in 1958 to 31.1 percent in 1975.[9] As the principal
voice of labour in the province, the Federation was also rising to new levels.
The affiliated membership, reported at 16,169 members in 1957, showed steady
gains, rising to 27,882 members by 1968 and 44,545 members by 1975. The
"new unionism" of the times led workers to believe that the unions could
produce benefits for all citizens. In a Labour Day tribute in 1960, a local
weekly newspaper in northern New Brunswick captured these expectations
in a cartoon with the title "Getting to the Top with an Experienced Guide!";
it showed "Organized Labour" as the lead climber advancing up the side of
a mountain called "Higher Living Standard."[10]

Whitebone vs. MacLeod

When the Federation's first "merged convention" met at the Lord Beaverbrook Hotel in Fredericton in 1957, the event was considered a new beginning for the organization, and Fredericton Labour Council President W. Arthur MacLean presented Whitebone with a new wooden gavel for the occasion. Following adoption of a new constitution, Whitebone stated that "this is the starting point of bigger and better things."[11] Mayor William Walker of Fredericton, who was elected that year with labour support, endorsed the Federation's effort to "obtain economic justice for those you represent." Premier Hugh John Flemming also acknowledged the importance of the Federation, and Minister of Labour Arthur Skaling, the veteran union member, reviewed the record of the provincial government and stated: "Present high wage levels, shorter hours, pension plans and other benefits are convincing evidence of your growing strength. The growing body of social legislation indicates the extent of your influence in public affairs."[12]

There was less self-congratulation when Angus MacLeod, the former president of the New Brunswick Council of Labour, addressed the delegates. There was "much propaganda about the prosperity in the Province," he said, but he warned against

OFFICIAL PROCEEDINGS OF THE

1st MERGED CONVENTION

NEW BRUNSWICK FEDERATION OF LABOUR, C.L.C.

FREDERICTON, N. B.
AUGUST 26th, 27th, 28th, 1957

THE MERGER When the New Brunswick Council of Labour merged with the New Brunswick Federation of Labour in 1957, there was continuity as well as change. Source: NBFL *Proceedings*, 1957.

concluding there was little left for labour to achieve. He pointed to the recent shutdown at the Milltown cotton mill and the near-idle dry dock in Saint John as examples of wasted opportunity and governmental failure: "No concrete action will come until we of the Labour movement take some definite action to remedy the situation." In all their history, MacLeod told the delegates, "there have been no advancements, no benefits, obtained by working people without a struggle and sacrifice." Whether it was workers' compensation or unemployment insurance or any other benefit or reform, "We have not been handed anything by governments or any group without a struggle. . . . We are not going to be given anything unless we fight for it, one way or another." He also urged delegates not to accept the claim that workers in the province and the region did not have the right to a standard of living comparable to workers in other parts of Canada: "The sorry part of it is that in many cases the Labour movement has accepted that. . . . But have any of us ever heard an employer saying that 'My business is not entitled to the same percentage of profit on my investment as that of a similar employer in Upper Canada'?"[13]

Two years later, MacLeod replaced Whitebone as president. At the Federation meetings in Edmundston in September 1959, there were few signs that Whitebone's leadership was in question. His presidential report drew attention to the enactment of the province's Hospital Care Insurance Act and to the continued need to improve laws such as the Vacation Pay Act, which still excluded many workers from even one week's paid vacation. He repeated the Federation's appeal for union rights for public sector workers. He spoke too at length on developments in Newfoundland, where the provincial government had adopted "the most vicious type of anti-labour legislation ever enacted in this country" in order to break a strike by the province's loggers, represented by the International Woodworkers of America. In response to the Escuminac Disaster, when thirty-five men and boys were lost at sea when their fishing boats were overcome in a storm on Miramichi Bay, he offered condolences to the widows and children and appealed for donations to the Fishermen's Disaster Relief Fund: "Labour has close kinship with these hardy people." A collection was taken up at the convention and matched from Federation funds.[14]

The only issue that provoked extended debate was a resolution on political action. Some controversy had been expected, as the Canadian Labour Congress was preparing the ground for the creation of a "New Party" to replace the CCF with a political party that would be a more effective voice for Canadian workers and other "liberally minded" citizens. When the convention opened at the New Royal Hotel in Edmundston, a civic welcome was delivered by Mayor Harry Marmen, who in 1944 had been one of the most successful CCF candidates in the history of the province. The most notable guest speaker was Stanley Knowles, the longtime CCF MP from Winnipeg who was now a CLC vice-president and travelling across the country to promote the "New Party." Knowles had a union background as a printer (and his mother had grown up in Saint John, the daughter of a domestic servant), but he was best known as a contemporary of Tommy Douglas, Canada's most successful socialist politician, with whom he had been a fellow student at Brandon College in the 1920s. In his address to the delegates, Knowles argued that the union movement had a large social responsibility: "Labour is not just a group seeking its own ends, but across the years has been a social force winning better conditions for all the people of the country." Political action was required because the unions must work both "economically and politically": "In the labour movement we have so much to do that we must not tie one arm behind our back." Delegates were well aware that, as Knowles pointed out, most of the resolutions on the Federation agenda related to issues that required political action. The real controversy was whether unions could achieve the best results by supporting existing parties or by formal affiliation to a new party. When the Resolutions Committee presented a statement in favour of continuing to "take a non-partisan part in politics," a 90-minute debate followed. When a roll call vote was taken, the resolution of non-partisanship was approved by a vote of 83 to 31.[15]

Whitebone was with the majority on this issue, but the following day the delegates unexpectedly voted to replace him as president. Many were obviously wondering if Whitebone was ready to provide continued leadership into the decade of the 1960s.[16] Meanwhile, MacLeod had shown himself to be an informed and experienced advocate. The fact that MacLeod had opposed the "non-partisan" resolution served notice on the "old" parties not to take labour's support for granted. MacLeod defeated Whitebone by a small margin, a vote of 64 to 57. After twenty-seven consecutive years in office, Whitebone was suddenly cast aside. Delegates could see a few tears in his eyes as he reminisced briefly about the history of the Federation and stated his pride in their achievements: "We have made a big contribution and we have gained a position of respect and prestige, not only in the labour movement, but with the general public." [17]

1959 Angus MacLeod (seated, second from left) became president of the Federation in 1959. Other executive members included (seated, from left) W. A. MacLean, Fredericton; James H. Leonard, Saint John; Charles A. Malchow, Bathurst; and (standing, from left) Frank W. Murray, Saint John; Ralph J. Boyd, Moncton; Michael J. Kenny, Newcastle; and Rolland Blanchette, Edmundston. Source: *Telegraph-Journal* Archives.

MacLeod's own term of office proved to be surprisingly short. By the time of the next convention, one delegate was stating that the past year had set the union movement back twenty years, and "as a result organized labour has lost its position of respect in this province."[18] This was an exaggeration, as MacLeod and other officers continued to promote the Federation's views on public issues and lobby the government to act on their resolutions. MacLeod's report as president reviewed several legal controversies, including one in which union certification was withheld after the employer appealed to the province's Supreme Court. He also noted that unemployment was rising and that governments should not be allowed to ignore these needs: "If private enterprise cannot provide employment at decent wages for all willing and able to work, then it is the responsibility of government at all levels to do so."[19]

The biggest surprise in MacLeod's term of office was his decision to accept nomination in the 1960 provincial election as one of the four Liberal candidates in Saint John. In election publicity that summer, the Liberals took full advantage and described him as a "labour candidate on the Liberal ticket." MacLeod was quoted as stating that the Flemming government had taken no action on labour's most important demands but that the Liberals would deliver results: "I have been given the assurance by my fellow candidates that the major demands of labour will be enacted and it is for this reason only that I offer as a Liberal candidate in the election on behalf of the working people."[20]

MacLeod's claim that if elected he would "speak officially for labour" in the legislature was partly a response to the failure of the Progressive Conservatives, since the death of Skaling in May, to include an identifiable "labour" candidate on their slate in Saint John. MacLeod himself may have been hoping to become minister of labour in a Robichaud government. The announcement of his nomination prompted Whitebone to write directly to CLC Secretary-Treasurer Donald MacDonald to state that MacLeod's actions had created "a terrific furore among our people here" and that he needed to know whether the CLC approved of this and "if so, how does this square with Congress' attitude towards the proposed new party, to say nothing of Mr. MacLeod's open support of the said new party." There was no direct response from Ottawa, but in an internal memo MacDonald noted: "We should not make any statement thru Jim but I think we should consider issuing some sort of release or circular stating the CLC endorses no candidates in N.B., or at least no Liberal candidates."[21] There were no CCF candidates at all in the provincial election that year. In Saint John, MacLeod proved his appeal by receiving a final count of 8,846 votes, a substantial result for a labour candidate of any description, but in this case not enough to win election. Even with four seats in Saint John, the voters supported the incumbent Conservatives, even as the Liberals came to power with a strong majority.[22]

MacLeod's position was increasingly awkward by the time of the Federation convention in Campbellton at the end of the summer. It was expected that Whitebone would attempt to reclaim the presidency. Then, to MacLeod's embarrassment, the delegates learned that the Federation's financial affairs were in disarray. There was no report from Secretary-Treasurer James Leonard, who had not performed his duties for several months and had left the province; instead, an auditor appointed by the CLC reported that irregularities and missing documents made it impossible to give the Federation a clean financial bill of health. The auditor noted that prior to the convention, MacLeod had personally made restitution of $2,300 to the accounts, which covered all but $50 of the funds that were not accounted for by himself and the secretary-treasurer. At the start of the convention, MacLeod addressed the delegates in a closed session, taking personal responsibility for the situation. According to the convention report, "He said the Federation had had a busy year and he had no apologies to make in this regard. He knew what he had done was wrong and asked that the delegates think of his record and exercise forbearance in their criticism of him." Then he turned the chair over to one of the veteran vice-presidents, Michael Kenny of Newcastle, and departed for Saint John.[23]

Whitebone's return to office was opposed by two candidates. Both represented a younger generation of union members who wanted to continue the transition to new leadership. One of them was a local leader from Dalhousie, Aurèle Ferlatte, who had joined his first union, the Canadian Seamen's Union, when he served on Canadian merchant vessels during the Second World War.

He returned to the province after the end of the war and became an active member of the International Brotherhood of Pulp, Sulphite and Paper Mill Workers at the International Paper mill. Meanwhile, in Fredericton, Phillip Booker was a local youth who had worked in the lumber industry before going into the air force in 1939; he later joined the Fredericton police and was active in the labour council as well as in the police union, which became a local of the National Union of Public Employees. At the start of the 1960 convention, Booker introduced the union's national director R.P. Rintoul, who had presented a charter to the New Brunswick Division of NUPE at their convention in Bathurst a few days earlier. Both Ferlatte and Booker were already playing their part in provincial labour history and had substantial support, but neither was able to defeat Whitebone. In a three-way contest, Whitebone received a majority of the votes on the first ballot.[24]

None of this controversy helped to advance the "New Party." When the New Democratic Party was founded in August 1961, only a handful of New Brunswick union delegates attended the Ottawa convention. Later the same month there was more heated debate at the Federation meetings in Moncton. The Resolutions Committee failed to endorse any of the resolutions submitted in support of the NDP, and many delegates lined up at the microphones to speak their piece. Ferlatte pointed to the recent provincial election results: "Where are the Labour men in the Liberal party? There was not one elected. We are a vast majority in the population but we are not represented in the political parties. Every government is made up of lawyers, doctors and professionals." Normand Bourque of Moncton stated that "when the pioneers organized unions they were called idiots, but today we are unionized. Today we enter another field, and who can say we should not have our rights in politics." Fred Hodges of Saint John added: "All that is being asked is that we endorse the New Democratic Party and if we do not endorse it all Canada will be laughing at us tomorrow." On the other side of the debate, Ken Hussey of the paper mill workers in Bathurst noted that his union's constitution prohibited "political or religious agitation" at union meetings. Yvon LeBlanc of the Moncton machinists argued that labour's role should be to strengthen the union movement by promoting the training and education of members, not to build a political party. Vice-president Kenny stated that individuals had every right to be politically active, but "by endorsing the New Party, all they do is make a political machine of the Federation, which it was never intended to be."[25]

As chair of the convention, Whitebone was determined to avoid deepening the conflict. At the next morning's session, he objected to the report of the previous day's debate in the *Telegraph-Journal*, which had stated that the Federation was "split" and that the issue was "too hot to handle." In fact, said Whitebone, there had been an orderly debate, which was not about "affiliation" as such but about endorsement of the new party. This was a somewhat misleading distinction, as the original resolutions had called for the Federation to encourage member unions to affiliate to the party. However, the Resolutions Committee seized on this approach, and the delegates were asked to adopt a substitute resolution to support the "principles and policies" of the NDP "without direct affiliation."[26] Whitebone then indicated that there had been sufficient discussion on the previous day and ruled further debate out of order. A few hands were raised against the compromise, but to Whitebone's satisfaction, the resolution was adopted. As he subsequently explained, the NDP's policies were "almost identical to those the Federation has adopted from time to time through the years and I fail to see how the Federation could not endorse its own policies." Despite Whitebone's skillful handling of the issue, the *Telegraph-Journal* reported the Federation had failed to support "a resolution more favorable to the new left-wing party," and the next day's headline stated: "New Party Fails to Get Full Support in N.B."[27]

By this time, the new Liberal government was already beginning to address some of labour's expectations. The Minister of Labour, Kenneth J. Webber, was not a union man like Skaling, but he had grown up in a union town, St. Stephen, and worked there as a customs officer prior to his election. At the 1961 convention, he boasted that one of the first laws passed by the Robichaud government was the Female Employees Fair Remuneration Act, which prohibited an employer from paying women workers at a lower rate than a man doing the same work. In 1965 he was also able to report that the province's minimum wage standards no longer discriminated between male and female employees as they had in the past; however, it remained the case that different minimum rates applied in several sectors.[28] The Robichaud government also passed a number of small amendments to the Labour Relations Act that had far-reaching consequences. One provided that municipal employees now fell within the scope of the legislation "without option on the part of a municipal authority." This had the effect of making collective bargaining rights available to all municipal employees, including those working for hospital and school boards. Another amendment permitted both employers and unions to file charges concerning violations of the act, effectively spreading responsibility for the labour relations system beyond the departmental bureaucracy.[29] On a more critical note, Whitebone stated in 1961 that some three hundred employees had lost their jobs when the Liberals took power and the Federation planned to pursue test cases in order to challenge a "vicious and outdated institution which perpetuates the old belief that 'to the victors belong the spoils.'"[30]

Whitebone continued to lead the Federation until he retired again as president in 1964, at seventy years of age. During these last years, he considered the leading issue for labour to be the unacceptably high levels of unemployment and underemployment in the province, and he repeatedly called for new public works and new resource development. Another of Whitebone's continual concerns was the lack of good, affordable housing in the province, and in 1962 he pointed to the new model town of Oromocto, adjacent to the expanded Canadian Forces Base Gagetown, where the government had taken on a major project to provide low-cost quality housing.[31] In 1963, Whitebone reported that revisions to the Workmen's Compensation Act had been accomplished, which he claimed made it the best such legislation in Canada. Meanwhile, a range of new issues was also appearing on the Federation agenda. In 1962, the Resolutions Committee brought forward a call to amend the Labour Relations Act to prevent the hiring of strikebreakers during labour disputes. There were resolutions calling for a comprehensive national medicare plan, rent controls, improved vacation pay, and better compensation for silicosis victims. Another committee called for preparation of a union label shopper's guide, which was published the following year, in both English and French editions. There was also support for a meeting of officers from the labour federations in all the Atlantic Provinces, with a view to strengthening regional cooperation among labour organizations.[32]

At the Edmundston convention in 1964, Mayor Fernand Nadeau (later a provincial minister of labour) announced that Whitebone was to be proclaimed an honorary citizen of the "république" of Madawaska in recognition of his service to the province. In his address, Whitebone took the opportunity, as he had done many times before, to point out the leading place the Federation had come to occupy in the public life of the province over the past half-century. This achievement must be preserved, he said, and it would always be necessary to guard against those who aimed at "curtailment of union rights and functions and rendering our organizations impotent and ineffective." Looking ahead to the election of new officers, Whitebone encouraged members to find personal fulfillment in the responsibilities of leadership: "There is no more rewarding service than that rendered to the working people, and to be chosen to represent and serve them is a privilege and an honour not to be considered lightly."[33]

New Members

Meanwhile, the face of the Federation was changing in several ways in the early 1960s. In the 1962 election of officers, for instance, Frederick Douglas Hodges was chosen as one of the two trustees, the first delegate of Afro-Canadian origins to hold office in the history of the Federation. In 1969, he became a vice-president and served until 1975. A descendant of the Black Loyalists who came to the province in the eighteenth century, he was named for one of the great black civil rights leaders of the nineteenth century. Hodges grew up in an all-white neighborhood in west Saint John and was one of the few blacks to attend Saint John High School. He left school before graduation in the 1930s to work as a freighthandler for the CPR. At that time he was unable

to become a member of his own union, which required that black members belong to separate lodges. When the union finally abolished the colour bar at the end of the Second World War, he became in 1946 the first black member of the local Brotherhood of Railway and Steamship Clerks. Almost at once Hodges started to attend labour council meetings, where longtime members gave him a welcome reception. In 1964 he replaced Whitebone as president of the Saint John and District Labour Council and held the office for ten years. In 1974 he ran as a labour candidate in municipal politics and served three terms on Common Council.[34]

Another important pioneer was Dorothy Power, one of the slowly increasing number of women delegates at the conventions. In 1964 there were only twelve women delegates, a small group who accounted for only 7 percent of the total number. Power herself first attended in 1961, as a delegate for Local 636, International Typographical Union, in Moncton. She had worked originally as a telephone and telegraph operator for CN during the Second World War but was forced to leave because the railroad refused to employ married women after the war. She then went to work as a typesetter for the daily newspapers in Moncton, where she was employed for thirty-eight years.

The ITU had long followed a policy of equal pay for men and women members, and Power became active at all levels of the union, eventually serving as Canadian chair for the Communication Workers of America. At the Federation meetings, Power initially failed to win election as a trustee in 1962, and when she offered again in 1963, there was a tie vote. The chairman decided against her on the toss of a coin. Power was finally elected by acclamation in 1964, making her the first woman officer of the Federation in more than forty years. Later she was also elected president of the Moncton and District Labour Council, the first woman to hold this position. Meanwhile, in order to advance the status of women within the Federation, in 1963 delegates from Moncton Local 51 of the National Union of Public Employees proposed the election of a vice-president-at-large, to be held by a woman officer, in order to "give women of the province direct representation on the Executive Council." This was opposed by the delegates, including Frank Crilley of the Saint John and District Labour Council, who was usually considered a man of the left within the politics of the Federation. Crilley argued that there was "no need of extending extra advantages to our sister delegates, as the female delegates are equal in every respect to any male delegate, and we have always fought for equal rights for women."[35]

This was a mixed welcome, but over the course of the next decade, the number of women delegates increased significantly, reaching a total of fifty-four in 1975 — more than four times as many as in 1964 though still only 14 percent of the total delegates that year. There was also more attention to the issues that women brought to the convention meetings. In 1967, delegates listened to an address by Grace Hartman, the new national secretary-treasurer of the Canadian Union of Public Employees, on "The Role of Women in the Trade Union Movement." Women were in the work force to stay, said Hartman: "Women have become an integral and necessary part of Canada's working force — they are essential to its economic growth. But if they are to reap the due rewards of their labours they must also become an integral and vital part of the trade union movement." The following year the Federation approved a constitutional amendment that added "age" and "sex" to the organization's statement of purposes: "To encourage all workers without regard to race, creed, age, sex, colour, and national origin to share in the full benefits of union organization." In 1970 the Federation endorsed a resolution supporting the right to maternity leave without loss of benefits or seniority. In 1971 the Federation called on the province to provide assistance to daycare centres, and in 1973 they called for legislation to regulate daycare standards.[36]

The visibility of Acadian union members was also on the rise within organized labour during these years. The most prominent Acadian during the Whitebone era was Rolland Blanchette, one of the longtime leaders of Local 29 of the International Brotherhood of Pulp, Sulphite and Paper Mill Workers at the Fraser mill in Edmundston. He was elected a regional vice-president continuously from 1955 to 1976. Blanchette was often a delegate from the Edmundston and District Trades and Labour Council, which was established in 1947 and strongly supported by the millworkers and railway unions. Although the vast majority of local union members and officers were French-speaking, the labour council considered the outside union movement to be a primarily anglophone milieu, for English remained the language of record in their own minutebooks until 1977.[37] In Dalhousie, a community with more equal numbers of anglophone and francophone workers, another strong local of the paperworkers was instrumental in gaining ground for Acadian workers. With Aurèle Ferlatte as president, Local 146 challenged the traditional job hierarchies and favouritism that limited Acadians to the ranks of unskilled and semi-skilled labour. The union also succeeded in ending the exclusion of Acadian women with clerical and secretarial skills from employment on the mill's office staff. One industrial relations specialist has noted that once the union had demonstrated that they were prepared to go on strike to end discrimination in hiring practices, there was a visible change in the attitude of management, who learned to "handle ethnic problems intelligently." Ferlatte himself served as a vice-president of the Federation in 1961 and 1962 and became regional vice-president for Atlantic Canada when the Canadian Paperworkers Union was created in 1974.[38]

MATHILDA Mathilda Blanchard attended Federation meetings as a guest in 1967 and later as a representative of fish plant workers on the Acadian Peninsula. A fierce advocate for the rights of francophone members, she was elected a vice-president in 1977, the first woman to hold this office since 1922. Source: *Telegraph-Journal* Archives.

Another notable Acadian presence at the Federation meetings was the Caraquet union organizer Mathilda Blanchard, whose presence raised issues of gender and ethnicity both. She attended for the first time as a guest in 1967. President Lofty Mac-Millan welcomed her warmly and noted that she was bringing new members into the union movement through her work with fish plant workers on the Acadian Peninsula. Blanchard, who had worked as a hairdresser in Caraquet for many years, was drawn into union activity by her customers, who often told her about their low pay, working conditions, and other grievances. Blanchard was familiar with the potential of union organization and told delegates that she had first joined a union as a young woman when she was working in Windsor, Ontario, in the 1940s. The Maritimes needed strong unions, she stated, in order to counteract the effects of poor wages and poor conditions: "I believe, I sincerely believe, that if New Brunswick and the Maritime Provinces are so economically backward — we hear that all the time — it's because the labour movement was not strong enough before in these parts." Blanchard's comments were greeted with applause, and in response to MacMillan's advice to add comments in French, she repeated her statement in her mother tongue. She also added the observation that there was not enough French spoken at the meetings. A similar comment was made by Québec Federation of Labour President Louis Laberge, who noted the large number of francophones in attendance as well as the efforts of the Federation to address the issue: "Il y a je pense plus de délégués canadiens-français à cette convention ici que nous avons de délégués de langue anglaise au Congrès de la FTQ, et pourtant nous avons la traduction simultanée, et je sais que vos officiers y pensent très sérieusement et que le seul empêchement jusqu'à cette date ç'a été tout simplement la question financière." After several minutes in French, however, Laberge returned to "la langue de Shakespeare" for most of his speech.[39]

By 1972, the Federation was making some progress on bilingualism, as several reports and documents were prepared in both languages, and this was the first convention to feature simultaneous translation. A committee chaired by Blanchette called for continued improvements in bilingual services, and their report was adopted by the convention. By this time, Blanchard was in attendance as a representative of the Canadian Seafood Workers Union, together with several women delegates from the fish plants on the Acadian Peninsula. In a discussion of plans for a full-time executive secretary for the Federation, Blanchard argued that the position should be designated as bilingual and that she did not want to see the Federation of Labour divide into separate organizations based on language. A crude remark from the back of the hall —"you smell like fish anyway"— led Blanchard and four women delegates to walk out in protest: "If we cannot get French, we're getting the hell out." They returned later in the day, and President Paul LePage attempted to calm the waters by stating that the Federation was already well ahead of the provincial government in providing bilingual services. The issue remained a lively one into the 1980s, as did the unresolved status of women within the Federation.[40]

In the expanding labour activism of this period, a long-overdue breakthrough arrived in the woods, where unions had failed to have a lasting impact despite the earlier work of organizations such as the New Brunswick Farmer-Labour Union. Efforts resumed with the organization of the Restigouche Woodsmen's Union in 1949, which soon represented men cutting wood for more than a dozen contractors supplying International Paper at Dalhousie. However, when they attempted to expand to other mills, the union faced resistance from employers who continued to benefit from some of the lowest wages, longest hours, and most dangerous conditions in the Canadian woods. Workers tried to shore up their position in 1953 by joining the United Brotherhood of Carpenters and Joiners, as Lumber and Sawmill Workers Local 3012. This did not produce results until ten years later, when the union won the right to bargain for workers employed in the woods by the Fraser mills at Newcastle in 1963 and Atholville in 1964 as well as workers at Bathurst Power and Paper, South Nelson Forest Products, and other mills. By the end of the decade, Local 3012 represented almost 2,500 woods workers in the province, more than one-third of the work force in the woods. Their collective agreements covered not only the usual issues of wages, hours, seniority, and grievances, but also many of the conditions of work in the woods, such as supplies for camps and kitchens, the care of chainsaws and horses, and the use of equipment and clothing. A study of the arrival of unions in this sector has noted that by the 1960s the long years of substandard conditions had created serious labour shortages and that the acceptance of unions was a belated attempt by employers to improve the appeal of woods work.[41]

One of the more dramatic struggles of the early 1960s was the campaign to win recognition at the large new Irving Oil refinery in east Saint John. In 1960, soon after the refinery opened, the employees voted overwhelmingly to join the Oil, Chemical and Atomic Workers International Union, the union that represented workers at other Canadian refineries. The first agreement signed by Local 9-691 was relatively weak, and by 1963, with the refinery boasting high productivity and low costs, the union was determined to bring wages up to the standard in the industry. This would require much more than the additional 15 cents an hour that Irving proposed, an offer based on the company's stated position that local workers should expect low wages: "No major departure from the economic position of this area should be undertaken solely for the purpose of meeting this industry pattern."

The strike started in September 1963 and did not end until the following March. In a province where the Irving empire employed as many as one in ten workers, this was described as a David and Goliath battle. The strikers, some of whom had union experience from other refineries, did not lack determination. But when they called for a boycott of Irving gas stations, the courts issued injunctions to prevent picketing, and when they submitted radio advertisements, local stations refused to accept them. The strikers turned out to march in the street, demonstrate in the Loyalist cemetery, and burn K. C. Irving in effigy. When the union negotiator arranged a compromise settlement, the members voted by a ratio of four to one to reject it.

This struggle in Saint John attracted attention around the province and across the country, and the union appealed for donations and solidarity: "Are you going to allow that a group of workers be slaughtered by an employer whose trade union notions are those of feudalism?" A strike by Irving truck drivers at more than a dozen locations in Québec raised the stakes for the company, and in the end there was an agreement in which improvements in the wage scale were disguised as "merit" pay. The union also, without publicity, paid a $2,000 settlement to compensate Irving for damage to his reputation during the strike. It was a bitter struggle, but Premier Robichaud did his best to draw a positive picture of the outcome: "I personally am delighted that the parties have overcome the differences which separated them, and hope New Brunswick may continue to enjoy the progress to be obtained through harmonious relations in labour."[42]

Most of the union growth in the late 1950s and early 1960s was in the industrial sector among traditional blue-collar workers, but the unions were also breaking ground in new areas. When the Retail, Wholesale and Department Store Union launched a campaign at grocery stores in the fall of 1958, organizer Walter Kensit pitched a tent in King's Square in Saint John to draw public attention to their efforts at the Dominion store there. By Christmas the union had thirty-three members, and Local 1065 was chartered on 6 January 1959. The Labour Relations Board failed to grant certification, however, until the union also organized the other two Dominion stores in Saint John. Within the next few years the RWDSU was certified to represent workers at several retail establishments across the province, including the Dominion stores in Moncton, Newcastle, Bathurst, Dalhousie, Fredericton, and Edmundston. The union also faced much employer resistance in this sector. In Moncton, a long campaign at Eaton's, one of the most anti-union employers in the retail sector in Canada, failed to win a majority of the employees. In other cases, there was some hard-earned success. When workers at the Sobeys stores in Saint John joined the union and received certification in July 1968, they did not gain a first contract until March 1969. They were on strike most of that winter, and unions showed solidarity by picketing Sobeys stores in other parts of the province.[43]

Public Employees

The unions took on their biggest union challenge in the public sector. Although provincial government employees were not entitled to union rights under the existing Labour Relations Act, there was some progress at other levels. Slowly but surely, workers were signing up in unions in the province's municipalities, school boards, and hospitals. As organizer for the National Union of Public Employees, Lofty MacMillan often met resistance from local elites. When recruiting union members in hospitals at Dalhousie, Campbellton, and Chatham, he found it useful to travel with a box of papal encyclicals on the Labour Question in order to refute claims that unions were contrary to Catholic teaching. Even then, success in forming a union local was only the beginning. When hospital workers at the Hôtel-Dieu de l'Assomption in Moncton met at the Carpenters' Hall and organized Local 821 of NUPE in November 1960, there was vocal opposition from the hospital, which was run by a Québec-based religious order, the Soeurs de la Providence. The union won certification by a bare majority of one vote in 1961, and then it took another year to secure a contract. When a conciliation board finally recommended a settlement in 1962, the hospital did not accept the agreement until the union threatened to go out on strike the next day. Local 821 went on to play an active part in the Moncton and District Labour Council and the Federation of Labour. As MacMillan later recalled, it was a difficult struggle that produced a strong local: "A union that has never had a struggle doesn't create the leaders who come out of a struggle."[44]

These kinds of local breakthroughs were taking place across the province, and by 1964 the Canadian Union of Public Employees, created by a merger of two older organizations in 1963, had thirty-nine locals in New Brunswick. They represented 2,500 public employees who had received certification and signed collective agreements with local governments, hospitals, and school boards.[45] The future status of these workers was complicated by the reorganization of public services recommended by the Robichaud government's Byrne Commission in 1964. After more than three years of study, the report recommended sweeping changes that would equalize the tax burden across the province and establish common standards in health, education, and other public services. For New Brunswick workers, there was much to welcome in the Byrne Report. However, as Whitebone pointed out at the 1964 convention, the most significant omission was that almost nothing was said about the place of the workers and their unions in this revolution in provincial administration. It was estimated that some 20,000 workers employed by municipalities, school boards, and hospital commissions would now become employees of the provincial government. Since the Labour Relations Act did not recognize civil servants as "employees" within the meaning of the law, their status as workers with union contracts and rights was uncertain. Would they now lose their right to be recognized as union members?[46]

These questions coincided with the Federation's need to choose a successor to President Whitebone at the 1964 convention. There were three candidates, but when the votes were counted, delegates had chosen the organizer who was closely associated with the cause of public employees, John Francis MacMillan — commonly known as "Lofty" due to the height that allowed him to tower over most of his fellows.[47] A Cape Bretoner who was born in the coal-mining town of Port Hood in Nova Scotia's Inverness County in 1917, he had left school at sixteen and gone into the mines, where he joined his first union in 1934. Soon afterwards he was attending an international convention of the United Mine Workers of America, where he was presented to the legendary president John L. Lewis as the youngest delegate in attendance. MacMillan went into the navy during the Second World War, serving as a stoker on harbour patrol vessels in Halifax and Saint John. When he was discharged in

LOFTY He started in the coal mines
as a youth in Port Hood, but after
service in the Royal Canadian Navy
he joined the police force in Saint John
and rose to leadership in the local
. union. MacMillan (1917–2006) became
Federation president in 1964. His work
as an organizer of public sector unions
led to the enactment of the Public
Service Labour Relations Act in 1968.
Source: Provincial Archives of New
Brunswick, New Brunswick Federation
of Labour fonds, MC1819, box 192.

Saint John at the end of the war, he joined the police
force. By 1947, he was president of the Saint John
Policemen's Protective Association, whose history
went back to its original charter from the Trades
and Labour Congress of Canada in 1919. When the
National Union of Public Employees was organized
in 1955, the union joined as Local 61. MacMillan
later became the NUPE representative in Saint John
and then regional director for the Canadian Union
of Public Employees.[48]

As Federation president, MacMillan's most urgent mission was to protect the interests of public
employees in the ongoing changes in provincial
administration. At the 1964 convention, Alexandre
Boudreau, a member of the Byrne Commission who
was also Director of Extension at the Université de
Moncton, told delegates that "it might have been
an oversight" on the part of the commission not to
safeguard the rights of labour: "Perhaps it was an
exaggerated confidence in the intelligence of our political leaders, I didn't feel we had to."[49] MacMillan
knew that labour could not make such assumptions. Existing rights needed to be protected, but
MacMillan also recognized that this was a strategic moment of opportunity to secure union rights
for all public employees who had been repeatedly
denied it in the past. The Federation had supported
this principle for many decades. As early as 1919, it
was asserted in the Federation's Reconstruction Programme, and Whitebone defended the same principle
when the province's collective bargaining legislation
was enacted in the 1930s and 1940s.

Under MacMillan's watch, the campaign continued. At the 1965 convention in Moncton, delegates voted unanimously to call for bargaining rights for all provincial civil servants, including those working for provincial boards and commissions. CLC President Claude Jodoin was in attendance to state that governments, regardless of party, should not lag behind but set an example in providing rights for their employees. A strange situation at the New Brunswick Liquor Commission was discussed in detail. The province had earlier agreed to declare the Liquor Control Board an "employer," but when store clerks and warehouse workers applied for certification, they were rejected by the Labour Relations Board on the grounds that the "employer," under revised legislation, now had a different name. As a result, the workers still had no rights. Also, one employee explained, managers were asking workers to sign a form letter undertaking not to join CUPE Local 963: "You know, nobody can be dictated to, in New Brunswick. They have been, but if we follow it up, I don't think that we can be dictated to." MacMillan drew an unfavourable comparison when he claimed that civil servants in emerging economies in east Africa had more union rights than workers in New Brunswick: "We should be taking some of the people in the Civil Service and sending them to Tanganyika and Kenya in order to learn what the trade union movement has done in those countries." He also expressed confidence that the desired reforms would be achieved: "It has been a long hard fight to get those benefits for the civil servants, and it will be a little longer. But we will get them."[50]

The agitation lasted another two years. "We had rallies all over the province. These included the civil servants, the secretaries, clerical workers, liquor store workers, highway workers, public works, forest rangers, the general broad scope of public employees," recalled MacMillan. "We also had a policy of getting to the local MLAs. We kept on the backs of them all the time. We figured you're not going to get the legislation passed, if you just present briefs to the cabinet." The unions kept a close watch on legislative reforms and took every opportunity to advance their case. MacMillan has recalled that, when the school boards were being reorganized, he had to stop the minister of education in the lobby of the Lord Beaverbrook Hotel to

FRIEND OF LABOUR
In the 1960s, the reform-minded Premier Louis J. Robichaud looked to the ranks of labour for support in his campaigns for modernization and equal opportunity. In 1968 he examines a union brief with Federation President Paul LePage, former president J. F. "Lofty" MacMillan, and Federation secretary-treasurer Valerie Bourgeois. Source: *Telegraph-Journal* Archives.

show him the amendments needed to maintain union contracts in the new school districts.[51] Another ad hoc adjustment in 1967 forced the province to amend the Civil Service Act to end the prohibition on the employment of married women, which was considered acceptable at the municipal level but had been prohibited under provincial law.[52] A select committee of the legislature was named to study changes to the Labour Relations Act, and the Federation and CUPE submitted briefs, as did the Civil Service Association of New Brunswick, the New Brunswick Association of Registered Nurses, and the New Brunswick Teachers' Federation. However, meetings were few and far between and progress was slow. MacMillan feared that many of the Federation's suggestions were being ignored.[53]

Then, in June 1966, Premier Robichaud appointed a one-man royal commission to provide advice. This was a turning point. Union leaders were aware that the selected McGill University specialist in industrial relations, Saul

Frankel, would write a positive report with a practical plan for implementing collective bargaining in the public service. In supporting this appointment, Robichaud's principal advisor on the issue, the former Saskatchewan civil servant Donald Tansley, reassured the premier that civil servants in Saskatchewan (where Tansley had worked for the CCF government) had enjoyed normal union rights since 1945.[54]

The Federation and CUPE, as well as the teachers, the nurses, and the Civil Service Association, all participated in hearings in August and September 1966, and when the report was released in July 1967, there were no surprises. The recommendations outlined a plan for the extension of union rights to all provincial employees and proceeded from the general principle that collective bargaining had become an accepted feature of the democratic way of life:

> Collective bargaining in one form or another is characteristic of the political process in a society that allows its members a wide area of freedom. Men have interests that they seek to satisfy, and they tend to form themselves into groups or associations based on common interests in order to compete more effectively for a share of the goods and values available in a given society. Because these goods and values are relatively scarce in relation to the demand for them, the competition sometimes generates tension and conflict. If democratic societies are viable and enduring it is not because they seek to suppress this competition, but because they succeed in developing institutions and procedures that help to reconcile differences and provide ways of resolving disputes.[55]

On the basis of these recommendations, a Public Service Labour Relations Act was announced in the Speech from the Throne in February 1968. When he introduced the bill, Minister of Labour H. H. Williamson stated that the purpose was to give employees of the government the same rights as other workers in the province. This would allow for a "planned and professional approach" to labour relations in which basic principles of due process and fair treatment would prevail: "All public service employees will be treated equitably, both in relation to each other and to the community." This would also serve to promote "a public service which has the best possible employees with a high morale because they are working under conditions which they themselves have had a part in creating."[56]

In detail, the new act resembled the Labour Relations Act and was in effect a parallel constitution for the conduct of labour relations in the public sector. The new law covered some 25,000 to 30,000 workers — including those working for departments, commissions, school districts, and hospital boards. Where union contracts already existed, these would continue in force, but the act was a new opportunity for many workers who had only recently become provincial employees when the province assumed responsibility for the hospitals in 1966, and for the schools in 1967. Workers who wanted to join unions would now have the right to do so and to negotiate with their employer — which was defined as the province's Treasury Board. A separate Public Service Labour Relations Board was created to grant certifications. The negotiation of province-wide agreements was an important consequence, as it guaranteed that standards would apply to all workers covered under a contract, and this would do much to reduce internal regional disparities within the province. One important provision in the act was the result of a conversation between MacMillan and Robichaud. When the premier said he did not want to see picket lines in front of public buildings in the event of a strike, MacMillan replied that the only way to achieve this would be to prohibit the use of strikebreakers. As a result, section 102 included a restriction on picketing during strikes and a prohibition on the use of strikebreakers.[57]

When the bill received final reading in December 1968, the ground had been well prepared, and Robichaud pronounced the legislation "long overdue." Although public service collective bargaining was not one of the original objectives of Equal Opportunity, Robichaud recognized that it was among the most important achievements of his government. What he failed to state more explicitly was that the enactment of this reform was made possible by New Brunswick workers who organized themselves into unions and insisted on their rights, thus forcing the government to introduce measures that it did not originally foresee undertaking. Besides the workers who were affiliated to the Federation of Labour through their unions, other workers in the public sector would also have new opportunities. In the case of the nurses and teachers, for instance, their exclusion from the provisions of the Labour Relations Act was in effect reversed by the new law in 1968 and the subsequent changes that produced a new Industrial Relations Act in 1971. Many years in the making, the enactment of the Public Service Labour Relations Act was a major success for the Federation. As MacMillan later recalled, "That era changed the face of the province of New Brunswick."[58]

Development and Underdevelopment

While public employees were gaining ground throughout the province, the most concentrated geographic zone of new union activity in the 1960s was in northern New Brunswick. The huge local deposits of lead, zinc, and silver had been known since the early 1950s, when these strategic raw materials attracted the attention of the American government and multinational corporations. Further development of this resource, with the condition that processing of the ores be carried out in the province, was one of the biggest ambitions of the Robichaud government. When he announced plans for a $50 million industrial complex in 1961, Robichaud predicted thousands of new jobs. Once Brunswick Mining and Smelting began operations, the area surrounding Bathurst entered a boom period. Bathurst was incorporated as a city, and the population rose from fewer than 5,500 people in 1961 to three times that by the end of the decade. At the peak of expansion in the mid-1960s, there were as many as 1,500 jobs for workers constructing the facilities, and another 2,500 or more in the mining and smelter operations. Robichaud supported the expansion of these operations through a series of provincial guarantees and tax concessions. He had also recruited K.C. Irving as a major investor to reduce American control and later brought in Noranda Mines to undercut Irving's influence. By 1970, the province was producing more than 500 million tons of ore per year, with an annual value of $90 million.[59]

The need for strong union representation in this sector was apparent from the start. Already, in the summer of 1965, there was trouble among construction workers at the Belledune smelter and Brunswick mine sites. Members of an independent labourers' union were bargaining with one of the contractors to establish an eight-hour day and a five-day week (they were working 9.5 hours, five days one week and six the next) and to win rates of $1.60 an hour (in place of $1.32). When the province failed to appoint a conciliation board, 350 labourers went on strike at the end of August. Operations came to a halt as another 800 carpenters, millwrights, electricians, welders, riggers, pipefitters, plumbers, bricklayers, and others refused to cross the picket lines. One man was injured by a truck loaded with a bulldozer belonging to Irving Equipment when it crossed the line at Belledune, and two men spent a night in jail after they were charged with intimidation on the picket line. The next day a judge granted an injunction to prohibit picketing. Meanwhile, the RCMP was patrolling the sites, and union spokesman Réjean Charlebois was considering a call for a general strike. After seven days, the strike ended in a stalemate and negotiations resumed, but labour relations remained tense.

There would be another four work stoppages at the Belledune site over the next year and several at the Brunswick mine as well. Many of these were wildcat strikes, not authorized by the unions but provoked by workplace grievances such as the dismissal of individual workers or the failure to remove unpopular supervisors. A notable feature of these strikes was the solidarity between workers belonging to different unions, when electricians, plumbers, carpenters, bricklayers, and other trades refused to cross picket lines. When Charlebois spoke at the Federation convention in September, he appealed for support in a common cause: "We've got to fight that battle, and I'm asking your financial support and your prayers to beat the big lion. And if we beat him, this will be good for you people, for your children going to school right now, and for all the future of New Brunswick. But if we get beat once more now, we'll stay with the low wages another 15 to 20 years. We'll never pick up with the par of the country."[60]

NORTHERN MINERS The opening of new mineral resources in northern New Brunswick in the 1960s drew thousands of workers into new industrial employment, where they struggled to establish principles of union recognition and collective bargaining: "If we get beat once more now, we'll stay with the low wages another 15 to 20 years. We'll never pick up with the par of the country." From left: Marcel Gallant, Lawrence Vienneau, Daniel Comeau, Ulric Roy. Source: Centre d'études acadiennes Anselme-Chiasson, E-15596.

The most important union to emerge from the mining boom in the north was the United Steelworkers of America, one of the pioneer industrial unions representing hard rock miners and smelter workers in Canada. In 1965 they sent an experienced organizer to staff the Local 5385 office on St. George Street in Bathurst. Born in 1926 at Sault Ste. Marie, Ontario, another blue-collar town that depended on forest and mining operations, Paul LePage had worked at the Algoma steel plant for eighteen years and had held several posts on the local union executive. It was also important that he came from a francophone family, which gave the union a much-needed bilingual presence in northern

New Brunswick. As one of the first graduates of the union-sponsored Labour College of Canada in 1963, LePage belonged to a new generation of working-class leaders who were familiar with the complexities of the modern industrial relations system as well as those of internal union politics. In dealing with disputes, LePage was considered a "good negotiator" and a "straight shooter" who regarded a properly enforced collective agreement as the best guarantee of good relations with employers. LePage's abilities, as well as the importance of developments in the Bathurst area, were both recognized when he joined the Federation executive as vice-president for Gloucester.[61]

By the time of the 1967 convention, Lofty MacMillan had taken on his next challenge. It was hardly a retirement. His appointment as director of organization for CUPE was recognition of MacMillan's talent as an organizer, and over the course of the next decade, he would help to make CUPE the largest union in Canada. He was sent on his way to Ottawa with thanks for his "untiring efforts on behalf of the working man" and with the hope that "he will not forget that he comes from the Maritime Provinces."[62] Meanwhile, the Federation needed a new president. Stalwarts Frank Crilley of Saint John and Aurèle Ferlatte of Dalhousie were nominated, but they stood aside in order to support the election of LePage. Although LePage was less polished in style than Whitebone and not as dynamic a speaker as MacMillan, the delegates were choosing an experienced organizer and administrator committed to building the Federation and expanding the influence of the unions.

When the 1968 convention was called to order at the Collège de Bathurst a year later, LePage was able to tell delegates that the Federation was in good condition and that numbers were continuing to rise: "Unions are here to stay, and this the employers must recognize. When all employers recognize this, we will increase our productivity, have better wages, better conditions of employment, and more labour stability in our province."[63] One of his first priorities, however, was to keep up the pressure for the province to participate in the medicare programme for hospital and physician services enacted by the federal government in 1968. This issue was of special interest to LePage, who had been one of the founders of a union-supported group health centre in Sault Ste. Marie. Under the leadership of the CLC, the provincial labour federations were among the most vocal supporters of the full universal programme that was recommended by the royal commission headed by Justice Emmett Hall in 1964. On the evening prior to the opening of the 1968 convention, the issue was pushed to the fore when speakers for the provincial Liberals, Progressive Conservatives, and New Democratic Party were invited to explain their positions. Like other labour groups, the Federation was disappointed that all of Justice Hall's recommendations were not accepted by the federal government, but it continued to lobby for prompt action to meet national standards. When the province's Medical Services Payment Act was adopted in December 1968, the Federation had done its part to ensure that New Brunswickers would benefit from one of the major social reforms in Canadian history.[64]

Meanwhile, in a political landscape where the provincial government seemed to be pursuing moderately social democratic policies, the New Democratic Party was not gaining traction. The provincial CCF had dissolved in favour of the NDP in December 1962, but the new party attracted little support during the Robichaud years and only a handful of unions took out formal affiliation. By 1970, there was a renewal of interest among labour supporters. The leadership was taken on by a youthful union activist from the Miramichi, J. Albert Richardson, who had worked in the mines in New Brunswick and Manitoba and was now a representative for the Canadian Food and Allied Workers. The election campaign that followed in October 1970 included public ownership of the forest industry and telephone system, the adoption of public auto insurance, and the creation of 50,000 new jobs. However, the results were disappointing. The Robichaud government was replaced by the Progressive Conservatives under Richard Hatfield, and the NDP's thirty-one candidates received less than 3 percent of the vote.

The party was also facing claims that its programme was too conservative for the times, a challenge similar to that issued to the federal NDP by the "Waffle" movement for "an independent socialist Canada." At a provincial party convention in Saint John in September 1971, a group known as the New Brunswick Waffle proposed adoption of a manifesto under the title "For a Socialist New Brunswick." Few labour leaders in the province were prepared for this highly charged critique of New Brunswick capitalism or for the claim that the achievement of limited reforms served only to "reinforce basic power relationships" within the capitalist system. Much to the surprise of many Waffle supporters themselves, however, the convention voted by a one-vote margin to endorse the manifesto. Several labour delegates immediately walked out. During the period of internal crisis that followed, prominent labour leaders, including LePage, urged the federal NDP to intervene. Party leader David Lewis, who had won the leadership against a surprisingly strong bid by Waffle leader James Laxer, was happy to do so. By November, a special convention had reaffirmed Richardson's leadership, and the Waffle group soon broke up in disarray.[65]

In the short run, this internal conflict did little to strengthen the NDP in the province, but there were efforts at the Federation's 1972 convention to renew support for the party. An extended two-page resolution, introduced by a Moncton local of the Canadian Brotherhood of Railway, Transport and General Workers, stated that "alternating between a Liberal Administration and a Conservative Administration for the past one hundred years has produced nothing but economic chaos and social unrest" and that it was time to "bring about in the Province of New Brunswick a government responsible to the needs of the working people." Delegates, labour councils, and affiliates were invited to affirm their support for "a broadly based political party which was committed to the principles of social and economic justice for all and special privilege for none." The NDP was described as the party that "consistently supports labour's legislative objectives," and several themes were listed: "Canadian control of our economic affairs — full employment — protection of our environment — more emphasis on the quality of life — better social security — human rights and improved health services — low cost auto insurance — and recognition of the right of senior citizens to enjoy their twilight years in dignity, comfort and security." As in the original debate on support for the NDP a decade earlier, however, it was recognized that some union members were committed by their union constitutions or by provincial legislation to "a non-political role" and that their independence must be respected. The resolution provoked a lively debate and carried on a standing vote.[66]

Certainly, the old problems of under-development and regional disparity had not disappeared by the early 1970s. The situation was especially alarming in northern New Brunswick, where the boom of the previous decade was coming to an end. In late 1971, there were widespread layoffs, including shutdowns in the paper mills, mining operations, and fish plants. This, in turn, was drawing the whole north into a severe downturn, and there was concern that governments were shifting their attention to growth centres such as Moncton and Saint John. The Federation launched a campaign of protest in December, and local unions in Gloucester, Restigouche, Madawaska, and Northumberland appealed to the province for a moratorium on layoffs. They also called on the federal government to designate northern New Brunswick as a special area

★ NO ADMISSION CHARGE ★   ★ ADMISSION GRATUITE

A Songfest Of Folk & Union Songs
In Support Of The
DAY OF CONCERN

CHANTONS
NOTRE AMITIE

EDITH BUTLER of New Brunswick
Acadian Songstress fér 'Canada at Osaka
Vedette De La Radio & TV

PERRY FRIEDMAN of Toronto
Just returned from Europe where he starred on Radio & TV
and made recordings. Both artists are devoting time & talent with:

CALIXTE DUGUAY
JACQUES SAVOIE
THE WARD SISTERS
DEREK KNOWLES

and other New Brunswick artists

Thursday, January 13 — 8 p. m.

Auditorium
College De Bathurst

Jeudi, 13 Janvier

En Marge De La Journée D'inquiétude
Chantons Notre Amitié—
Chantons Notre Folklore

DAY OF CONCERN In 1972, the Federation joined forces with local unions and community leaders to sponsor protests against shutdowns in the fisheries, paper mills, and mining operations of northern New Brunswick. A concert prior to the Day of Concern attracted prominent Acadian musicians such as Edith Butler. Source: Provincial Archives of New Brunswick, New Brunswick Federation of Labour fonds, MC1819, box 111.

for assistance from the Department of Regional Economic Expansion. The Federation's efforts focused on a massive public demonstration in January. A veteran Mine-Mill organizer, Ray Stevenson, was assigned to coordinate a Day of Concern in Bathurst. The plan was to build a local common front through a Citizens Coordinating Committee, co-chaired by Federation vice-president Eric Pitre of Bathurst and lawyer Frederick Arsenault of the

Gloucester County Barristers Society. On Thursday, 13 January, a free public concert —"Songfest of Folk and Union Songs," also advertised under the heading "Chantons notre amitié"— aimed to "tune up" the community for the event. The show featured the star Acadian folksinger Edith Butler, who interrupted a tour of the United States in order to participate, and labour troubadour Perry Friedman, who was supplied by the steelworkers union. Local artists Calixte Duguay, Jacques Savoie, the Ward Sisters, and Derek Knowles also performed.[67]

On the cold early Sunday afternoon of 16 January, thousands of marchers assembled on the downtown boulevard and nearby streets. At 1 p.m., with Bathurst Police Chief J. J. O'Neil as parade marshal they proceeded across the causeway, led by Canadian and New Brunswick flags and a band of drummers.

COMMON FRONT On 16 January 1972, the Day of Concern in Bathurst protested the failures of economic development in northern New Brunswick. Thousands of marchers proceeded across the harbour causeway, led by Canadian and New Brunswick flags and a band of drummers. The mobilization attracted national attention. Source: Centre d'études acadiennes Anselme-Chiasson, E-16014.

Three of the seven sections in the line of march were filled by union members; others included public officials, clergy and religious orders, chambers of commerce and professional groups, firemen and police, and community organizations ranging from the long-established Knights of Columbus to the much newer militants of the Conseil régional d'aménagement du Nord-Est (CRAN). At the Collège de Bathurst, people crowded into the gymnasium while others listened on loudspeakers in other halls. The proceedings were also broadcast on a local radio station, CKBC. Dozens of union leaders and public figures sat on the stage, including presidents of local unions, officers of the Federation, and representatives from the national offices of the steelworkers, machinists, paperworkers, and the CLC. The organizers had also succeeded in attracting major political figures to attend. Premier Hatfield was there with most of his cabinet, and so too were the leaders of the provincial Liberal and New Democratic parties. Among the federal politicians were NDP leader David Lewis, Progressive Conservative leader Robert Stanfield, and Jean Marchand, the former Québec union leader who was now minister of regional economic expansion as well as one of Prime Minister Pierre Elliott Trudeau's closest colleagues. Estimates of the crowds ranged as high as 10,000 in number, and LePage later described the event as "the largest undertaking ever taken by our Federation."[68]

LePage gave the first major speech, stating that this was not just a "narrow sectional" union protest but one that involved "every section of our community" in addressing "the shattering effects of economic stagnation and crisis upon every section of the communities, our region and our entire province and people." The forest industries, he charged, had been allowed to slide into inefficiency while subsidies supported new plants elsewhere; and the mining industry was failing to develop the smelting and refining capacity needed for long-term development. LePage demanded that public assistance to the resource industries be protected by giving the Canadian taxpayers dollar-for-dollar equity in ownership and profits. In short, this was "public investment on the basis of protected equity for the Canadian people," and he argued that there was nothing unprecedented in such government intervention, which had been taking place since the days of John A. Macdonald's National Policy and was continued when public funds were used to build up industry during the Second World War. At last it was time to recognize the same urgency in developing the mining and forest resources of New Brunswick: "The regional disparities and inequalities that exist, and we in New Brunswick and in the Atlantic provinces know the results of this in our bones from bitter experience, are the result of national policies that have maintained these disparities. It IS time for a New Deal from Ottawa and it is this new deal we are proposing." LePage ended by referring to the promise of $10 million in emergency aid announced by Marchand and Hatfield a few days earlier and warned: "When a person has a broken leg, you do not put a bandaid on it to cure it. I hope I will be forgiven if I use the language we sometimes hear at the bargaining table when a company has made an initial and limited offer: 'well that's fine . . . you have recognized the justness of our proposals . . . but let's really get down to brass tacks and have a look at what is really in that bag you have there.'"[69]

For many in the crowd, however, the most memorable speeches were the ones that were interrupted. When NDP leader David Lewis spoke, encouraging workers to take political action, he did so only in English and there were cries of "En français! En français!" Premier Hatfield received the same treatment, and as other speakers took their turn, there was a rising chant of "On veut Mathilda!" Mathilda Blanchard (the local union leader was assigned a seat on stage but arrived from the back of the hall) was invited to address the crowd. Pointing her finger at Marchand, Blanchard denounced Ottawa's modernization programmes for favouring growth centres in the south and ruining the resources of the north. She also called for nationalization of the mines, pulp mills, and fishing industry and warned that "union leaders do not necessarily speak for the workers." Marchand had the last word, speaking rapidly and entirely in French. His message was that he had no "foolish promises" and that the federal government would continue to use its established regional development policies to find lasting solutions to the unemployment problem.[70]

REGIONAL DISPARITY Federation President Paul LePage delivered one of the major addresses at the 1972 Day of Concern, appealing for more responsible development policies: "The regional disparities and inequalities that exist, and we in New Brunswick and in the Atlantic provinces know the results of this in our bones from bitter experience, are the result of national policies that have maintained these disparities. It IS time for a New Deal from Ottawa." Source: Centre d'études acadiennes Anselme-Chiasson, E-16016.

Those were frustrating answers, and so too were the apparent divisions within the Federation's carefully constructed common front. The language of anti-corporate populism, as articulated by LePage and Lewis, was not enough for the occasion. The discontent, especially among a generation of students and youth facing an uncertain future in their home region, was accelerated by the growth of Acadian nationalism, which a few weeks later resulted in the founding of the Parti Acadien. For all their dedication to holding governments to account, the Federation of Labour in this context seemed to be, as Richard Wilbur later put it, a "conservative-minded" force.[71]

In the weeks after the Day of Concern there was continued agitation, as the high number of unemployment claims and the centralization of administration in Moncton caused delays in the processing of files. In February, a group of unemployed workers occupied the Unemployment Insurance Commission offices in Bathurst and on the second day of their sit-in were joined by students. Police ejected them all from the building, and thirteen people were arrested. In another protest, demonstrators threw rocks and mud, and broke doors. In collaboration with the labour council and the CLC, the Federation opened an office to assist workers with their claims and to convince the Unemployment Insurance Commission to introduce emergency measures to speed up the processing of files. Commenting on the involvement of students and other young activists over the previous weeks, LePage expressed his anxieties in these terms: "Our concern lies in the fact that college students form part of a moving population which disperses following graduation leaving the results of their radicalism to be resolved by workers' organizations. Problems facing workers must be resolved through utilizing the strength and resources of the trade union movement; community problems require joint efforts but the action must take place within a structured framework acceptable to all participants."[72]

Looking Forward

In the wake of episodes such as the New Brunswick Waffle and the Day of Concern, the Federation leaders continued to look for ways to balance the demands of militancy in support of their members while also maintaining influence with the provincial government. As in the working alliance between MacMillan and Robichaud in the 1960s, LePage enjoyed a cordial relationship with Premier Hatfield, whom he recognized as a "Progressive" within the limits of Progressive Conservative party traditions. The Federation continued to insist on its right to name labour representatives to provincial bodies and enjoyed influence through appointees to the New Brunswick Safety Council, the Public Service Labour Relations Board, the Industrial Relations Board, the Employment Standards Advisory Board, the Human Rights Commission, and the New Brunswick Research and Productivity Council, among others. In 1973, LePage reported that the Industrial Relations Board, under University of New Brunswick Dean of Law George McAllister, was following "a very enlightened approach towards labour relations problems in the Province."[73]

Two years later LePage was less satisfied, noting an increase in challenges to the certification of unions, which he described as a form of "adversary legalism": "Not only have certain lawyers in the Province continually offered their services to management as reputed union busters and constantly appeared before the Board in this capacity in opposition to applications for certification, but the same element have made it a practice to encourage management to appeal Board certification orders to the Supreme Court of New Brunswick." Nonetheless, the status of the Federation was at a high level, said LePage, and their message was clear and consistent: "Organized labour through collective action simply seeks a fairer redistribution of the benefits of increased productivity, protection against the adverse effects of inflation, a better working environment and improved social and economic conditions for all workers, whether organized or unorganized, active or retired."[74] When a spokesman for the Department of Labour stated that labour unrest in the province had reached unusually high levels during the past year and that many of the strikes were illegal walkouts, LePage had nothing reassuring to say.

"UNIONS ARE HERE TO STAY"
Paul LePage (right), Federation
president from 1967 to 1980, is
shown here with Premier Richard B.
Hatfield. LePage (1926–2000) saw
labour as a partner of business and
government in raising provincial
standards but never failed to warn:
"Unions are here to stay, and this
the employers must recognize."
Source: *Telegraph-Journal* Archives.

Instead of discussing "man-days lost," he replied, the Department of Labour should consider measuring strikes in terms of "loss of income" by the workers. He also added: "We are not a bunch of strike-happy wing-dings, but when we have an ever-increasing cost of living, we have had to take action."[75]

The Federation did not hold a regular convention in 1974, and there were more than enough issues to consider in 1975, including a set of four major policy statements on food prices, housing, pensions, and wages and incomes.[76] There was also a heated debate on support for a provincial takeover of the New Brunswick Telephone Company, on the grounds that such a profitable monopoly should benefit the people of the province. Delegates repeated their support for public automobile insurance and called on the province to take over the operation of private nursing homes as well. A resolution from the Newcastle-Chatham and District Labour Council proposed that the province take over control of the resource industries —"and the profits derived from these resources be used for the benefit of the people"; however, this wording was set aside by the executive and replaced by the more moderate demand that the government "more effectively control the Province's natural resources to ensure we derive maximum economic and social benefit."

On some issues, delegates were especially cautious. They voted against a resolution to support the right of women to seek an abortion, and a resolution opposing capital punishment was referred back for amendment, with the majority later voting in favour of life imprisonment without parole for convicted murderers. There was a resolution supporting identification cards for the purchase of liquor, adopted after delegates heard an account of a Liquor Commission employee convicted of selling liquor to a minor. The use of ex parte court orders in labour disputes was again denounced as "government by injunction," and Premier Hatfield and other members of the legislature were condemned for staying at the Lord Beaverbrook Hotel while a strike was in progress there. There was also a debate over a letter sent by the Federation executive to a veteran union man who lost his leg in an industrial accident at the paper mill in Saint John. He had been asked to refrain from further public criticism of the Workmen's Compensation Board; the issue, brought to the floor by paperworkers delegate Larry Hanley (it was his father's case), was referred to the CLC ombudsman. At the end of the convention, one reporter in attendance summed up the busy hum of activity, calculating that by the third day the 341 registered voting delegates had faced more than 160 resolutions as well as the four policy statements, nineteen documents, and numerous other reports, speeches, and debates. The microphones in the Grand Salon of the Hotel Beauséjour were always busy: "There were harangues and pleas, threats and conciliatory remarks, words that provoked outbursts of applause and words that were forgotten before the speaker could say them."[77]

For many delegates, the most notable event at the 1975 convention was the visit of César Chávez, the charismatic American union leader who was appealing to Canadians to boycott California grapes and lettuce. When Chávez was introduced, he received a standing ovation and was accompanied by rhythmic clapping as he came to the podium. "How many of you take a union for granted?" he asked. "How many of our brothers and sisters in this convention take the idea of having a union for granted?" In a short speech, he told delegates that the farm workers had been fighting for a union for more than fifty years and that the United Farm Workers were at last having some success. Recent changes in state law were at last making it possible for farm workers to secure recognition of their union; they had survived Richard Nixon in Washington and Ronald Reagan in California, he said, "and now we are on the verge of winning."

They were also winning thanks to international support for their boycott, especially in Canada. They were stopping sales in Ontario and Québec, and Chávez explained that it was important to stop Dominion Stores, the only major distributor that had failed to respect the boycott, from dumping surplus produce in places such as New Brunswick. Following his speech, Chávez led the delegates and other supporters on a march down the road to Champlain Place in Dieppe, where they gathered in front of the Dominion store with placards reading "Viva la causa!" and "Boycott Grapes!" Together with LePage, Chávez was invited to meet with the store manager, who explained he had no authority to change store policy but would phone Toronto to report the situation. "I've picketed more Dominion stores than I can count but this is the first time I've ever been inside one," Chávez said afterwards. He added that he was pleased with the demonstration of support and was also amused by the cooperation of local police during his visit: "When I return home and tell them I had a police escort from the airport, they'll never believe me."[78]

The visit by an international figure such as Chávez helped delegates understand that they were participants in a larger struggle for social justice that reached well beyond their own borders. In his own way, Chávez was also helping New Brunswick union members understand how much they had already accomplished in their own province. By 1975 much had happened to strengthen the place of labour in New Brunswick. The total number of union members had tripled since the early 1950s, and these gains had taken place among blue-collar and white-collar workers, in both private and public sectors. Although union membership was still predominantly male, rapid changes were taking place: women made up 19 percent of union members in 1970 and 27 percent five years later. Moreover, by 1975 almost one in three workers in the province were members of unions.[79] The Federation itself was also gaining strength. Secretary-Treasurer Alvin Blakely reported a total of 268 affiliated locals, of which thirty had joined since the previous convention. More than half the delegates were from Moncton and Saint John, but there were more than twenty-five communities represented in all, and the number of women delegates and francophones had also increased significantly. There was room for more members, and Blakely did not hesitate to point out that some eligible locals in the public service and railway and building trades had not affiliated. The merger of the rival federations could be counted a success,

SOLIDARITY The legendary California farm workers' leader, César Chávez, spoke to delegates at the Moncton convention in 1975: "How many of our brothers and sisters in this convention take the idea of having a union for granted?" He then led a march to the local Dominion store to support the farm workers' boycott. The photograph shows the store manager (left) listening to questions from Paul LePage (back to camera), with Chávez (at centre) standing by. Source: Centre d'études acadiennes Anselme-Chiasson, E-19587.

and the Federation could claim accurately to represent the majority of union members in the province. With 44,545 affiliated members, the Federation was larger than ever before and so too was its influence.[80]

In the years ahead it would be important to remember that this new level of unionization was achieved through a long history of efforts by countless men and women whose names are rarely prominent in the historical record. At the 1975 convention, one veteran local member recalled his own history as an "agitator" and "organizer" over more than fifty years. Bill Touchie was seventy-eight years old and had started work in the Miramichi woods at the age of thirteen. After fighting in the Great War, he joined the ranks of several successive unions, including the One Big Union, the New Brunswick Farmer-Labour Union, the United Brotherhood of Carpenters and Joiners, and the Union of National Defence Employees. During his lifetime, he said, he had helped to organize thirty-seven different union locals, and if he was twenty-five years younger, he would do it all again: "Not to start a revolution, but to stir things up a little." When he called a meeting, he explained, it was best to begin with a simple appeal: "'Come here brothers and sisters, there's something here that just isn't right.' And then I'd tell them to sign up for the union. I'd like to do that until my last breath."[81]

THE BIG CHILL The climate for workers changed after 1975 as governments and employers turned to policies that undermined union rights and labour standards. The unions were often out in the cold, but the Federation continued to promote alternatives to the corporate agenda, defend workers' rights, and support the cause of social justice within provincial society. Source: *Telegraph-Journal* Archives.

FIVE

"On *the* Line" 1976–1997

Days of Protest

They marched from all corners of the city. Early in the morning on Thursday, 14 October 1976, thousands of union members came out into the rainy streets and brought the city of Saint John to a standstill. One group started at the entrance to the dry dock on Bayside Drive and marched across the Courtenay Bay Causeway. Others gathered at the Reversing Falls Bridge and the Harbour Bridge on the west side and crossed from there. The largest contingent proceeded up Thorne Avenue to City Road and Garden Street, led by Federation of Labour President Paul LePage, Canadian Labour Congress Secretary-Treasurer Donald Montgomery, and Larry Hanley, a young activist from Local 601 of the Canadian Paperworkers Union who was the coordinator for the protest. Stopping traffic, the demonstrators marched towards the

centre of the city, joking, singing, and shouting slogans, their banners carrying
the names of dozens of local unions and their hand-lettered signs spelling
out the messages of the day: "We're Out to Fight Controls," "Where Are Our
Freedoms?" "What Happened to Price Controls?" and "Why Us?" When they
arrived at King's Square, their numbers were 5,000 strong, and they filled
the street as they continued down the hill to assemble in front of City Hall.[1]
Smaller demonstrations were organized by labour councils across the province. There were marches of 1,500 workers in Moncton and Edmundston,
1,000 in Newcastle, 400 in Bathurst, 350 in Fredericton, 200 in Campbellton
and Dalhousie. In addition to those who were in the streets, thousands more
stayed off work. Overall, reports phoned in to the Federation offices that day
indicated that about 24,000 members of affiliated unions remained off work
and almost 10,000 workers participated in demonstrations.[2]

These New Brunswick workers were among the more than one million workers who participated in what has been described as Canada's first
country-wide general strike. Organized by the Canadian Labour Congress,
the "Day of Protest" was directed at the programme of wage controls introduced by the federal government twelve months earlier. Under this plan, all
wage agreements were limited to increases of 8, 6, and 4 percent in each of
the programme's three years. This was the government's answer to what they
saw as wage settlements that were too favourable to workers. Prices had been
rising at more than 10 percent per year, and unions had been bargaining hard
to keep up; when possible, they were also cutting into corporate profits and
making gains in real wages, tipping the balance of the national income away
from corporations and towards wages and salaries. The "anti-inflation" plan
claimed it would restrain prices as well as wages but exempted key items such
as housing, energy, and food. In practice, the controls were about weakening
the bargaining power of unions. They were administered by a board that
policed all collective agreements, intervening in provincial jurisdiction under
a loose constitutional interpretation of the federal government's peacetime
emergency powers. The restrictions on collective bargaining came as a shock
to those who had taken the prime minister at his word when he campaigned

against wage controls in the 1974 election on the grounds that they were unfair and unenforceable. Moreover, the announcement alarmed those who considered Pierre Elliott Trudeau to be a friend of labour, a reformer whose 1972 Canada Labour Code had endorsed collective bargaining as a legitimate means of providing "a just share of the fruits of progress to all." Suddenly the promise of his famous "just society" was evaporating, and the 1976 "Day of Protest" served notice that Canadian workers would defend past gains and continue to seek a greater share of the country's wealth.[3]

In New Brunswick, where Premier Richard Hatfield was one of the first provincial premiers to support Trudeau's plan, the most immediate opposition came from unions that were in the middle of contract negotiations. An instructive example was provided by Canadian Paperworkers Union Local 30 and International Brotherhood of Electrical Workers Local 1888, who were completing an agreement with Irving Pulp and Paper at their Saint John mill. The paper industry as a whole had been earning unprecedented profits in the early 1970s, and employers were eager to gang up on the new independent paperworkers union, which had separated amicably from the American-based international union in the industry. In this case the Irvings, despite their anti-union reputation, preferred to sign an agreement: "He figured what he was doing was fair to his employees," recalled CPU veteran Paul Young; they wanted to "do their own thing" rather than join the "cartel" in fighting the union. When the contract was signed in November 1975, it provided a 23.8 percent increase in the first year and 2 percent in the second year. By this time three other paper mills in New Brunswick, including the MacMillan Rothesay mill and St. Anne–Nackawic and Miramichi Timber Resources, were also on strike, and the CPU hoped that the Irving settlement would set the standard for their 50,000 members across the country. The agreement exceeded the guidelines, however, and the situation became even more confusing in December when the Anti-Inflation Board announced that the Irving workers would nonetheless be allowed a 14 percent increase. The company appealed the decision and continued to pay the higher rates in the new contract until they were finally forced to comply and were fined $25,000 for defying the controls. This was the first major episode of resistance

CITY HALL Saint John and District Labour Council President George Vair speaks to the crowds in front of City Hall during the 1976 Day of Protest. In the front row to the right are protest coordinator Larry Hanley, Donald Montgomery of the Canadian Labour Congress, and Paul LePage of the New Brunswick Federation of Labour. Source: Saint John and District Labour Council.

DAY OF PROTEST Demonstrators filled the street as they proceeded down the hill from King's Square in Saint John on 14 October 1976. They were marching in the Day of Protest against the wage controls imposed by Prime Minister Pierre Elliott Trudeau a year earlier. Source: Saint John and District Labour Council.

to the wage controls in New Brunswick. It showed that workers would continue to bargain for the settlements they wanted, and sometimes they would succeed.[4]

Throughout the winter months, local unions and labour councils continued to agitate against the controls, and on 5 May the Federation of Labour organized a major protest at the legislature in Fredericton. With 3,000 supporters cheering approval, President LePage read an "Anti-Inflation Declaration" to the crowd, calling for "fair and equitable solutions to inflation" and taped the document to the doors of the legislature. Later that month, the Canadian Labour Congress met in Québec City and adopted a policy statement, under the title "Labour's Manifesto for Canada," that called for a balanced solution to the problems of managing the economy based on more participation for labour in social and economic planning. They also adopted a short "Program of Action" that authorized the CLC to call "a general work stoppage, or stoppages, if and when necessary" in order to restore collective bargaining rights. The idea of a general strike was strongly supported by CUPE's Lofty MacMillan, the former NBFL president, who ran unsuccessfully for the CLC presidency.

LePage returned to New Brunswick saying that a national strike was on the way, and when the Federation held its annual convention a few weeks later in June, he described the controls as "the gravest threat to free collective bargaining and the trade union movement since organized labour gained the legislative right to bargain collectively." The Saint John and District Labour Council, which had already organized its own Wage Controls Committee and was holding public meetings and protests, submitted a resolution calling for a general strike against wage controls. There was much support, although one delegate urged caution, warning that "if labour entered a confrontation with the government by calling a general strike, it could be the 'War Measures Act' of 1970 all over again." Others preferred to voice support for the New Democratic Party, whose new federal leader Ed Broadbent remained consistent in denouncing the controls. The general strike resolution passed almost unanimously, and LePage noted that they were the first provincial federation to endorse the plan. The most dramatic moments in the June convention came when provincial Minister of Labour and Manpower Rodman

Logan addressed delegates on the need for a "cooperative relationship" with the provincial government. When he finished, he was dressed down by LePage: "By entering into the Federal Government's programme of wage and price controls, your government has undermined free collective bargaining and changed labour's course from cooperation to civil disobedience."[5]

A year later, at the Federation meetings in May 1977, LePage counted New Brunswick's participation in the Day of Protest a success: "With approximately one-half of our 45,000 membership off the job and almost one-quarter actively participating in demonstrations, it is safe to say that trade union members in New Brunswick have not and do not accept wage controls." LePage also underlined the historic importance of the event —"one million trade union members off the job in support of a single cause was unprecedented in the annals of Canadian trade union history."[6] The impact on government policy was more difficult to measure. By the time of the Day of Protest, Trudeau had already announced that the controls would not be extended, and when the province's new Minister of Labour and Manpower, Paul Creaghan, addressed delegates at the 1977 convention, he agreed that "the time has come to discontinue wage and price controls."[7]

Ultimately, the controls were brought to an end six months early in 1978. George Vair, who was president of the Saint John and District Labour Council at the time of the Day of Protest and has written a detailed account of local events, concluded that the government achieved few of its stated objectives: "When the controls ended, the inflation rate was 9.4 percent. The programme had been successful in transferring millions of dollars of negotiated wages out of the pockets of workers and back into the coffers of corporations." Apart from the bureaucratic costs of administering the programme and considering hundreds of appeals, there were also the political costs. By the time of the 1979 federal election, union members were mobilizing under the slogan "Wage controls. Remember?" The Liberals lost the election and Trudeau prepared to go into retirement. Meanwhile, workers had drawn lessons from the experience that prepared them for a long round of attacks on union rights and economic standards in the years ahead. They would be on the line again.

Moderates and Militants

At the Federation conventions in the 1970s, LePage regularly called on the province to provide more encouragement for collective bargaining by strengthening labour laws and denying government assistance to anti-union employers. There were plenty of examples, including a flagrant situation at the Japanese-owned Cirtex Knitting plant in Caraquet, which opened in 1974 with substantial federal and provincial assistance. When the Canadian Seafood and Allied Workers were certified to represent the workers, there was no contract, and a long strike followed. In January 1976, the company decided to sign an agreement with a different union, literally leaving members of the officially recognized union out in the cold. By the end of the year, the company had decided to close doors permanently. When Mathilda Blanchard reported on the struggle at the 1977 convention and thanked the Federation for supporting the strike fund, she received a standing ovation. She was also elected as one of the Federation's vice-presidents.[8]

On the other side of the province, there was another example of the trouble workers were having in securing first agreements. Workers at a new plywood mill in McAdam operated by the Georgia-Pacific Corporation voted heavily in 1977 for the Canadian Paperworkers. After gaining certification, they faced a multinational corporation that refused to deal with the CPU. The company took their objections twice to the Industrial Relations Board and then to the Court of Queen's Bench and the Supreme Court of New Brunswick. At the 1978 convention, Aurèle Ferlatte, now the CPU's Atlantic region vice-president, appealed for support. In response, the Federation urged the province to suspend the company's woodcutting rights and the federal government to discontinue its regional development grants. By this stage, having exhausted all avenues of evasion, Georgia-Pacific agreed to begin negotiations.[9]

The 1978 Federation convention was notably raucous. It began with what the *Telegraph-Journal* described as "a stinging attack" on the provincial government for failing to reduce unemployment, raise standards, and protect workers' rights. After reviewing the province's many failures, LePage concluded that "the time is long overdue where organized labour in this

province becomes far more active politically" and called for the election of New Democratic Party governments both provincially and federally. Although many delegates wore NDP buttons, no specific resolutions concerning support for the party were considered. However, when Premier Hatfield's latest minister of labour and manpower was introduced — the third minister to hold the post in three years — there was a request from the floor not to allow Lawrence Garvie to speak. LePage ruled the motion out of order. Some twenty delegates walked out, and others interrupted the speech with boos and jeers. Garvie carried on, thanking the Federation for continuing to propose reforms to provincial labour laws and "the responsible attitude of the Federation which it has demonstrated in its deliberations."[10] The incident confirmed the growing tensions between the Federation and the province. With the exception of the next minister, Mabel DeWare (who was invited to speak in 1981), this was the last occasion on which the minister of labour addressed the Federation convention.

LePage also came in for criticism in 1978 when the Campbellton-Dalhousie District Labour Council called for the withdrawal of the Federation president from the Industrial Relations Board. Their concern was that membership on this quasi-judicial board that administered the Industrial Relations Act and other laws limited the president's freedom to criticize anti-union employers. Others argued that service on the board enabled the president to be more fully informed about cases and to better defend workers' interests. The resolution was defeated, but a long debate took place a year later on a resolution to prohibit all officers from sitting on the Industrial Relations Board. This too was defeated. Following the 1978 convention, LePage was bitterly offended when Blanchard, who was defeated as a candidate for re-election as a vice-president in 1978, charged that the Federation was too much of a "one-man show and the man's name is Paul LePage." She had been especially critical of LePage for failing to defend the Cirtex workers more effectively as a member of the Industrial Relations Board.[11]

By 1980, LePage was ready to step down. With the exception of White-bone, he was the longest-serving president of the Federation. Although sometimes out of step with more militant members, LePage was always re-elected by acclamation, and none doubted his skill in managing the Federation's affairs. During his time in office, the affiliated membership had more than doubled, to a historic level of more than 48,000 members at the end of the 1970s. On behalf of the delegates, vice-president Tim McCarthy paid tribute to LePage in these words: "All he ever brought this federation is credibility, and all he has ever done is good for the working people of this province." LePage's achievements also included increased cooperation with the other federations of labour in the region and the creation of ARLEC, the Atlantic Region Labour Education Centre, based at St. Francis Xavier University, to provide training for rank and file union activists. As the 1980 convention came to a close, delegates presented LePage with a set of golf clubs, gave him a standing ovation and broke into a singing of "Solidarity Forever."

PHIL BOOKER He had worked in the woods before joining the Royal Canadian Air Force during the Second World War. In the 1950s he helped build the policemen's union in Fredericton. Booker (1919–2009) became Federation president in 1980: "Public employees are being used as scapegoats by governments. . . . Canadians can take things up to a point, and then they don't take anymore." Source: Provincial Archives of New Brunswick, New Brunswick Federation of Labour fonds, MC1819, box 192.

As usual, LePage did not mince words: "I've been called a dictator, and I guess that's true to a certain extent. But you've got to be either a leader or a follower, and you've got to be a bit of a dictator to be a leader." He also recalled his arrival as a stranger to the province more than twenty-five years earlier and said: "Now there's not too many places I can go in this province where somebody won't stop me on the street and say 'Hi, Paul.' I am one of the most fortunate people in the world."[12]

At least three names were mooted to succeed LePage, and each of them did become president of the Federation over the next several years. Tim McCarthy was a vice-president for Northumberland-Kent, and Larry Hanley was vice-president for Saint John-Charlotte; both worked at paper mills represented by the CPU. McCarthy declined nomination, and the thirty-one-year-old Hanley finished second to Phil Booker, the longtime vice-president for the Fredericton area. His labour credentials went back to the embattled early days of the Fredericton police union in the 1950s, where he was president of the local; after seventeen years on the force, Booker became a staff representative for the Canadian Union of Public Employees in 1970. He has recalled that the day he accepted the CUPE position, he was offered an unexpected appointment as deputy chief of police, but he never regretted his decision to stay with the union. Booker's election flyer underlined the importance of his background as a public employee: "At this point in our province's history, it is the public employee who is being hit hardest by management.

Public employees are being used as scapegoats by governments to remove blame from themselves. And the politicians use that myth to charge us more taxes. But then they cut back the services we used to receive. This is the fight in our society right now — for all of us." Booker later told the *Telegraph-Journal* that he planned to follow a steady course: "I'm a moderate, neither a hawk nor a dove. I wouldn't call this a cautious approach. I'd call it a mature approach." Booker left no doubt he would be a staunch defender of union rights, including the right to strike when other solutions failed: "It's certainly in the best interest of Canada as a democracy for workers to have that right. Canadians can take things up to a point, and then they don't take anymore."[13]

Like LePage, Booker faced frustrations. Once more there was a dramatic example of an employer who was able to defeat workers who wanted union representation. It happened in Dalhousie, usually considered a strong union town. When workers at the Sobeys store there joined the Retail, Wholesale and Department Store Union, they were unable to conclude a first contract and were forced to go on strike in December 1980. As one worker recalled, "they thought it was quite funny that we would try to organize. And they tried to break us, and we wouldn't. We were very strong." Two months later, Sobeys decided to close the store on the grounds that it was not a "viable" operation. At the 1981 convention in Moncton, Booker reported on the Federation's support for a province-wide boycott of all non-union Sobeys stores and led a march to the store at Highfield Square.[14]

Although there would be no first-contract legislation for New Brunswick workers, Booker had some success in advancing labour's legislative goals. He was especially pleased with the appointment of a new Occupational Health and Safety Commission with a mandate to improve the regulation of workplace conditions; three of the six commissioners were to be nominated by the Federation. He also noted amendments to the Workmen's Compensation Act that provided for the use of workers' advocates in hearing cases and also increased benefits, expanded coverage, and improved the definitions of "industrial disease" and "pre-existing conditions." Many of these changes followed the recommendations of a study committee on which the Federation was represented by Ed Levert of the Steelworkers and Larry Hanley of the Paperworkers. Booker also expected soon to see the province enact an overdue employment standards code and amendments to the Industrial Relations Act. In the light of this progress, the executive decided to invite the current Minister of Labour and Manpower to address the 1981 convention. Before she spoke, however, DeWare was forced to wait at the head table and listen to a debate on whether labour should refuse to participate in consultations that were loaded in favour of government and management.[15]

One trying internal situation for organized labour in Canada was also coming to a head at this time. That was the suspension of the building trades unions from the Canadian Labour Congress for non-payment of dues. The dispute had little to do with conditions in New Brunswick. Indeed, the 1980 convention had taken steps to provide for a separate vice-president-at-large to give the building trades stronger representation on the executive. However, the CLC suspension, which took effect only a few weeks before the 1981 convention, rendered twelve unions ineligible to participate in the Federation, including mainstays such as the Carpenters and the Electrical Workers. When a motion from the floor asked that the disputed delegates be seated as observers, Booker ruled the request out of order, stating that this would constitute a form of recognition. His ruling was sustained by a standing vote, with about one-third of the delegates opposed. The exclusion of the building trades proved a lasting setback for the Federation. These were among the oldest and strongest union locals in the province, and the Federation was losing almost 10,000 members as well as 18 percent of its annual revenue. Before the end of the 1981 convention, delegates passed an emergency resolution calling for the resumption of negotiations. However, the CLC seemed to underestimate the impact of the suspensions on smaller provincial bodies such as the Federation and was not prepared to make any allowances. The Fredericton and District Labour Council, for instance, was advised by the CLC that it was entirely out of order for them to allow participation of "persons whose parent organizations are intent on destroying the Congress."[16]

As in 1980, the contest for president matched Booker against Larry Hanley. This time the younger man won by a reported margin of eight votes. Delegates seemed to be closely divided on whether they preferred Booker's moderate ways or Hanley's more militant message. Hanley belonged to a new generation who had come of age in the 1960s. Born in Saint John in 1948, he grew up in the culture of the union movement. His father had been a member of the old Canadian Seamen's Union and then worked at the sugar refinery and the paper mill. At one stage, when the elder Hanley was blacklisted in Saint John, he moved the family to Alabama to find work. That was during the early days of the civil rights movement in the United States, and the younger Hanley returned to New Brunswick with a well-developed social conscience. He went into the Rothesay paper mill after high school and was soon recognized as a leader in his union local. He attended courses at ARLEC and the Labour College of Canada and was elected president of the Saint John and District Labour Council in 1977. As early as 1972, Hanley identified himself as a critic of the existing union establishment. As he put it in a union newspaper, he was keen to recapture the

LARRY HANLEY The son of a veteran Saint John trade unionist, Hanley (1948–2006) belonged to a new generation of union leaders who came of age in the 1960s and 1970s: "The labour movement as I understand it, originated to create a life worth living as a man, not as a servant or a serf to industry." He was elected President of the Federation in 1980. Source: Courtesy of Mary Hanley.

labour movement's sense of mission: "The labour movement as I understand it, originated to create a life worth living as a man, not as a servant or a serf to industry. Was it not meant to be a step or even a path to human dignity and rights? We have created in our labour movement a highly centralized authoritarian administration: the same type of administration that industry and even government of today have perfected." As president of CPU Local 601, Hanley was proud of their success in achieving wage parity with west coast workers in the industry. In addition, he had a lasting concern with workplace safety and workers' compensation that owed much to the bureaucratic obstacles his father encountered after losing his leg in an industrial accident.[17]

Convention delegates knew that Hanley was the key organizer behind the well-planned Day of Protest in Saint John in 1976. They were also aware of his part in a campaign against the export of nuclear fuel supplies to Argentina. This was a notable example of support for workers in a distant country who appealed directly for support from Canadian workers, and the response in New Brunswick owed much to Hanley's passion for international solidarity. In May 1979, he accompanied Enrique Tabak, a member of the Group for the Defence of Civil Rights in Argentina, to the Federation convention, where Tabak delivered a moving appeal for support in their struggle to defend union rights in Argentina against the military dictatorship. Delegates gave him a standing ovation and passed a resolution calling for the restoration of human, civil, and union rights and the suspension of nuclear sales to Argentina. On 3 July 1979, Saint John longshoremen refused to load a shipment of heavy water bound to supply a CANDU reactor in Argentina. The "NO CANDU

NO HOT CARGO On 3 July 1979, Saint John longshoremen refused to load a shipment of heavy water bound for Argentina. They were supporting the Federation's appeal for the restoration of human rights and the suspension of nuclear exports to Argentina. The picket line received support from social and human rights activists, including (left) Keay Halstead, Ten Days for World Development, and Ann Breault, Catholic Women's League. The protest forced the military dictatorship of the time to release more than a dozen political prisoners. Source: *Telegraph-Journal* Archives.

for Argentina" campaign resulted in the release of more than a dozen political prisoners and the abandonment of a second Canadian nuclear reactor sale to Argentina.[18]

The election of Hanley was reported in the newspapers as a "militant takeover," and Hanley did not resist the description. Delegates had been calling for "more militant action" from their Federation, he said, adding that he wanted to make the Federation "a little less of an institution to the average worker": "We will be a visible force at any legal strike or other action by the unions in the province. We will strive to get closer to the workers and establish solidarity within the Federation." Hanley was among the delegates who supported seating the building trades as observers, and, in the interests of labour solidarity, he wanted to keep the door open for their return. He also planned to "stay away from the banquet circuit" and spend more time "where it counts — with the workers." An editorial in the *Telegraph-Journal* cast a skeptical eye over the convention and the election of Hanley, warning that "militancy and solidarity" must be balanced by "responsibility and accommodation." In an interview with the newspaper, Hanley explained that "militancy is not a bad word in the trade union movement" but that confrontations could be avoided where there was respect for labour's rights: "When there is a total lack of respect, that's when you have confrontation."[19]

Hanley had no success in bringing the building trades back into the fold, but as expected, he focused much attention on the labour councils, which he saw as a strategic local level in plans for greater provincial solidarity. The NBFL executive held joint meetings with the labour councils and encouraged them to establish "action committees." In Fredericton the Federation sponsored a Day of Action against high unemployment and high interest rates, and in Chatham they collaborated in a Miramichi Day of Concern about local economic conditions. At the 1982 convention, the executive was expanded to include presidents of the seven labour councils. Fears that labour would withdraw from all contact with the provincial government were exaggerated, as Hanley and other officers met regularly with government officials and submitted briefs on several issues. The new Occupational Health and Safety Act was amended to strengthen the right of workers to refuse unsafe work, and a new Employment Standards Act consolidated the laws governing working conditions in the province. Looking ahead, the Federation produced a list of major amendments to the Industrial Relations Act required "to minimize employer interference in the right to organize and to streamline and simplify the process of obtaining certification of a new union." Meanwhile, the Federation had been invited to sit on several new boards, including the Advisory Council on the Status of Women.

More troubling was the province's decision in January to use emergency powers to end a legal strike. The federal government had done the same more than a dozen times since 1950, most recently against postal workers in 1978, but this was the first use of such powers in New Brunswick. The situation involved a strike by non-teaching school board employees, members of CUPE Local 1253, and as a result the province was in this case acting as both employer and lawmaker. The 1982 convention called for repeal of Bill 18 on the grounds that such legislation was in violation of the new Canadian Charter of Rights and Freedoms, which appeared to protect union rights under the constitutional guarantees for "freedom of association." The shift from "consent" to "coercion" in labour relations was threatening to become a widespread trend in labour relations; back-to-work legislation had been used across Canada only three times in the 1950s and a dozen times in the 1960s, but more than forty times in the 1970s. Two former presidents took the time to speak to the issue. Paul LePage argued that the general public must be convinced of the importance of protecting the right to strike for all workers. Lofty MacMillan, also in attendance at the 1982 convention, told delegates that it was time to put in power a government "that will respect the working men and women of this province."[20]

The most dramatic events of the year took place at the St. Anne–Nackawic paper mill, where union officers were jailed for their part in a local sympathy strike. The mill, which was located on the upper reaches of the headpond created by the Mactaquac hydroelectric dam on the St. John River, was considered one of the success stories of economic development in the 1970s.

The mill's four hundred workers were vigorously represented by CPU Local 219, which played an active part in community life and helped make the single-industry town more a labour town than a company town. When thirty office workers at the mill, who were members of the same union and had been working without a contract since the previous August, went on strike on 29 May 1981, millworkers refused to cross the picket line. The company appealed to the provincial Court of Queen's Bench for an injunction ordering them to return to work. When workers refused to obey, Local 219 officers Doug Homer, Tim Noel, and Glen McGuire were jailed for contempt of court. The Federation immediately organized a demonstration outside the York County Jail in downtown Fredericton, where Hanley stated that the Federation "has long expressed concerns over the willingness of the courts to involve themselves in industrial relations matters which are best handled by labour relations boards." He also sent telegrams to Premier Hatfield and leaders of the Liberals and the NDP calling for legislation to give workers the right to respect legal picket lines. The crisis continued on 22 June, when the millworkers again went out to support the office workers and were joined by two hundred additional union members from across the province. This time one of the officers, Tim Noel, was sentenced to ten days in jail. Work did not resume until 3 July, when the office workers finally secured a settlement. The union meanwhile faced fines of $40,000, and the company filed a claim for $900,000 in damages arising from the shutdown. The Supreme Court of Canada later denied the company's claim for damages, but the events confirmed that under existing labour laws, workers who respected picket lines and engaged in expressions of labour solidarity did so at the risk of court orders, fines, and imprisonment.[21]

In another sector of the economy, the Federation was lending support to the long fight for collective bargaining rights for inshore fishermen. The organization of the Maritime Fishermen's Union at Baie Ste. Anne in March 1977 was the latest round in centuries of struggle to break the hold of merchants and processors over the price of fish. This time the fishermen would have the support of organized labour. When they were invited to the Federation

MARITIME FISHERMEN'S UNION Founded at Baie Ste. Anne in 1977, the MFU opened a new round in the centuries-old struggle to break the power of merchants and processors over the price of fish. Source: Courtesy of Raymond Léger.

of Labour meetings in 1977, the MFU already had nineteen locals in New Brunswick, mainly among Acadian workers in the southeast and northeast. The new union soon discovered that the fish processors and lobster plants were unwilling to negotiate with them. And under existing labour laws, fishers were not considered "employees" and their union did not have the right to apply for certification. The Federation's endorsement, as well as that of the CLC, gave the MFU political and financial support, and in 1982 the Hatfield government finally agreed to enact the Fisheries Bargaining Act, which established a system of collective bargaining in the fisheries. Like the Public Service Labour Relations Act of 1968, this measure extended union rights to large numbers of previously excluded workers. As Sue Calhoun writes, it was a "major victory": "The union had begun the fight in 1974, and since then, there had been committees, studies and reports nearly every year that had recommended collective bargaining for fishermen. After eight years, fishermen in New Brunswick finally had the right to negotiate the price of fish." The campaign included a mix of mobilization, publicity, lobbying, and direct action. The turning point may well have come on the wharf in Caraquet in September 1979, when the MFU led a five-day protest against the season opening of the herring stock to the large seiners that left little for the inshore boats to harvest. When the RCMP used tear gas to break up the occupation of the wharf, the Federation supported a "day of solidarity" at the Caraquet arena. Fisherman Herménégilde Robichaud and MFU executive secretary Gilles Thériault were later convicted of public mischief for their part in the local "herring war." Calhoun concludes that the events at Caraquet showed that the MFU was dedicated to the fishers' interests and had public support: "Of all the battles that the union had fought and would fight, it was the one that strengthened and increased the membership, that won over the public."[22]

Hanley's lively term as President came to an end at the 1982 convention. Although his dedication and skill were evident, there were signs early in the convention that his return to office was not assured. In a debate on a resolution to resume annual briefs to the cabinet, Hanley left the chair to oppose the motion: "We are really talking about a question of philosophy," he said.

UNION RECOGNITION The RCMP breaks up an MFU demonstration on the wharf at Caraquet in September 1979. The Federation supported the long campaign for union recognition, which was achieved with the enactment of the Fisheries Bargaining Act in 1982. Source: Centre d'études acadiennes Anselme-Chiasson, E-15751.

TIM MCCARTHY Born in Ireland,
McCarthy was a skilled worker who
became president of the paperworkers
local at one of the mills on the Miramichi. As Federation president from
1982 to 1991, he was a soft-spoken
but forward-looking leader, calling on
members to "take action to ensure a
united and strong labour movement that
will meet the needs of present and future
workers." Source: Provincial Archives
of New Brunswick, New Brunswick
Federation of Labour fonds, MC1819,
box 192.

"Do we go out and talk to our workers in the street
or do we do it through press conferences with Hatfield?"[23] Despite concern that this might signify a
return to a "cap-in-hand" approach to government,
the resolution was adopted by a seven-vote margin.
The election of president was also decided by the same
margin, as Hanley was defeated by Tim McCarthy,
president of CPU Local 689 at the Boise Cascade
paper mill in Newcastle. Having served as a vice-
president since 1969, the soft-spoken McCarthy
was the senior member of the Federation executive. Born in County Cork, Ireland, in 1929, he had
trained as a pipefitter and later as an electrician. He
came to Canada in 1955 and worked on construction at Williams Lake, British Columbia, where he
met and married a woman from Newcastle. They
moved east, and McCarthy worked first at Heath
Steele Mines before taking employment at the paper
mill, then known as Miramichi Timber Resources.
McCarthy was active on the labour council and
served several terms as a town councillor in Newcastle. His victory over Hanley was described in the
newspapers as a return to a "moderate" approach, but
McCarthy insisted that his "personal style" should
not be considered a sign of weakness. There would
be "consultation" and "dialogue," but the labour
movement would not be abandoning other tools,
including protests and demonstrations. For his part,
Hanley said he believed that his leadership had helped
to reinvigorate the Federation and renew the involvement of "rank-and-file" members.[24]

Strengthening Participation

By the 1980s, the Federation was prepared to address at least one historic weakness by directing more attention to the needs of women workers. This was a result of the activism of women themselves, who were entering the labour force in large numbers and also joining unions. By 1984, for instance, women accounted for 41.2 percent of the work force in the province and 33.4 percent of union membership.[25] The participation of women within the Federation was also rising to a new level. The 106 women delegates at the meetings in 1984 accounted for 27 percent of the delegates, a significant increase over the situation as recently as 1976, when the 42 women were only 14 percent of the total. In addition to the many women members in the public sector unions, especially in the hospitals and schools, a large number of women fish plant workers had joined the Canadian Seafood and Allied Workers, and five locals from Caraquet and Shippagan were represented at the 1982 convention. Also, a new Union of Bank Employees sponsored by the CLC was having some initial success, much of it the result of organizing work by Moncton's Kathryn-Ann Leger. As Linda Dufour, who worked at the local branch of Central Trust, explained at the time of the Edmundston convention in 1982, issues such as job security, salary, staffing, turnover, and promotion provoked them to join the union: "We have no regrets. We feel more secure."[26]

Women who worked in the province's nursing homes, which were funded by public monies but privately operated, were also joining unions. By 1981, workers had won union certification at more than twenty of these establishments across the province. In rural Queens County, employees faced unusually extreme conditions at the Bethel Nursing Home at Mill Cove. When Jean Moss and other workers invited CUPE organizer Joan Blacquier to meet with them, Blacquier recalled that "the air was blue" with stories of long hours, low wages, little training, missed pays, paternalism, intimidation, and abusive treatment. They also told her about practices that endangered the health and safety of the residents. All this was taking place under the aegis of an independent evangelical minister whose family owned and operated the nursing home, the gas station, motel, restaurant, and general store as well as a funeral home. To Blacquier's surprise, it took only a few days for the women to collect more than enough signed union cards to organize CUPE Local 2464 and apply for certification in January 1981; a vote was held in February and a certification order issued in March. Signing a contract was another matter, and the local went out on strike at the end of August.

The impasse did not end soon. Members and families parked cars and trucks along the Trans-Canada Highway to block access to the home, and truck drivers were warned by CB radio not to make their usual stops at Mill Cove. Injunctions later limited the picket line to six people and two cars, and the new union members settled in for a long siege, supported by small strike pays and contributions from the Federation and other supporters. Meanwhile, sworn affidavits concerning irregularities in financial practices and nursing care at the home were submitted to Premier Hatfield by Jean Moss and by a doctor and a registered nurse who had previously worked at the home. Following an inspection, Minister of Health Brenda Robertson ordered the home closed, and the one hundred residents were relocated by ambulance to hospitals. The Federation and CUPE called for expropriation of the home. Instead, the province arranged for a purchase by new investors, and the new Mill Cove Nursing Home reopened in September 1982. It had taken a full thirteen months on the line, but the workers finally had a contract. In this local battle, a small group of workers helped consolidate the place of unions in the province's nursing homes. They also demonstrated that unions could succeed in winning public support and respect for low-paid women workers. As Phil Booker, who regularly stood on the picket line from midnight to 8 a.m., later recalled, "This local, from the time it started, I think, as a crew had probably more guts than I ever saw in people in a local before or since."[27]

In addition to organizing workers in places such as Mill Cove, Blacquier, who was CUPE New Brunswick's first woman staff representative, also played a leading part in advancing the place of women within the Federation. A Women's Committee, originally announced by Paul LePage, began work in October 1980. When Blacquier, as chair, gave the committee's first report in 1981, she explained that their goals were to increase the participation of

WOMEN'S COMMITTEE The Federation took up the cause of pay equity soon after a Women's Committee was established in 1980. Members of the committee in 1986 were (from left) Delalene Pickering, Pierrette Cyr, Mariette Richard, Marina Grant, Mona Beaulieu, and Valentine Ward (chair). Source: *Telegraph-Journal* Archives.

women in the labour movement, to raise the awareness of women's issues, and to push for legislation in areas such as maternity leave, daycare, and equal pay for work of equal value. At this time Blacquier was also elected Federation vice-president for Carleton-York-Sunbury, the first of her five terms. In 1984, Kathryn-Ann Leger, who had succeeded Blacquier as chair of the Women's Committee, was elected vice-president for Kings–Westmorland–Albert and also served five terms. After these pioneers had shown the way, women would no longer be limited to an occasional presence on the executive.

The participation of women was underlined when the 1984 convention considered a constitutional amendment to establish a vice-president for women's issues. As in the past, this proposal sparked a heated debate, with a number of delegates objecting to "tokenism" and "special treatment." Tom Appleton of the Energy and Chemical Workers Union in Saint John opposed the amendment on the grounds that "what we're saying here is that the previous executives have failed to do their jobs"; an hour later he returned to the microphone to say that his views had been changed by the debate and asked for unanimous support for the proposal. For her part, Leger said she was not surprised by the long debate, as many men and women delegates "are still not informed on women's issues," and the distinction between "equal pay for equal work" and "equal pay for work of equal value" was an example of one issue that required considerable public and membership education. The amendment passed without a recorded vote, and a CUPE delegate from the hospital local in Edmundston, Mona Beaulieu, was elected to fill the new post.[28] Recognizing the place of women in the Federation also came to the fore at this time in a discussion of the name of the Federation. Delegates from CUPE Local 821 at the Georges Dumont Hospital in Moncton proposed that the official name in French be revised in order to signify the inclusion of both female and male workers. The change was approved in 1986 and the term "Fédération des travailleurs et travailleuses du Nouveau-Brunswick" came into common use in the 1990s.[29]

In the following years the committee's work focused on holding conferences and workshops for members and preparing information on issues such as sexual harassment and abuse, parental leave, child care, health and safety, pensions, benefits, and the supposed "flexibility" of part-time work. In 1985 the Committee also took issue with a new television film, *Labour of Love*, which the CBC described as a "romantic, fictional comedy" about a strike on the Miramichi; on behalf of the Federation executive, Tim McCarthy wrote CBC President Pierre Juneau to condemn the film for "its poor portrayal of the Miramichi area, its people and their way of life, as well as for the degrading manner in which it depicted organized labour, women and local service organizations."[30] By 1986 the Women's Committee was focusing on the issue of pay equity. They objected to the province's "blatant omission" of pay equity from a discussion paper of more than a hundred pages on changes to the Employment Standards Act and argued that "the undervaluation of 'women's work' is tantamount to segregated minimum wages." In a statement released for International Women's Day, 8 March 1987, the Committee argued that "equal pay for work of equal value is a fundamental right which is covered under section 15 of the Charter of Rights and Freedoms." This was the beginning of a major campaign, to be directed at both public and private sectors. The 1987 convention unanimously endorsed "equal pay for work of equal value" as a priority.[31]

The discussion of gender balance in the Federation's official name in the French language was also a reminder that the organization was committed to a policy of bilingualism. The growing level of Acadian participation, particularly through the affiliation of union locals in the north, in the fisheries, and in the public sector, placed new demands on the Federation. By 1986, the Federation estimated that its affiliated members included 25,249 English and 13,595 French members. For some years the Federation had taken steps to deliver services in French as well as in English, and a policy of practical bilingualism had taken root within the organization. Beginning in 1972, the conventions offered simultaneous translation, and in 1975 the resolutions were available in both languages. There were formal declarations in 1979, when a constitutional amendment provided for publication of the Constitution and policies in both languages, and Article 1 was amended to recognize the right of members to use both languages at the convention and at executive or committee meetings. In 1980 the Federation made all convention documents available in both languages for the first time, and all briefs, press releases, and newsletters were subsequently made available in both languages. The updated edition of the Constitution in 1984 confirmed that "Fédération des travailleurs du Nouveau-Brunswick" had equal status as the official name of the organization. As president, Paul LePage often assured delegates that he could respond to members in either language. However, this was more difficult for his successors, as neither Booker, Hanley, nor McCarthy was bilingual. The election of a bilingual secretary-treasurer was one informal solution, as was the case earlier when Valerie Bourgeois held the position during Lofty MacMillan's presidency, and the same applied when Jean Thébeau held the office in 1980–81.[32]

The progress was slow, however, and at the 1985 convention, which took place in Edmundston, delegates from the labour council in Moncton called for a special meeting to examine the problems of increasing Acadian participation.

An "NBFL Conference on Issues Facing Acadian and Francophone Workers" took place in Fredericton in March 1986, with Richard Mercier of the CLC as keynote speaker and simultaneous translation throughout. With sixty-four delegates in attendance, including McCarthy and other officers, the discussion ranged broadly. The workshops considered issues such as delays in building a community college in Dieppe and the need for a workers' rehabilitation centre in the north of the province. They noted too that francophones in the province were disproportionately affected by low incomes and that provincial labour laws remained an obstacle to higher levels of unionization. The province was asked to provide funding for language training for union leaders, and delegates pointed to the need to re-establish a daily French-language newspaper in the province since the shutdown of *L'Évangéline*.

A number of recommendations addressed the functioning of the Federation itself: translation services at executive council meetings, a bilingual assistant to the executive secretary, nomination of bilingual representatives to provincial boards, more Federation activities in the north, more weekend courses for union members in both languages, and more francophone speakers at conventions. Delegates also reported a perception that, when translation services were available, there were sometimes not enough headsets and that some members did not take the trouble to listen to speakers in French. The idea of separate federations for French and English workers was raised but rejected as an option that would undermine union solidarity in the province.[33]

Although they had not achieved a "fully bilingual federation of labour," McCarthy told the Federation meeting in Moncton a few months later, he was pleased with the results and the steps being taken. The latest was the addition of a vice-presidency for the Acadian Peninsula. However, he considered a proposed "co-presidents" arrangement unworkable and suggested it might be better to elect two vice-presidents, one from each language group. From McCarthy's point of view, attention to the needs of francophone members was part of a larger strategy of building labour solidarity: "Workers can ill-afford to be divided over language or any other issue for that matter."[34] Gilles Thériault of the Maritime Fishermen's Union spoke in support of a resolution submitted by the Acadian Peninsula labour council calling for a co-presidency. Unfortunately, said Thériault, there was a "communication problem" within the Federation. "It is not in the spirit of division that we bring this," he said. "We just want to fully participate in the federation." For example, he noted that while it was possible for a unilingual anglophone to become president of the Federation, it would be virtually impossible for a unilingual francophone to function as president. Other delegates, both English and Acadian, shared Thériault's concerns, but few were prepared to support the proposal for two presidents. "If we don't stop dividing, we're going to be conquered," stated Ronald Paulin of the Bathurst paperworkers, who earned a standing ovation when he added: "If we put more energy into fighting management and the jeezless government, we'd all be winners."[35]

While the proposal was defeated, the debate helped confirm the commitment to serving members in both languages. Four of the twelve officers elected in 1986 were Acadians, although one of them, Blair Doucet of the Steelworkers in Bathurst, had been raised in an English-speaking environment and did not consider himself bilingual. The election of another Acadian president (Melanson had been the only one to date) was still some years away. However, the partnership between an anglophone president and a francophone secretary-treasurer was re-established when Maurice Clavette of the Paperworkers in Edmundston (who replaced the incumbent provisionally in 1986) was acclaimed to the post in 1987 and served until 2001. In addition, in 1987 the Federation was able to secure the loan of a francophone executive assistant from the CLC for a two-year period before later hiring a more permanent staff member. The visibility of the Federation among francophones was enhanced by efforts to include Edmundston in the rotation of convention locations, which had been limited to Moncton in recent years. Delegates met in Edmundston three times during the 1980s (1982, 1985, 1989) and with similar frequency in the 1990s, experiences that helped to introduce hundreds of union members to a francophone community with strong union traditions. On one of these occasions, a local reporter observed that although most of the discussion at the convention was in English, "les délégués étaient visiblement heureux d'avoir passé trois jours dans la République du Madawaska."[36]

Language issues certainly remained secondary for the large numbers of both anglophone and francophone workers represented by Locals 5385 and 7085 of the Steelworkers, who were engaged in a long struggle at Brunswick Mining and Smelting in northern New Brunswick that started in the summer of 1990. Although this was the largest and most productive lead and zinc operation in Canada, the 1,500 unionized workers had settled for minor increases in wages in the 1980s and were determined to make gains in the next round and reduce the contracting out of work to non-union companies. In addition, health and safety were a major concern, as a study released in June 1990 found that 69 percent of the workers tested had hearing loss and 24 percent had high levels of metal in their blood. When strikes started at both the mine and the smelter, the courts issued injunctions limiting the number of pickets to no more than six at any location, which enabled the company to continue operations at a low level using replacement workers and contractors. When a train was blocked from reaching the mine site, the union was fined $4,000, and there would be even larger fines against individuals and the locals during the following weeks. This led to the establishment of a picket line by the spouses and partners of striking workers, who told reporters: "Comme nos maris sont limité dans leurs actions par une injonction, nous avons décidé de les remplacer et nous avons l'intention de maintenir nos piquets de grève et de bloquer l'acces aux sites jusqu'à ce que nous obtenions des résultats positifs"; the injunction was soon amended to include "any person aware of the injunction." The strike, which lasted until the following May, had a huge impact on the local economy, but the union succeeded in maintaining community support, in part by ensuring that statements were issued in both languages. One, for instance, was addressed not only to union members but "à tous les citoyens de la région Chaleur qui croient à la justice — l'honnêteté — les droits et la liberté."[37] Another reminded the community that the company "has forgotten that the resources belong to the people of the province" and "are not willing to share their wealth with the community at large."[38]

Plan of Action

Over his nine years as president, McCarthy earned the respect of members for his dedication to strengthening the Federation and bridging differences between moderates and militants. Hanley challenged him unsuccessfully in 1983, and Brian Murphy, a Steelworkers delegate from Bathurst, ran against him in 1985, but otherwise McCarthy was acclaimed to office until he stepped down in 1991. Although he rarely raised his voice and was attentive to procedural detail, McCarthy proved to be an able organizer and a strong defender of union rights. As one delegate remarked, McCarthy seemed to have "the ways of a bureaucrat but the heart of a trade unionist."[39] His patience was sorely tested during his years in office. Membership numbers remained stable, just short of the 40,000 members often mentioned in news reports, but instead of advancing their agenda for reform of labour laws and renewal of the union movement, the Federation was repeatedly called upon to resist attacks on the status of workers and unions.

It was alarming to find that governments often seemed to be leading the way. Since the end of wage controls in 1977, organized labour had bargained hard to "catch up" with rising prices. Meanwhile, the federal government in 1982 brought in wage controls that were directed at employees in the federal public service but expected to set an example for other employers. Existing contracts were arbitrarily extended for an additional two years, and any scheduled increases were limited to 6 and 5 percent for that period.[40] In New Brunswick, the Hatfield government followed the lead by announcing "voluntary" guidelines, a prescription that sounded less severe but had a chilling effect on negotiations with provincial employees. Meanwhile, employers in the private sector were showing more reluctance to deal with unions, and some were taking advantage of opportunities to hire replacement workers and avoid contract negotiations. The situation did not improve with the election of Brian Mulroney's Progressive Conservative federal government in 1984 and Frank McKenna's Liberal government in New Brunswick in 1987, who in due course proved to be more determined than their predecessors to weaken employment standards, reduce public services, and limit the influence of unions. When McCarthy reported to the Federation's 1985 convention, he warned that there were challenging times ahead: "Labour is increasingly under attack by big business, conservative governments and other right-wing elements who seek to make unions the scapegoats for society's ills."[41]

It would take more than resolutions to meet this challenge. When the 1986 convention met in Moncton, under the theme "Workers' Options," the Federation adopted an "action plan" for informing, organizing, and mobilizing union members. It started with a package of legal reforms needed to stabilize the labour relations system. At the top of the list was "first agreement arbitration" to ensure that workers who chose to join a union were not prevented from achieving a first contract. There was more. Certification should be speedy when there was majority support for a union. The hiring of replacement workers during strikes should be fully prohibited. Equal treatment for full-time and part-time workers should be guaranteed. Equal pay for work of equal value should be legislated. Workers' compensation should be reformed to provide the right to return to work and receive training as needed. In the medium term, solidarity within the union movement should be strengthened, and in the longer term, support for the New Democratic Party should be encouraged because it was "the only proven vehicle for Canadian working people to achieve their legislative goals." The "action plan" also recognized the need to reach a broader public. Delegates would need to "take our message back to the membership" and build an understanding that "the solutions we're fighting for will make a difference to them and other working people." To achieve this, unions needed to make more effort to educate their own members and to convince the public that unions were serving the general interest.[42]

In Moncton itself there was an obvious example of how the unions could help defend community interests. The city's largest industrial employer, the Canadian National Railway, was threatening to shut down operations, eliminating 1,200 jobs directly and another 800 related jobs. On behalf of the Federation, McCarthy had already written the Minister of Transport in 1985 to warn about the severe consequences of such a plan, and the Federation was a leading participant in the local "Save Our Shops" campaign. Petitions went forward to each of the Atlantic premiers calling for unity in defence of the railway shops as an economic engine that injected tens of millions of dollars into the regional economy every year. Another petition called on Parliament to stop any moves to downgrade or close the Moncton operations. A flyer entitled "Your Voice Could Save 2000 Jobs" warned that closing the shops would be the end of Moncton's "proud, century-old heritage as a great railroad town" and would destroy a tradition of achievement and expertise among local workers, "dismantling a team of hundreds of experienced skilled workers, including boilermakers, blacksmiths, carmen, electricians, machinists, pipefitters, and sheet metal workers."[43]

"SAVE OUR SHOPS" The shutdown of the railway shops in the 1980s was a major blow for workers in Moncton and marked the abandonment of the railway and other public enterprises as instruments of national policy: "The CNR was designed and has traditionally been used as an instrument of cultural, political and economic development in Canada." Source: Provincial Archives of New Brunswick, New Brunswick Federation of Labour fonds, MC1819, box 192.

The situation received close attention from one of the visiting speakers at the 1986 Moncton convention who was now one of the most prominent labour leaders in Canada. Valerie Bourgeois had started work as a machinist's apprentice at CN in 1952, and was active in IAM Local 594 as well as the labour council and the Federation (he was secretary-treasurer from 1963 to 1969). After working for the union in Montréal and Ottawa, he was elected IAM vice-president for Canada in 1985. When he spoke to the delegates, Bourgeois focused his attention on the plan to remove Moncton's "historic right" to the railway shops as part of the Maritime provinces' contribution to the Canadian economy: "To say such a move is scandalous and irresponsible is an understatement. It is economically unsound, socially reprehensible, and politically stupid." He congratulated the "Save Our Shops" committee for mobilizing public support, but warned that downsizing, shutdowns, and backdoor forms of privatization were "but one part of the current insane ideological rush towards 'laissez-faire' by our conservative government": "Throw in deregulation, abolishment of generic drugs, major cutbacks of such programmes as unemployment insurance and medicare funding, to name just a few things, and you have Brian Mulroney's vision of a new Canada." Instead, the IAM took the view that, as a Crown corporation, the CNR was always "more than a business" and should promote local development rather than aggravate unemployment and regional disparities: "The CNR was designed and has traditionally been used as an instrument of cultural, political and economic development in Canada." After passing a resolution of support, the four hundred delegates then marched down Main Street to the CN Terminal Building, chanting "Save Our Shops" and singing new words to an old union song: "The shops belong to Moncton,/They shall not be moved." The CN workers attracted wide support, and Moncton's Progressive Conservative MP Dennis Cochrane stated in Parliament that closing the shops was "totally unacceptable and will not be tolerated," but in the end his government did nothing to stop CN from making the fatal announcement and starting to wind down operations.[44]

The potential of a well-organized campaign was also demonstrated when the Federation supported a province-wide boycott of Coca-Cola products in 1987–88. For several years Brunswick Bottling, who distributed Coke products from plants and warehouses in Edmundston, Saint John, and Moncton, had been attempting to evade provisions in their union contract, especially by laying off experienced workers and union activists. In 1987 the company showed little interest in renewing the collective agreement, and when the members of RWDSU Local 1065 went on strike that spring, the company continued operations with pro-company employees and new replacement workers. The Coke strike became a major test for union rights, including the right to participate in union activities without fear of losing employment. With support from the Federation, the striking workers took their message to shopping malls, grocery stores, and ferry terminals, and sympathetic union workers asked to have Coke machines removed from workplaces and lunchrooms. To help raise funds for strike pay, the Federation adopted an innovative "adopt-a-striker" campaign under which unions supported individual workers with strike pay of $100 a week. In another well-publicized tactic, the Federation sponsored a touring "Anti-Scabmobile" that travelled from town to town to spread the boycott and raise funds. As the conflict dragged on from May into December, labour councils and local unions organized Christmas parties for the strikers and their families. The long strike also drew attention to the need for the province to consider prohibiting the use of replacement workers during legal strikes. A large crowd demonstrated at the opening of the legislature in

1988 and presented Minister of Labour Mike McKee with a petition bearing more than ten thousand signatures in support of "anti-scab" legislation.

With no solutions in sight, in May 1988 McCarthy, together with union representatives, appealed directly to the Canadian Labour Congress, which was meeting in Vancouver. With support from Buzz Hargrove of the Canadian Auto Workers, they convinced all the unions representing Coca-Cola operations in Canada to support a national boycott of Coke products unless the dispute was settled within thirty days. After CLC President Shirley Carr announced this decision to the convention, she received a telephone call from Coca-Cola headquarters in Atlanta. Over the next several weeks, the corporation stepped in aggressively in order to avoid a national boycott, which also threatened to become international, by forcing Brunswick Bottling to sell out to their own distribution branch. In the negotiations that followed, it took only five hours to reach an agreement — with all workers rehired, seniority rules preserved, and a raise in pay. This was a remarkable achievement for a relatively small group of eighty workers who were on the picket line for fourteen months. Their determination made a difference, and so too did the support they received locally, provincially, and nationally. As one striker's wife recalled: "The support we received during the strike was excellent. It was a lot better than I expected. I thought we were going to go through the strike and everybody would back away saying it is not their fight. That's not the way it turned out. We got excellent support. We got a lot more support than we anticipated because we were fighting for our rights." At the end of the conflict the Federation of Labour prepared a certificate entitled "Strength and Solidarity," which was presented to all strikers: "Your courage, militancy and solidarity, and that of your family, has become an example for all workers in our province. You are an integral part of modern labour history."[45]

The campaign had raised the issue of replacement workers once again, but overall "the plan of action" was not winning the day. With employers taking a "you're lucky to have a job" attitude, McCarthy warned delegates at the 1987 convention, it was not time to be complacent about defending union rights. Several labour councils had organized public events on labour law reforms, workers' compensation, and technological change, but others had not. It was also important, he added, to continue advancing new priorities, especially the retraining of workers to meet technological change and the establishment of pay equity principles in provincial legislation.[46] At this time, several steps were taken to improve the functioning of the Federation. Delegates endorsed a plan to elect the president and other officers for two-year terms in order to improve continuity in their work. A more controversial reform came to the floor when delegates debated a plan to require all affiliated union locals to become members of their local labour councils, on the grounds that this would strengthen grassroots participation in the union movement. The measure was defeated, and when the issue was revisited in 1988 it was again defeated, but closely, on a standing vote of 85 to 74.[47]

Federation leaders were also hopeful about changes in New Brunswick politics. With the Hatfield government drifting towards collapse in 1987, the prospects were uncertain. For some years there had been signs that voters were taking a larger interest in social democratic politics. In 1978, the Parti Acadien demonstrated the ability of a left-leaning party to attract support when Armand Plourde, an activist priest in Kedgwick, came within 170 votes of winning a

COKE BOYCOTT During a strike against the distributors of Coca-Cola in the province, the Federation supported a boycott and campaigned for fair labour laws to prevent employers from using replacement workers during labour disputes. Federation President Tim McCarthy listens as striking worker Steve Frost addresses supporters in Moncton in 1988. Source: Provincial Archives of New Brunswick, New Brunswick Federation of Labour fonds, MC1819, box 192.

seat in Restigouche West. In the NDP itself, J. Albert Richardson had stepped down as party leader in 1976 but continued to strengthen ties with organized labour as Federation secretary-treasurer from 1981 to 1986. His successor as party leader, Kent County teacher and environmentalist John LaBossière, helped broaden the party's appeal. The same was also true of George Little, a Saint John area high school teacher with a Scottish background who became leader in 1980. Little's polished platform style and his command of social democratic ideas made him a popular speaker at the Federation conventions throughout his term. In 1982 the NDP finally made a breakthrough in the Tantramar riding by electing Bob Hall, a teacher who was also mayor of the village of Port Elgin. A second member, Peter Trites, was elected in a 1984 Saint John by-election but later left to sit with the Liberals. The NDP achieved a new level of support in these years, and in the 1982, 1987, and 1991 elections attracted more than 10 percent of the provincial vote. At the 1987 convention, McCarthy was pleased to note that almost half the party's candidates were trade unionists. There was no hope of the NDP forming a government, he added, "but it would be really sweet to hold the balance of power."[48]

Meanwhile, at the federal level the Mulroney government's plans for a free trade agreement with the United States were ringing alarm bells for organized labour. The CLC's executive vice-president Nancy Riche had already warned the Federation in 1986 that the government was going down a dangerous road that threatened Canadian sovereignty at many levels. From labour's point of view, the "level playing field" advocated by the Americans was a danger to social programmes such as unemployment insurance and medicare as well as to regional development efforts to assist industries and communities. With the government embracing a continentalist free-market ideology, a wave of restructuring, privatization, and deregulation was expected to follow. Collective bargaining itself would also be directly affected as employers tried to impose inferior American wage and benefit packages on Canadian workers. In many ways the free trade debate was raising old questions about the relationship between business and government in managing economic and social policies in Canada. The statement adopted by the Federation in 1986, with its mix of social democratic and nationalist ideals, called for an alternative approach with a better balance: "Free trade is not a substitute for economic leadership. Governments federally and provincially have a responsibility to intervene to create viable economies which serve the interests of working people and are not totally dependent on the market mentality. Canadians must be free to choose their economic future rather than have it imposed on them as a result of businesses pursuing their self-interest in a continental market."[49]

The 1988 election was widely understood by Canadians as a referendum on the free trade agreement, with the Liberals, under John Turner, and the NDP, led by Ed Broadbent, both making strenuous arguments against closer integration with the American economy. The election was still months away, however, when the prime minister and his entourage arrived in Moncton in May for the annual meeting of the provincial Progressive Conservative Party. There they faced a large crowd protesting government policies in general and the shutdown of the CN shops in particular. In the dense bottleneck of protesters, politicians, and police in front of the Beaver Curling Club, the prime minister's wife was badly jostled. In the same melee, veteran CN employee and former Federation secretary-treasurer Greg Murphy was tackled by police forces, wrestled to the ground, and arrested; he suffered cuts and bruises and was taken to hospital suffering from chest pains. Mila Mulroney herself was winded by the incident and later said she had been elbowed in the stomach. Other observers claimed she was hit by an anti-privatization placard.

The prime minister was not slow to lash out at organized labour for a deliberate attack on his wife, and MP Dennis Cochrane and Liberal candidate Mayor George Rideout called for union leaders to apologize to the prime minister. The police found no evidence to lay assault charges. However, Murphy himself later took legal action by charging that the city police were responsible for "an unprovoked and unjustified attack on an innocent protester." In this he had the support of the Federation, which provided legal aid for his case. A Federation statement blamed poor security and unnecessary force for causing an unfortunate incident: "Damaged reputations, personal anguish and negative publicity have followed unfounded accusations by

Prime Minister Mulroney and other elected officials that labour protesters were responsible for assaulting his wife and violently attacking women and children."[50] Although the protesters were defended by the CLC's Shirley Carr and other labour leaders, the bad publicity offended the Federation's image of itself as a responsible participant in a legitimate public protest. It also contributed to the polarization of opinion in the country. While the opposition parties won a majority of votes in the November election, the government was returned with a reduced number of seats. In New Brunswick the results divided evenly between Liberals and Conservatives, a loss of four seats for the government. The NDP, with almost 10 percent of the vote, again failed to win a seat. In Moncton, the final CN layoffs took place just as the election campaign officially began, and Cochrane was among the defeated MPs. As union leaders had warned, within a few years Canadian National was one of the major public corporations, including Air Canada and Petro-Canada, that were turned over to the private sector.

The questions raised in debates about the economic future of the province and the country could not be easily answered. The unions alone did not have the power to force governments and corporations to make social and economic decisions that were responsive to the needs of workers and their communities. To achieve more, organized labour needed allies, and the Federation was an active participant in groups such as the New Brunswick Health Coalition and the Atlantic Coalition for Fair Unemployment Insurance. In 1985 they assisted the Provincial Alliance in protesting cutbacks in government services, which included handing out "Demerit Awards" to cabinet ministers "who have shown contempt for the citizens of New Brunswick by attempting to dismantle and destroy those social programs, services and working conditions which New Brunswickers have fought long and hard to achieve."[51]

Some alliances also raised difficult questions for union members, especially in establishing the balance between economic development and environmental protection. In the 1970s, for instance, delegates debated the spruce budworm spray on several occasions, and in 1987, despite concerns voiced by Saint John unions, they voted against the construction of a second nuclear power station at Point Lepreau. By 1990, the Federation had established an ad hoc committee on the environment, with two members sitting as Federation representatives on the board of directors of the Conservation Council of New Brunswick; the following year it was added to the list of standing committees, with a mandate to promote knowledge of environmental issues among union members.[52]

When social and economic issues were debated at the broadest level, there was also interest in the ideas of the supposedly more "conservative" elements in civil society such as the churches. The social gospel, a major influence on early-twentieth-century labour and social reformers, enjoyed a revival in the late 1970s and 1980s. An influential document issued by the Catholic bishops of Atlantic Canada in 1979 under the title "To Establish a Kingdom of Justice" quoted a recent pastoral message: "The riches of Canada are unequally shared. This inequality, which keeps so many people poor, is a social sin." The document also identified regional disparity and underdevelopment in Atlantic Canada as moral issues and drew attention to the wide range of social movements, including the trade unions, whose history and activity demonstrated "the tenacious versatility of our people" in the struggle for social justice.[53]

When the Social Affairs Commission of the Conference of Catholic Bishops produced "Ethical Reflections on the Economic Crisis" in 1983, the Campbellton-Dalhousie and Saint John labour councils presented resolutions welcoming this widely circulated appeal for the assertion of ethical priorities in economic life: "This option calls for economic policies which realize that the needs of the poor have priority over the wants of the rich; that the rights of workers are more important than the maximization of profits; that the participation of marginalized groups takes precedence over the preservation of a system which excludes them." Again, the labour unions were endorsed as key figures in this struggle: "Labour unions should be asked to play a more decisive and responsible role in developing strategies for economic recovery and employment. This requires the restoration of collective bargaining rights where they have been suspended, collaboration between unions and the unemployed and unorganized workers, and assurances that labour unions will have an effective role in developing economic policies."[54]

McKenna vs. the Unions

When Tim McCarthy announced his retirement as Federation president in 1991, he found it difficult to end on a note of optimism. It had been a difficult year. More than four hundred members of the paperworkers union at the Irving Rothesay mill had been on the picket line for eleven months, and the Federation launched a province-wide boycott of Irving products before the strike was finally settled in February 1991. In the north, the steelworkers had been out since July and did not reach an agreement until May 1991. At Sussex, members of the United Food and Commercial Workers were locked out by Dairytown Products in January, and their jobs were taken over by local replacement workers and professional strikebreakers. "The past year has been a trying one for many in the labour movement in New Brunswick and across Canada," McCarthy concluded. "Attacks on workers by government and the many labour disputes in our province make this year's convention theme, 'Changes! Solutions! Actions!' most appropriate. For together, we must examine the adverse changes that have taken place in recent times, seek solutions to the problems and challenges facing us, and finally take action to ensure a united and strong labour movement that will meet the needs of present and future workers."[55] CLC Secretary-Treasurer Richard Mercier thanked McCarthy for his years of service as president and warned that he was retiring too early. He also singled out McCarthy's success in promoting cooperation between language groups in the Federation: "The manner in which you have insured that anglophones and francophones of New Brunswick work together for their brothers and sisters is nothing short of remarkable. Those who are looking for models of cooperation between the two groups do not have to go far."[56]

The choice of a new president involved two candidates from northern communities, Blair Doucet of the Steelworkers Local 5385 in Bathurst and John McEwen of the Paperworkers Local 263 in Dalhousie. Doucet had served as a vice-president since 1985, but McEwen's longer experience since 1973 as vice-president for Restigouche helped win his election. McEwen's biography revealed another example of the local citizen-worker who was at home in the union movement. Born in Campbellton in 1941, McEwen graduated from high school in Dalhousie and went to work in the International Paper mill in 1961. There he became a member of the United Papermakers and Paperworkers, later one of the founding unions of the CPU. In the local, he occupied offices from shop steward to president, and like other activists across the region, McEwen attended courses at ARLEC and the Labour College of Canada. In 1972 he became president of the Campbellton-Dalhousie District Labour Council. He was also active in the NDP, credit unions, and special needs associations. In McEwen the delegates were choosing a seasoned union leader with strong workplace and community roots and a personal sense of the importance of solidarity among union members. As he once told union members, "The strength of the labour movement comes from within, and the belief that we are all brothers and sisters, ready to support each other in time of need."[57]

Meanwhile, the new provincial government, elected in the 1987 landslide, was receiving close scrutiny from the Federation. The new Liberal administration was dominated by a young Chatham lawyer who had grown up in a rural working-class family near Sussex. After going to St. Francis Xavier University and graduating from law school at the University of New Brunswick, Frank McKenna earned a reputation as a scrappy fighter on behalf of his clients, most notably in defending local boxing hero Yvon Durelle on murder charges. When he became party leader in 1984, McKenna had little familiarity with organized labour and would become the first premier in more than half a century to have never attended a session of the Federation of Labour before or after taking office. During his first term there was disappointment among union leaders with the lack of anti-scab legislation and doubts about the Liberals' commitment to pay equity and protection of casual workers, which they believed had been promised during the election campaign. Doubts only increased as the direction of McKenna's "Agenda for Change" became clearer. As biographer Philip Lee has noted, McKenna's background had prepared him for "the politics of self-reliance"; in power, this soon translated into an "entrepreneurial politics" in which the premier was the province's chief executive officer and New Brunswick was "open for business."[58]

JOHN MCEWEN A Dalhousie millworker originally from Campbellton, McEwen (1941–2004) became Federation president in 1991, at a time when the provincial government was launching a major attack on public sector workers: "The strength of the labour movement comes from within, and the belief that we are all brothers and sisters, ready to support each other in time of need." Source: Provincial Archives of New Brunswick, New Brunswick Federation of Labour fonds, MC1819, box 192.

By the time of the 1989 Federation convention, the new leader of the provincial NDP, Elizabeth Weir, was also making her impact. Trained as a lawyer, she had a strong union background in her own family, who were working-class immigrants from Northern Ireland; she taught labour law at the University of New Brunswick in the early 1980s, where she chaired the Collective Bargaining Committee of the faculty union before leaving to work as provincial secretary for the NDP in 1983. On becoming NDP leader in 1988, she demonstrated much of the same public presence and ready intelligence as her predecessor George Little.[59] Although McKenna was a Liberal, Weir was not slow to connect him to Prime Minister Mulroney for their common support of free trade and reduced social spending. She also told delegates that she could see the influence of British Prime Minister Margaret Thatcher and American President Ronald Reagan, who were commonly seen as the leaders of the new wave of neoliberalism in international capitalism.[60]

The Federation continued to resist this new turn in public policy. In 1990 the Federation adopted a policy statement entitled "Countering the Corporate Agenda"—"An agenda that would remake Canada in the image dictated by the largest corporations in this country. An agenda with no consideration for social and economic justice for ordinary Canadians." Besides failing to act on reforms, in 1990 McKenna was also accused of failing to protest the closure of bases at CFB Chatham and CFB Moncton or to defend seasonal employees and others affected by rising premiums and reduced benefits under the unemployment insurance system. The provincial government was also seen as a willing accomplice of the federal government in implementing the Goods and Services Tax, which came into effect in 1991 and would expand the scope of the provincial sales tax when the two taxes were "harmonized," as happened in 1997. Corporations in Canada were moving dangerously close to "zero taxes," charged McEwen in 1990, while the overall tax burden was shifting heavily to individuals earning lower and middle incomes. At the 1991 convention, a Federation "report card" assessing the McKenna record on labour relations, technological change, employment standards, pay equity, health and safety, and workers' compensation produced a near-failing mark of D.[61]

The situation worsened when the province started to cut spending. The province's financial dilemma was in large part due to reductions in the constitutionally mandated transfer payments that provinces received from the federal government. In effect, the federal government had decided to interpret its responsibilities narrowly and download fiscal problems onto the provinces. Some provinces were better able to absorb the cuts, but New Brunswick was not among them. Unlikely to change minds in Ottawa, the province decided instead to take aim at its own employees, even though the province's public sector workers were among the lowest paid in Canada. In 1991, Bill 73 was modestly called the Expenditure Management Act. The unions described it more accurately as a wage freeze. The plan was presented as a fiscal measure rather than a labour relations issue. Under the rationale that public spending must be reduced in order to avoid tax increases, save jobs, and eliminate the deficit, the plan was to delay all public sector wage increases for one year. The unions accused the government of duplicity in negotiating agreements through the normal collective bargaining process in 1990, knowing full well that they would soon bring in special legislation to exempt themselves from the agreements.

Soon after the legislation was announced, union members from all parts of the province arrived on 17 April for a huge demonstration in the front of the legislature in Fredericton. This included workers from CUPE and other affiliates, but the protest also attracted support from other public sector unions such as the New Brunswick Nurses Union, the New Brunswick Public Employees Association, and the New Brunswick Teachers' Federation. With some 4,000 to 5,000 protestors, the demonstration was described in the press as the biggest in the city's history. Federation president McCarthy told the crowd that "an insult to the public employees of this province is an insult to all workers in this province." In a similar vein, CUPE national Secretary-Treasurer Judy Darcy stated that public employees were already carrying their share of the burden, with most living on modest incomes and many below the poverty line; she accused the government of using "cheap tricks" to divide workers against each other. Premier McKenna, who was leaving for a business meeting in Saint John, took his share of abuse from workers gathering at the Lady Beaverbrook Rink prior to the main protest and later said he was not surprised by their reactions: "We knew it would be very controversial. It's what you could expect. They're frustrated and angry, and I'm the source of their anger. I don't blame them."[62]

After this, there was no hope the government would back down. Meeting in Edmundston in June, the Federation endorsed the newly formed Coalition of Public Employees. An emergency resolution charged the province with bargaining in bad faith and breaking legal contracts, contrary to provincial labour law and international labour conventions. As Federation Vice-President Bob Davidson of CUPE put it, "The government waited until it got the best deals from the unions, then hit us with the freeze, something that completely undermines our collective bargaining rights." After two hours of discussion and debate, there was unanimous support and a standing ovation. The Federation decided to produce anti-McKenna radio and television ads featuring the theme "Honesty. Not a lot to ask." President McEwen said that it would be necessary to "change the government's attitudes in dealing with workers . . . or change the government."[63]

When a provincial election took place in September, it was apparent that the McKenna magic was tarnished but that the opposition was badly divided. Elizabeth Weir had already won a reputation as an articulate, but unelected and unofficial, Leader of the Opposition. Thanks to hard work in building an alliance of labour, women, environmental, and anti-poverty activists in her riding, she succeeded in winning Saint John South for the NDP.

The Progressive Conservatives won only three seats, and the title of Official Opposition went to the eight members elected under the banner of the Confederation of Regions Party. This new party, whose main policy was their opposition to official bilingualism, attracted most of their electoral support in the region surrounding the capital city, where many public employees lived. It was a protest vote against the McKenna government, but it was hardly satisfying to Federation leaders to see the corrosive anti-French politics of COR become a lightning rod for concerns about cutbacks in government employment and public services.[64]

In the spring of 1992, the International Labour Organization was still investigating union complaints that the 1991 legislation violated international labour standards.[65] The provincial government did not wait for a decision before deciding to repeat the experiment. A new Expenditure Management Act, introduced as Bill 42, extended existing agreements in the public sector for two more years, with any pay increases limited to no more than 1 and 2 percent in the first years. Again, the province was singling out public employees for special measures, and the "exceptionalism" of 1991 now threatened to become normal practice. The Coalition of Public Employees returned to action, and their rallying cry focused directly on the premier: "In McKenna No Trust." They delivered that message on buttons, banners, and billboards as well as in radio and television spots and full-page newspaper ads. The theme was that McKenna was betraying the principles of "bargaining in good faith" and using his legislative power to overturn legal contracts: "The McKenna Government under the guise of financial responsibility, is dismantling the values that make New Brunswick worth living in. . . . Is this the kind of Government you deserve?"[66]

The union campaign framed the issue around the "honesty" of the government and launched a public debate that continued throughout April and May. The New Brunswick Government Employees Union repeated its argument that greater fairness in the New Brunswick tax system would go a long way to resolving the province's fiscal problems. The New Brunswick Teachers' Federation urged the government to "honour its commitments to its employees" and stated that they were preparing as usual for their upcoming

NO TRUST A Coalition of Public Employees attracted support from unions such as the New Brunswick Nurses Union, not at that time affiliated to the Federation. Their campaign portrayed the suspension of collective bargaining as a betrayal of New Brunswick values. The slogan was on buttons, banners, billboards, and t-shirts. Bottom (from left): Sheila Letterick, Linda Silas, Pat Rogers, Debbie McGraw; top (from left): Tom Mann, Mary Atkinson, Vivian Scott. Source: New Brunswick Nurses Union.

contract negotiations.[67] New Brunswick Nurses Union President Linda Silas, the daughter of a union millworker in Dalhousie, considered the government's proposition "a real insult" and stated that the nurses were prepared to go "as far as needed" to save their contract.[68] By the third week of May, members of CUPE and the Nurses Union had voted by large margins to go on strike unless the government withdrew its legislation.

Meanwhile, with UNB law professor Tom Kuttner acting as a mediator, Finance Minister Allan Maher had agreed to meet with a team from the two unions. While these negotiations were taking place and the strike deadline loomed closer, the controversial legislation passed final reading and became law. Following several overnight negotiating sessions, Kuttner arranged a compromise with the Nurses Union, under which they were able to hold onto significant scheduled wage increases by delaying implementation for fifteen months; the nurses decided to postpone any strike action and refer the proposal to their members.[69] CUPE, however, had no major pending increases at stake and was not prepared to compromise. When the strike deadline passed at midnight on Sunday, 31 May, the union rallied members to join picket lines in front of hospitals, schools, highway garages, liquor stores, ferry docks, and government offices.

In the middle of this crisis, the Federation of Labour opened its annual convention that Sunday evening at the Hotel Beauséjour in Moncton. The strike situation received priority. CUPE strike coordinator Bob Davidson presented a short video reviewing the past year's fight against the breaking of collective agreements, and Lofty MacMillan, who was by this time living an active retirement in Campbellton, followed with an appeal to delegates to support public employees in their battle with the government. The Federation executive then introduced an emergency resolution stating that the labour movement was prepared to mobilize financial, moral, and picket line support and, if it became necessary, escalate their support to include a general withdrawal of services — a diplomatic term for a general strike.[70] The debate was punctuated with loud applause, cheering and foot stomping, and the media turned out in force at a press conference to hear McEwen announce the decision: "Any attack by the McKenna government on public sector workers, whether it be by punitive measures or decertification of unions, will be interpreted by the federation as an attack on the labour movement as a whole. The entire provincial labour movement is now engaged in a struggle of critical importance."[71] McEwen later elaborated by contrasting the McKenna policies with those of his predecessors Louis Robichaud and Richard Hatfield and pointing out that CUPE had acted in good faith by negotiating minimal wage increases in recent years. According to McEwen, the province did not seem to understand its responsibilities under the collective bargaining system: "There is a difference between the members of the legislature serving as a government and the government acting as an employer. It is a slight nuance but an important one. It may be difficult for the government to wear the two hats, but it must do it and respect the difference between the two."[72]

While the Federation was announcing its support, on 1 June there was some hope of a settlement. A last-minute deal arranged by CUPE negotiators with mediator Kuttner was presented to an emergency meeting of more than two hundred local union presidents. After a heated debate, the proposal was voted down almost unanimously, an indication that the union's efforts to keep members informed of the issues at stake had produced results. With CUPE's new national president Judy Darcy now on the ground to assist, the confrontation was drawing attention across the country, and the union was preparing to bring in Canada's best-known labour leader, CLC President Bob White, to rally support among other unions.[73]

The province was also taking action. With the largest union in the province out on an illegal strike and public services in disarray, the government secured an injunction to prohibit mass picketing at government buildings. The province also took steps to apply for decertification of CUPE as a bargaining agent and threatened to sue the union for millions of dollars in lost sales at the province's liquor stores. McKenna told reporters that he was engaged in a high-stakes power struggle with the unions: "It comes down at this stage to who is going to manage the affairs of New Brunswick — the duly-elected government or the leadership of CUPE. It's my view that order must prevail and that as the government of the province of New Brunswick we have to stand on behalf of the people."[74] Speaking at the Federation meetings, however, NDP leader Weir warned that McKenna had made a political miscalculation: "If McKenna thought labour unions in this province would roll over and play dead, he thought wrong. Workers in this province saw the McKenna government's wage freeze for what it was, not just a grab at their pay-cheques, but a power grab for their collective bargaining rights."[75] McKenna had under-estimated the support for unions among the general public, and the attack on unions was part of the government's "real agenda" of removing the ability of New Brunswickers to resist the government's bottom-line business mentality.

In its last session, Weir charged, "the government gutted community school boards, gouged rural hospital boards, robbed small woodlot owners of their ability to make a decent living, cut hospital beds, eliminated teaching jobs, bilked the environmental trust fund, ripped up and shredded collective agreements and reduced injured workers' benefits."[76]

By this stage, McKenna was finally ready to listen to new advice. Although he did not see alternatives, there is some evidence that McKenna was troubled by his own chosen course of action. Some weeks earlier, in April 1992, when he was trapped in the air for several suspenseful hours on a small plane whose landing gear had failed, he included the following words in a short note to family members: "I regret the pain that I am causing our employees and others in New Brunswick. I really do care for them."[77] The key intervention came from Fernand Landry, a trusted friend to whom McKenna already owed much for his initial success in provincial politics. During McKenna's first term, Landry had served as deputy minister in the premier's office before leaving to teach law at the Université de Moncton; his spouse Aldéa Landry

"FREE COLLECTIVE BARGAINING" In the spring of 1992, public sector employees, including nurses and hospital workers, fought the Frank McKenna government to a standstill in order to defend their right to collective bargaining. At this picket line outside a Moncton hospital, the prominence of women workers was especially visible. Source: *Telegraph-Journal* Archives.

was an even more prominent power broker in opening doors for McKenna; she served as deputy premier and minister of intergovernmental affairs but was defeated in the 1991 election. Since the days when he lectured at the UNB law school when McKenna was a student there, Fernand Landry had also acquired professional experience as a labour arbitrator, and in 1992 he knew that McKenna was heading down a dead-end road. During that critical week in early June, he convinced the premier to sit down with CUPE national president Judy Darcy. In the Landry living room, they started to work out a deal that allowed both sides to claim success.[78]

Under the arrangement, CUPE was exempted from the wage freeze while agreeing to an additional contract extension that included an 18-month period without increases, followed by a 2 percent raise later. To assist the government in reaching an agreement, CUPE undertook to provide the province with an interest-free $700,000 loan; for its part, the government agreed there would be no disciplinary or punitive actions arising from the four-day illegal strike. While the province could claim that the solution was fiscally acceptable, CUPE was able to announce a major victory for the defence of union rights in New Brunswick. It was a complicated settlement, but CUPE had succeeded in fighting the government to a standstill, and the deal would be approved by the union membership. In effect, the principle of respecting the collective bargaining process was upheld by purchasing the government's acquiescence.[79]

In these tests of union rights and labour solidarity in 1991 and 1992, the Federation's support proved vital. Although the government preferred to deal with the unions one at a time, and even had some success in dividing the Coalition of Public Employees, the Federation by its nature had no specific collective bargaining goals. Instead, its mandate was to speak for the general interests of organized labour in the province. Federation President McEwen himself was from a major union that was not directly involved in the contract disputes at stake, but by rallying support among the unions and helping to present labour's case to the public, the Federation had helped to win a battle for the preservation of union rights.[80]

"Make It Fair"

The truce that followed was uneasy, and during the remaining years of the McKenna regime there was little sign that the old levels of guarded respect and negotiation between the Federation and the government would be restored. There were more than a few sources of friction. One amendment to provincial labour law increased the penalties for illegal strikes. Another allowed employers to request a secret ballot of union members on contract offers, without reference to the union officers. In another measure, school board employees were asked to agree to the contracting out of work covered by their contract. There was a rising sense of anxiety at Federation meetings, where the secretary-treasurer seemed to report a drop in membership almost every year and advised caution in expenditures. Leaders worried about the influence of the organization, and the 1993 convention took the trouble to reaffirm the Federation's main purpose in dealing with the government: "To secure provincial legislation which will safeguard and protect the principle of free collective bargaining, the rights of workers, and the security and welfare of all people. To promote workers' issues and ensure that the government of the day is clear on labour's position."[81] A year later, a less hopeful resolution stated that "the labour movement of this province is on the road to destruction" and that plans for a general strike, as discussed in 1992, might need to be reactivated. This was amended in favour of a potentially even more radical proposition — to build a practical form of solidarity among unions by creating a "common front in the negotiating of collective agreements."[82]

In these years, labour disputes seemed to be more frequent and to last longer, and the assault on public sector workers was followed by attacks on workers in the private sector as well. The most vexing was the Dairytown lockout, which by 1995 was in its fifth year. Although their products remained under a union boycott, the dairy was operating with strikebreakers and there were no signs of a settlement. Situations such as this led the Federation to renew the call for anti-scab legislation. At the 1994 convention, delegates heard from the president of the Quebec Federation of Labour, who explained the success of anti-scab laws in protecting workers' jobs and stabilizing labour relations. British Columbia and Ontario had also enacted similar laws, thanks to the election of NDP governments in the early 1990s. According to McEwen, a formal brief calling for such a law in New Brunswick was "favourably received" by the Minister of Advanced Education and Labour, but the premier spoke against it, which seemed to put an end to the discussion. Meanwhile, in March 1995, NDP Leader Weir introduced a private member's bill to prohibit the use of replacement workers during the course of a legal strike or lockout. Instead of being unceremoniously cast aside, Bill 21 passed first reading, which opened the door to a full airing of the issue before the Law Amendments Committee, including public hearings. This allowed various unions to make the case in more detail than usually heard by legislators. For instance, a brief from Local 1065 RWDSU included a list of more than twenty-five disputes since 1980 that involved the use of strikebreakers and the loss of almost 500,000 working days to New Brunswick workers. They also quoted Pierre Elliott Trudeau on the importance of the right to strike and summarized his view that it was hypocritical to defend strikebreaking as a "democratic" option, since workers could not go out on strike without majority support: "Si un groupe d'employés prend un vote de grève et que 70% de ces personnes votent contre la grève, les 30% qui ont voté pour la grève ne peuvent pas aller en grève."[83] In allowing the bill to proceed to this stage, the government was admitting the high level of concern about the issue. However, there was no further progress on Bill 21 or other reforms, as the legislature was dissolved and voters went to the polls at the end of the summer.[84]

For many workers in the province, the most disturbing measure taken by the McKenna government was a series of reforms to workers' compensation. This was a file that went back to the very origins of the Federation, when early labour leaders fought for the enactment of "no-fault" workers' compensation in which the income security of injured workers and their families was guaranteed by a relatively simple state-administered system of insurance. Employers accepted this as a cost of doing business, and in return for the insurance provided, workers gave up their right to take legal action against employers. By the early 1980s, the legislation had been updated and strengthened, and a separate Occupational Health and Safety Commission had been created, allowing New Brunswick to claim a model programme for both prevention and compensation with respect to workplace accidents.

Now, a Federation committee reported in 1993, "the cornerstones and founding principles are under attack and are being destroyed." The 1994 convention considered no fewer than ten resolutions objecting to recent changes, one of which declared that the board might as well be renamed the "Employers Compensation Board." In the first place, any injuries that resulted in less than four days of lost working time were excluded. Benefits were reduced in most cases from 90 to 80 percent of net income for the first thirty-nine weeks. The board was given more leeway to use its own judgment in weighing "the preponderance of evidence" in disputed cases. The very term "accident" was also redefined to exclude "disablement caused by mental stress," other than in acute or traumatic situations. Worst of all, workers could no longer be certain they were insured for lost earnings. A controversial "deeming" process was assigning disabled workers to "new" job categories based on an assessment of their abilities and training, at which point compensation benefits were discontinued whether or not workers actually obtained employment — an arrangement that seemed designed to exclude workers from their insurance benefits and transfer them to unemployment or welfare rolls. According to the Federation's Health and Safety Committee Report in 1995, this was a betrayal of the original philosophy of the programme: "The 'deeming' process is treating disabled workers like disposable commodities; throwing them on the 'bone yard'. The mental anguish and human suffering cannot be described in words." A resolution introduced by Local 263, Communications, Energy and Paperworkers, stated simply that the revised act violated "the original historic agreement between labour and business" and that the Federation should begin discussing a plan for a "worker controlled" compensation system.[85]

The province also seemed to be undermining the Occupational Health and Safety Commission, a body that the Federation considered to be one of its major achievements. In the Federation's view, the policy of "Prevention

Foremost," including the right to refuse unsafe work, was best promoted by a separate agency in which labour had a strong voice. The decision to place the commission under the authority of the Workmen's Compensation Board seemed likely to weaken the mandate for health, safety, and prevention. The dilution was evident when a new merged Workplace Health, Safety and Compensation Commission came into being on 1 January 1995, and the Federation received only one of the three labour seats on the nine-member board. One part-time representative could hardly address all the complex issues of compensation and prevention that came before the board, and the Federation threatened to withdraw unless at least two representatives were provided.

"FIGHT FOR THE LIVING!" Unveiling of the Day of Mourning monument at Miramichi, 28 April 1995, to honour workers killed or injured on the job. The open honour roll on the front is accompanied by a famous labour slogan, "Fight for the Living! Mourn for the Dead." Attending the ceremony were (from left): Ed Coleman; Paul Young; Tim McCarthy; Paul Stewart; Allan Goodfellow; Dick Martin, secretary-treasurer of the Canadian Labour Congress; Raymond Léger, president of the Miramichi and District Labour Council; Elizabeth Weir, Leader of the New Brunswick New Democratic Party; NBFL President John McEwen; and Ian Donovan. As a member of the provincial legislature, Weir introduced the province's Workers Mourning Day Act, which was adopted in 2000. Source: *Miramichi Leader* Archives.

In a few short years, the Federation charged in 1995, the New Brunswick government had implemented changes that reduced the number of successful claims from more than 10,000 in 1992 to fewer than 5,000 in 1994 and gave the province a programme with the country's worst benefits for workers and lowest payments by employers — and a 1994 surplus of $40 million.[86]

While the government was refusing to back down, there was rising interest in the newly invented Day of Mourning tradition. In 1984, the Canadian Labour Congress declared 28 April an annual day of remembrance for workers who had suffered death and injury as a result of workplace conditions. In the following years the tradition spread across the country as well as internationally.[87] With the Federation fighting to defend the compensation system and safeguard health and safety policies, local labour councils built on public concern about these issues and gathered support for Day of Mourning memorials in their communities. They were remarkably successful in raising funds from unions, municipal governments, and other supporters, and in 1995 monuments were unveiled in civic squares and public parks in Edmundston, Moncton, Newcastle, and Bathurst. Later there would also be monuments in Shippagan, Atholville, and Saint John. Each had its own distinctions — there was an honour roll on the banks of the Miramichi and a granite stone shaped like a tear on the main street in Atholville — and several carried a famous labour slogan, attributed to the labour organizer Mother Jones: "Fight for the Living! Mourn for the Dead!" These memorials paid tribute to the many hundreds of workers who had died or been injured on the job in New Brunswick over the years. In the long run, the annual commemorative ceremonies also raised public awareness, including among schoolchildren and younger workers, about the importance of health and safety in the workplace.[88] Although the Parliament of Canada gave official recognition to the Day of Mourning in 1991, New Brunswick declined to enact similar legislation in 1994. At the request of the Federation, NDP Leader Elizabeth Weir later succeeded in introducing a Workers Mourning Day Act, which was passed by the legislature in 2000.[89]

Meanwhile, the Federation was also reconsidering the direction of its leadership. Although he was nominated for another two-year term as Federation president at the 1995 convention, there was no enthusiasm for the re-election of McEwen. Certainly he had some successes to report, notably in planning a provincial Workers' Investment Fund, along the model of the Fonds de Solidarité du Québec. This was to be a venture capital fund governed by labour representatives and limiting its investments to opportunities within the province. Although no large returns were expected, there would be tax benefits for workers who were in a position to invest. More generally, McEwen was frustrated by the Federation's failure to have more success in defending workers against the onslaught by government and employers. Although they had even held a special conference on "Building Union Solidarity" in 1994, he worried that the Federation was failing to "walk the talk and turn our rhetoric on solidarity to reality." It was not clear how best to build solidarity, however. When a proposal for a general strike against the decertification of unions was debated, McEwen feared this would only divide the Federation. In 1995, he was also discouraged by the latest budget introduced by the Liberal government in Ottawa, which was swept to power in 1993 on a wave of repudiation of the Mulroney policies. Instead, Jean Chrétien's Liberals, with Paul Martin as Minister of Finance, were now embarked on what McEwen called a "slash and burn approach to a lot of good public programmes and services." New Brunswick was soon to lose a thousand federal jobs as a result of the latest cuts, and the ARLEC labour school was likely to be another casualty.[90]

There was enough discontent with McEwen's leadership to produce a nominee from the floor at the 1995 convention. Blair Doucet, the Steelworkers delegate from Bathurst, nominated a candidate from Saint John who was becoming well-known in CUPE and had made a strong showing as an NDP candidate in Saint John West in 1991. Bob Hickes joined his first union when he was seventeen years old and went on to work for the Saint John School Board as a carpenter for twenty years. Like other local activists, he came up through the ranks of his union, CUPE Local 380, and in 1991 he became a vice-president, later president, of Local 1253, the province-wide Council of School District Unions. In 1992 he became president of CUPE New Brunswick. The election of Hickes as Federation president was unexpected, but it was clear that he belonged to the next generation of union leaders in the province, and it was hoped that in tough times he would be an effective spokesman for the labour message.[91]

In the summer of 1995, the most urgent challenge for New Brunswick labour was the strike at the Irving Oil refinery in Saint John, which had started more than a year earlier in May 1994. The conflict was precipitated by a company plan to lengthen the work week without paying overtime rates. This was clearly a departure from standards in the industry, and after going through all the required stages of mediation, Local 691, since 1992 part of the new Communications, Energy and Paperworkers Union, called a strike. With 264 union workers out the gate, Irving Oil took full advantage of the situation, securing a court injunction to prohibit aggressive picketing. Operations continued with a small force of managers, specialists, and non-union workers, and work on a major upgrading of the technology also proceeded without interruption. Although a boycott of Irving Oil products was launched in July, with support from the Federation, neither the union nor the province was able to bring the company back to the bargaining table until a year later, in May 1995. Instead of dealing with the union, the company offered severance packages to all striking workers, making it clear that they intended to reduce the work force by as much as half. In the hearings on Bill 21 in the summer of 1995, the strike served as an instructive example of the need for anti-scab legislation. Local 691 President Larry Washburn explained that this was no ordinary strike: "Deep and enduring resentment develops when striking workers learn that their jobs have been taken by neighbours, friends and co-workers. This kind of social poison should have no place in New Brunswick."[92]

After more than two years on the picket line, the workers would have a humiliating settlement. When the union filed charges with the Labour and Employment Board, it had no choice but to rule that Irving Oil had violated provincial law by negotiating in bad faith and must "make every reasonable effort to conclude a collective agreement." Former Dalhousie University Dean of Law Innis Christie, who had also chaired the Nova Scotia Labour Relations Board, was brought in as a high-profile industrial commissioner. But the union was not pleased with the results of his investigation. Christie announced that the union had lost the strike. Some strikers had accepted severance packages or taken work elsewhere, and more than 50 had crossed the line to return to work. Only 143 of the original workers remained on strike, and they were forced to accept a settlement that violated seniority rules and included the dismissal of 37 employees.[93] The number included union officers such as Washburn, who had more than twenty years' experience at the plant as an industrial mechanic. In this protracted test of strength in a worsening economic climate, Irving Oil had succeeded in rolling back union standards and setting worker against worker. The return to work even included "ideological re-education" in the form of a mandatory "reorientation" stressing "excellence" and "team spirit." The union was subsequently decertified, making Irving Oil the only non-unionized oil refinery in Canada.[94]

The strike was a defeat not only for Local 691 but also for the cause of labour solidarity in the province. Despite their size and numbers, the Communications, Energy and Paperworkers were unable to protect their local at the largest oil refinery in Canada. It was also a defeat for the Federation of Labour. The labour relations system that the Federation had helped to create over many years had failed to deliver a fair settlement, and the agitation for anti-scab laws had also failed to produce results. As Federation president, Hickes participated in mediation and lobbying, and brought CLC President Bob White to a large protest rally on the steps of the legislature. In one speech to a rally of two thousand union supporters at the Exhibition Park Raceway in Saint John in 1995, Hickes even warned that organized labour would shut down the refinery if necessary. Despite all their efforts, the appeal to labour solidarity had failed. As in the resistance to McKenna in 1992, the situation was of interest well beyond New Brunswick — but in this case there were alarming conclusions to be drawn. As one student of the strike has noted, this confrontation between a major union and one of the country's largest corporations demonstrated the dangerous chill in the labour relations climate across North America: "We are living in the age of roll-back, that is a time when the hard-won social and economic gains of the working class are eroded and stripped away. The two-year strike at the Irving oil refinery in Saint John illustrates the shift in the balance of power between labour and business in favour of the latter."[95]

The roll-back was also visible in the huge reductions in federal transfer payments to the provinces. In responding to the waves of economic change since the 1970s, both Conservative and Liberal administrations had accepted the assumptions of neoliberal ideology about the high cost and low value of public spending and the superior benefits of low corporate taxes and weak unions. The general mantra was that there were no alternative ways to manage the economy. Promises such as a guaranteed annual income and a federal day-care programme disappeared, and after the 1995 budget, federal transfers to the provinces dropped by about 40 percent in the space of three years. At the 1996 Federation convention, Hickes warned that these kinds of cuts would have a devastating impact on New Brunswick's ability to provide quality health, education, and social services and that the new scaled-down Canada Health and Social Transfer gave provinces more opportunities to reallocate funds and evade federal standards. The Canada Pension Plan was also being reviewed, with a view to encouraging workers to make their own arrangements for retirement income through private pensions and savings. At the same time, Unemployment Insurance (soon to be renamed Employment Insurance) was also under attack, with plans to reduce benefits and limit eligibility in preparation; many seasonal and part-time workers, especially women, would no longer qualify for support. Soon fewer than half the "insured" workers would still be able to expect support under another "insurance" programme that returned surpluses to general revenue. "Programme by programme," charged Hickes, "provincial and federal governments have chipped away at the programmes that make Canada a country envied world wide. When comparing Canada to other countries, often our competitive advantages are listed as a healthy, well-housed, well-educated population. Why systematically take away all of the advantages that make Canada the envy of others? Is this progress?"[96]

The Federation's protests made little headway, and it would not be an easy matter to turn attention from the "fiscal deficit" to the "social deficit." Yet in the winter of 1996, a mood of resistance was spreading in several parts of the province, notably among Acadians in the southeast and the north, where access to schools, health care, and services was always contentious and resource industries and seasonal workers were badly affected by the changes. The leadership in resistance to changes in Unemployment Insurance came from local coalitions led by trade unions, labour councils, and committees of unemployed workers, which also attracted support from municipal leaders and local clergy. They presented petitions, lobbied cabinet ministers, attended public meetings, and held their own public hearings as well. When MP Fernand Robichaud attacked Angela Vautour, one of the local protest leaders, at a public meeting in January, he was shouted down by a crowd of more than 500 people. In February, protesters organized demonstrations and marches in Tracadie, Moncton, Chatham, and Edmundston. In Bathurst, 4,000 people came out to hear CLC President Bob White and Bathurst

Bishop André Richard, who declared that rising unemployment was "an attack on human dignity and an assault on the poor." A demonstration at Campbellton attracted more than 2,500 people to what *L'Acadie Nouvelle* called "un rassemblement historique" that included English, French, and First Nations participants from both New Brunswick, the Gaspé, and the Magdalen Islands. When Prince Charles paid a visit to the Village Historique Acadien in April, demonstrators assembled at the gates, with one representative from a group called Les futurs sans-abri de Restigouche (The Future Homeless of Restigouche) delivering a protest speech while dressed in period costume.[97]

These agitations produced only small modifications in the cuts, but in the 1997 federal election, discontent with federal policies caused two notable breakthroughs in New Brunswick. Despite her lack of formal political experience, Angela Vautour had become a local hero in the southeast and scored a gain for the NDP in the Liberal stronghold of Beauséjour-Petitcodiac, where she defeated Dominic LeBlanc, son of the popular Acadian Governor-General Roméo LeBlanc. In addition, Yvon Godin, a popular local labour leader from the United Steelworkers who had helped rally union support for the unemployed, topped the polls in Acadie-Bathurst. The victory of Godin was especially satisfying and was considered one of the more telling results in the country; although the Liberals were returned to power with a reduced majority, Godin had brought down a powerful Liberal cabinet minister, Minister of Defence Doug Young, who in his earlier portfolio as Minister of Employment and Immigration had been a leading spokesman for the cuts to unemployment insurance.[98] Within a few months, the McKenna era in New Brunswick was also starting to come to a close, as the premier announced in October that he was stepping down. It had always been his intention to move on after ten years in power, but he left a distrustful public and a divided Liberal Party that went down to defeat in the next election.

For the Federation, this was an opportunity for new beginnings, but by the time of the 1997 convention, Hickes had decided that he was not able to continue as president due to the pressure of his workload with CUPE. Although repeatedly discussed over the years, a full-time presidency was well beyond the Federation's means. Indeed, the latest report showed an affiliated membership of 34,098 members, a drop of almost 5,000 in the previous five years. This was the result of shutdowns and reductions in employment as well as failures to win or maintain certifications or to attract new affiliates. In a changing economy, there would always be a need to organize workers, but even the simplest reforms to provincial labour law remained badly stalled. In February 1997, for instance, some one hundred locked-out workers from Allsco Building Supplies sat in the gallery at the legislature and watched the Liberals silently but unanimously vote down a bill to provide for first contract arbitration. When the 1997 convention prepared a new "Action Plan" for the years ahead, it was notable that many of the issues remained the same as ten years earlier. There was more to do, but to make progress on labour matters and on broader social issues, the Federation was going to need allies. In making this kind of strategic move, Hickes argued, the Federation could shore up public support for unionism and help lead the way on issues of common concern to all citizens of the province: "Labour must join forces with other social groups and tell our governments that we will not sit idly by and see our social programs destroyed. We owe it to our children and future generations of workers to stand up and be counted . . . to say NO to the corporate agenda and government policies that put the interests of the rich and powerful before the basic needs of people and communities."[99]

It was already happening. A province-wide Common Front for Social Justice had emerged out of the previous year's winter of protests, with the Federation as one of the founding partners. When it was formally announced in March 1997, the Common Front represented twenty-five labour organizations and social reform groups with a combined membership of 130,000 people, a significant number in a province of New Brunswick's size. It was notable that the labour groups included unions that did not belong to the Federation, such as the New Brunswick Building Trades Council, the New Brunswick Nurses Union, the New Brunswick Government Employees Union, and the New Brunswick Public Employees Association. The even larger number of social action groups ranged from the New Brunswick Senior Citizens Federation to the Fédération des dames d'Acadie, the New Brunswick Native Indian Women's Council, the New Brunswick Student Alliance, the Fédération des jeunes francophones du Nouveau-Brunswick, and the Conservation Council of New Brunswick. The Common Front would be co-chaired by representatives from both the labour and social members, initially Bob Hickes from the Federation and Steven Boyce of the Senior Citizens Federation.

Writing to Premier McKenna a few days after their first public event, Hickes and Boyce stated that "the objectives and the vision of this group are profound, seeking the establishment of a more humane society through a democratic and peaceful process. We believe that it is this kind of society that is presently threatened under your government, but we dare to hope that you still have sufficient compassion and understanding to realize that a large part of the population of New Brunswick can no longer cope with these 'cuts that don't heal.'"[100] According to a formal Mission Statement released on 11 March, the Common Front was concerned about "the erosion of the quality of life and of the democratic process" in the province, and their overarching aims were "to increase the value and the dignity of human work" and to "develop and promote alternative policies in order to create a society concerned mainly about human beings."[101] It was a compelling theme and consistent with the history of the Federation in seeking allies and supporting broad social goals. Even in hard times, the Federation was continuing to pursue its original mandate to protect and advance the interests of workers.

Source: Courtesy of Raymond Léger.

"Honour *the* Past. Build *the* Future"

Back in the ballroom of the Hotel Beauséjour in Moncton in 2011, it is almost one hundred years since the founding of the Federation of Labour. The delegates are sitting at their tables as President Michel Boudreau continues his report. He addresses the latest fallout from the global economic crisis and the continual rise in unemployment and underemployment in New Brunswick. Conditions are urgent in places such as the Miramichi, Bathurst, and Dalhousie, where major pulp and paper mills have closed and are being demolished. Many communities dependent on the forest industry are facing an uncertain future, and delegates do not need to be reminded of the struggles to stop shutdowns at Edmundston and Nackawic and to prevent the confiscation of workers' pensions by runaway corporations. The issue of reinvestment in the local economy is as old as the beginning of merchant capitalism in the fur trade and the fisheries in the seventeenth century, and the forest industry is the latest example of a staple resource whose returns have failed to bring the province long-term stability and prosperity. The same is true in a more general way for the workers who have invested their labour in developing the provincial economy and building communities only to find that too many employers and too few government policies are prepared to make the same investment in provincial society. As closures multiply in the industrial sector — the levelling of the historic shipyards in Saint John, to enable the Irvings to focus their attention on Halifax, is one of the latest clearances in the urban landscape — too many of the young, skilled, and educated workers of the province are going down the road in search of new opportunities.

Little of this needs to be spelled out, and Boudreau goes on to call for more investment in the province's future, better access to employment insurance and skills training, and stronger protection for workers' incomes and pensions. He discusses recent labour disputes and the Federation's continuing work for first contract legislation and higher minimum wages. He thanks delegates on the Education, Youth, Political Education, and Health, Safety and Environment Committees. He singles out the Women's Committee and the Coalition for Pay Equity, whose twenty years of effort have achieved an updated law extending pay equity principles to more workers — although it still fails to cover most women employees in the province. He also reminds delegates of the Federation's part in the "NB Power Is Not for Sale Coalition," a popular mobilization that was chaired by Tom Mann, a vice-president representing one of the newer affiliates; their campaign helped stop the sale of a major public utility owned by the people of the province: "It was a very sweet victory that demonstrated the importance of people coming together to make a difference in our province."

Boudreau adds that public services, including health care and education and even water supplies, remain under threat, and that the Federation is working with allies such as the Common Front for Social Justice, which is co-chaired by John Gagnon of the Bathurst labour council. "There are two competing visions of the economy," Boudreau tells delegates, and his message seems to echo John Davidson's old observation that workers understand the economy in ways that put human needs ahead of market efficiencies. The vision favoured by business, says Boudreau, focuses on reducing public services, weakening regulations, and removing taxes. The one championed by labour and our supporters, he says, is based on fairness and dignity and ensuring that all citizens are able to meet their basic needs.[1]

In the course of his report, the Federation president also congratulates delegates and supporters on a recent court decision. It is a case that started more than ten years ago with an appeal by the unions to the International Labour Organization and then led to hearings in the New Brunswick Court of Queen's Bench in 2006 and 2007. The judge's decision in 2009 forced the province to amend the law in order to recognize public sector "casual workers" as employees who are entitled to union representation, benefits, seniority, and other rights on the same basis as other workers. This was an important case for New Brunswick workers, and it was also notable because the outcome was influenced by a Supreme Court of Canada decision in 2007 that collective bargaining is protected by the provision for freedom of association in section 2(d) of the Canadian Charter of Rights and Freedoms. In these cases the courts were overturning earlier interpretations and recognizing that the rights of labour in Canada are historical ones, activated and acquired by workers in the course of a long progress of social reform. As the Supreme Court put it, collective bargaining has become "a fundamental aspect of Canadian society," and union rights are "the culmination of an historical movement."[2]

The story of the New Brunswick Federation of Labour is one part of that "historical movement" to establish the rights of workers. But history always produces new challenges, and much of the news in the first decade of the twenty-first century was raising questions about the relevance of unions. Some critics claimed that unions were too powerful, while others worried that they had lost their sense of social purpose. Union officers sometimes wondered whether unions had given up too much of their independence in return for an industrial relations system biased in favour of employers. Meanwhile, management strategies such as casualization, privatization, and contracting out undermined existing employment standards, and more part-time, seasonal, and temporary work made the workplace more precarious for workers and more difficult for unions to organize. The province's labour laws continued to resist reforms to promote union certification and first contracts, and there were few successes in organizing in the new call centres, or in the information technology sector and the tourist trade, that were often presented as the province's salvation. Once rising prices were taken into account, real wages had not increased since the struggles against wage controls in the 1970s, and the real minimum wage had fallen about one-third, deepening the poverty of the working poor. With the forces of free trade and globalization on the rise, it often seemed that New Brunswick workers were being pushed to join a competitive "race to the bottom."[3]

There was a general belief too that unions were becoming less important within the provincial economy. Downsizing and shutdowns had reduced employment in the core industrial and resource sectors that once provided most of the union membership. By 2010, this had produced a contrast between public sector employment, where two-thirds of workers had the benefit of union representation, and the private sector, where a combination of closures and cutbacks and the "Wal-martization" of labour relations had reduced union membership to less than 15 percent of the labour force. Even fewer part-time workers belonged to unions. There was also a troubling generation gap, as union membership was less than 7 percent among workers under twenty-five years of age. Among the provincial population there was even some resentment of the "union advantage" achieved by workers with steady jobs, collective agreements, benefits, and pensions. This inequity was readily exploited by politicians and employers, although many workers also recognized that unions helped to drive up wages and improve conditions even in workplaces where they were not present. In the face of all this, however, New Brunswickers were not giving up on unions. The number of union members in the province increased from 73,600 in 1997 to 85,400 in 2010. Although it was several points lower than in the 1970s and 1980s, as it was in most provinces, the rate of union density remained relatively stable at 27.9 percent in 1997 and 27.4 percent in 2010, only slightly below the national rate of 29.6 percent.[4]

The Federation of Labour itself was less successful in weathering the storms, and the appeal of provincial solidarities seemed to be dropping at the turn of the century. By 2004, Federation membership had fallen to 29,337 members, a loss of almost 10,000 in ten years and the lowest number in more than thirty years. The Federation now had few friends in government, and the once-influential Department of Labour had been renamed the Department of Training and Employment Development.[5] In shoring up the embattled house of labour, members would have to show the same determination that had brought them through difficult times in the past. At the 1998 Federation convention, President Tom Steep hopefully assured delegates that the provincial mood would soon be shifting, and he urged the Federation to remain true to its traditions of promoting social justice and seeking alternatives to the corporate agenda.

When Steep, who was president of the provincial highway workers union, CUPE Local 1190, did not stand for re-election at the end of his two-year term in 1999, delegates picked a well-known labour leader from Bathurst to serve as president. Blair Doucet had started work at Brunswick Mines in 1966, before his eighteenth birthday, and later served as president of Local 5385 of the United Steelworkers for fifteen years, leading the long strike there in the early 1990s. As a veteran of the mining operations in the north, Doucet had firsthand knowledge of the extreme conditions that unregulated capitalism was capable of imposing. He remembered a year when five of his fellow workers were killed in a rash of fatalities, and he devoted much of his energy as a union leader to improving health and safety standards in the workplace and establishing the legal right to refuse unsafe work. Doucet's view of unions was that they must speak for the people who cannot or will not speak for themselves. His version of labour history was concise but accurate: "History shows that it is possible to make advancements when unions come together in solidarity and workers decide it's time for action."[6]

BLAIR DOUCET A veteran of struggles for workplace health and safety, Blair Doucet (1949–2009) was President of the Federation from 1999 to 2005: "History shows that it is possible to make advancements when unions come together in solidarity and workers decide it's time for action." He also directed attention to the needs of young workers and was a founder of the Federation's Youth Summer Camp, which is named in his honour. Source: Courtesy of Danielle Savoie.

The political landscape in the province produced few encouraging results for organized labour. The end of the McKenna era in 1997 was followed by a two-year interval when Raymond Frenette and then Camille Thériault held office as Liberal premiers. When the election came in 1999, the province voted heavily for a change.[7] Bernard Lord's Progressive Conservative administration, however, did not improve the province's labour policies. There would be no progress on anti-scab laws, pay equity, or first contract legislation, and when the ILO issued its ruling on the recognition of casual workers in 2001, Premier Lord took no action. During the election, NDP leader Elizabeth Weir, who was returned as her party's only member, had already quipped that when she saw Bernard Lord's lips moving, she still heard Frank McKenna speaking.[8] The impression was confirmed when hospital workers went out on a legal strike in March 2001, leaving more than half their members on the job to provide essential services as required. Within hours, Lord called an emergency session of the legislature to impose back-to-work laws and a final settlement that included new classifications and regulations. Rather than submit to an imposed agreement, the New Brunswick Council of Hospital Unions accepted a settlement that was only narrowly approved by the frustrated membership.[9] The province's neglect of the Workplace Health, Safety and Compensation Commission also remained a source of frustration. McKenna's drastic reforms to the system would not be undone, but the government even failed to act on a series of minor improvements requested by the commission's board of directors. At the 2003 convention, delegates approved an emergency resolution authorizing the withdrawal of Federation representatives from the commission and urging the Building Trades Council and the Nurses Union to join the boycott, which did not end until after the Lord government was defeated in 2006.[10]

The Federation continued to identify the NDP as the preferred party of labour — and took pride in their working alliance with party leader Weir. She was invited to executive meetings, and the Federation was given representation on the NDP provincial executive. In election campaigns, the Federation promoted issues such as first contract arbitration, anti-scab laws, and pay equity, as well as health care, education, pensions, public automobile insurance, and child care, all of which were also among the themes in the NDP platform. Nonetheless, in 2003 the Lord government was returned with a bare majority over the revived Liberals; the NDP vote edged up to 9.7 percent, but Weir was again the only successful candidate. Her decision to leave provincial politics before the next election was a disappointment to Federation leaders, who recognized how ably she had held the fort through four successful campaigns. There had been a strain on the relationship in 2003, when Weir refused to overturn the nomination of a local candidate to whom the Federation objected, but there was no shortage of tributes when she retired from active politics in 2004. "She has been a special friend of labour during all these years," stated Doucet. "For labour, Elizabeth Weir will always be a giant and icon in the New Brunswick history of labour. Thank you Elizabeth."[11]

The eventual defeat of the Lord government in 2006 was in part due to the weakness of the NDP vote in that election. Weir's own seat went to a Liberal, and her successor as party leader, Allison Brewer, was not able to maintain the party's earlier level of support. With the NDP vote falling by almost half, the Liberals, under Shawn Graham, won a three-seat majority. The youthful Liberal leader's admiration for the legacy of Premier Robichaud in the 1960s was somewhat reassuring to labour, and his government proved sympathetic to renewal of the Workplace Health, Safety and Compensation Commission and, later, action on pay equity and the status of casual workers. He also added community college seats and nursing home beds, raised welfare rates and removed offensive regulations. However, Graham was unable to reconcile his own liberal instincts with the enduring neoliberal influence of McKenna, which led him to pursue quixotic aims such as "self-sufficiency" and the "energy hub" as solutions to provincial underdevelopment. With large numbers of citizens objecting to an unexpected plan to sell NB Power to Hydro-Québec, the 2010 election was a rout for the Liberals. There were few political benefits for the NDP, however. The new leader Roger Duguay, a former priest influenced by traditions of Catholic social activism, made a strong second-place showing in Tracadie–Sheila, but no members were elected. Some labour supporters even wondered whether the NDP campaign slogan —"The Voice of the Middle Class"— was calculated to distance the party from organized labour. The NDP made a modest recovery, achieving 10.4 percent of the vote, but the little-known Progressive Conservative leader David Alward, a former Lord cabinet minister, had no trouble securing a large majority.[12]

In 2011 there seemed to be more promise for the NDP in the federal election results. Since addressing the Federation meetings soon after his election as federal party leader in 2003, Jack Layton, on his mother's side a descendant of a New Brunswick Father of Confederation, had visited the province regularly. The party's success story in New Brunswick in 2011 continued to be Yvon Godin, who was re-elected for his fifth term as the MP for Acadie-Bathurst with almost 70 percent of the vote, a remarkable achievement in any part of the country. NDP candidates, including several Federation activists and allies, placed second in six of the nine other constituencies (Saint John, Miramichi, Fundy–Royal, Fredericton, New Brunswick Southwest, Tobique–Mactaquac) with votes ranging from 19 to 30 percent of the total.[13] It remained to be seen whether this would begin a lasting shift in political behaviour. For optimists, the election of an NDP government in Nova Scotia in 2009 seemed to confirm that Maritimers could be persuaded to invest in the political options of a social democratic party.

Throughout these developments, the Federation continued to look ahead. The convention themes set the tone: in 1998 it was "More Action — More Solidarity"; in 1999, "Our Vision — Our Fight." Then it was "Green Jobs for the New Millennium" (2000), "Action — Visibility — Solidarity" (2001), "Organizing Our Future" (2002), and "Our Federation, Our Future" (2003). A restructuring plan in 2003 broadened the executive council by giving direct representation to the affiliated unions and the labour councils, and also provided that the principal executive positions must include both women and francophone officers.[14] It was also decided to hold regular conventions every second year, reserving the alternate year for a mid-term conference on a specialized theme that would strengthen the delegates' knowledge of the issues facing organized labour. Another decision, often discussed in the past, was to appoint the elected president as a full-time employee. It had been clear for a long time that the presidency was in effect a full-time job, subsidized in many ways by the president's home union and taking up innumerable hours travelling the province to lobby politicians and participate in public events. Doucet would not be standing for re-election and spoke strongly in favour of the change.[15]

The diminished size of the house of labour remained one of Doucet's constant concerns throughout his presidency. He appealed to member unions to promote the Federation among their locals, and like his predecessors, he called on the Canadian Labour Congress to make membership in the provincial federations mandatory for the local unions of CLC affiliates. He also met regularly with potential members, such as the New Brunswick Nurses Union, to discuss the advantages of joining the Federation. "Our ranks are nowhere near what they should be," he told delegates in 2005. "Your Federation, Brothers and Sisters, must have more members, more revenue, if we ever expect to have enough clout with government to force our politicians to respect and act on our demands for fair labour laws and for social and economic justice for all New Brunswickers."[16]

One step in that direction was the formation of a New Brunswick Coalition of Unions, which was launched in February 2004. They warned that the provincial government must not continue down the road of restricting and removing labour rights: "The democratic right to join a union and to bargain better working conditions did not come easily. But because of past struggles all workers today have a better standard of living."[17] The most remarkable fact about the coalition was that it brought together labour organizations representing 65,000 workers, the great majority of the unions and more than 75 percent of the organized workers in the province. This alliance hinted at possibilities for renewal of the Federation. By the time Doucet completed his third term as president, the tide was beginning to turn, and Secretary-Treasurer Terry Carter was able to report 35,085 members in 2005. He concluded that "the potential to build NBFL membership to 50,000 is excellent provided we all do our part to make it happen."[18]

A major step in that direction was delivered by a union that originated in 1954 as a relatively weak staff association, the Civil Service Association of New Brunswick. When labour laws were under revision in the 1960s, the CSA supported the introduction of collective bargaining but considered the right to strike unnecessary. The transition from "civil servant" to "public employee" was marked by a name change in 1968, to the New Brunswick Public Employees Association. And in a time of "voluntary" controls and other restrictions on labour standards, the association took stronger stands on workplace and economic issues. When the NBPEA, in 1986, decided not to affiliate to what was then called the National Union of Provincial Government Employees, several units left and formed the New Brunswick Government Employees Union. Despite their rivalries with each other, and with CUPE, all of these groups participated in the Coalition of Public Employees during the confrontations of the early 1990s. By the end of the decade, under the presidency of their first woman leader, Debbie Lacelle, the NBPEA was ready to cooperate with other unions on a more permanent basis. They voted in 2003 to join the National Union of Public and General Employees, one of the largest unions in the Canadian Labour Congress. Following amalgamation between the NBPEA and NBGEU in 2004, they also agreed to a new name, the New Brunswick Union of Public and Private Employees, a step that marked symbolically the transition from "association" to "union." The New Brunswick Union, as it is commonly known, includes a wide range of members, from professional educators and community college employees to highway, natural resources, clerical and engineering staff, laboratory and medical workers, and technical inspectors; moreover, there are private sector workers at nursing homes, hotels, and Moosehead Breweries. Like other modern unions, the NBU endorses the ideal of activism among members; their executive director, Tom Mann, was often heard speaking on social issues and public policy. Old rivalries had to be set aside for this to happen, but by 2007 the NBU was ready, as Mann put it, "to take its place within the house of labour." Several NBU delegates attended the Federation meetings in 2007, and by 2009 they had joined in strength, adding 7,000 members to the Federation.[19]

Later the same year, another major provincial union also decided to join the Federation, in this case a union made up almost entirely of women workers. The New Brunswick Association of Registered Nurses traced its origins back to 1916, but it was during

NEW MEMBERS The New Brunswick Nurses Union had a long history of struggle for quality health care and recognition of the value of their members' work, often in solidarity with other unions. Marilyn Quinn was president of the NBNU in 2009 when the nurses joined the Federation. Source: Provincial Archives of New Brunswick, New Brunswick Federation of Labour fonds, MC1819, box 192.

the 1960s that the nurses began to take concerted action to improve wages and working conditions. When the Robichaud government rejected salary increases for nurses in 1964, they established a Social and Economic Welfare Committee and requested the right to collective bargaining. This was achieved under the Public Service Labour Relations Act, but in negotiating contracts the nurses still faced the patriarchal expectation that skilled women workers would perform professional responsibilities for wages well below those of other workers with similar training and experience — and of nurses in other provinces. In 1975 they protested poor contracts by booking off work in large numbers in a protest known as the "blue flu." The old Association gave way to the New Brunswick Nurses Union in 1978, and in 1980 the union conducted an effective campaign for public support under the slogan "The Nurse Is Worth It." In these actions the nurses, like women in other sectors of the economy, were redefining the value of women's work by stressing the skill and professionalism of their occupation as well as the older ideals of service and dedication. Although they pursued their own path, the nurses were aware of the benefits of collaboration with other unions and also participated in the campaign against wage freezes in the early 1990s. Interestingly, many nurses among the new generation after the 1960s were familiar with unions, having grown up in labour towns and union families; Marilyn Quinn, a Saint John nurse who became president of the union in 2004, was the daughter of a CN brakeman and conductor in Newfoundland. Attending the Federation meetings initially as guests and observers, the Nurses Union voted at their 2009 annual meeting to join the Federation of Labour. This decision added more than 6,300 members by the time of the Federation's 2011 convention.[20]

These developments reversed the membership decline in the Federation. In 2009 the number of affiliated members was up to 39,473, and in 2011 Secretary-Treasurer Danny King was able to report 47,163 members. This was a benchmark, as it once again established the Federation's claim to represent a majority, albeit a small one, of the province's more than 85,000 unionized workers. Moreover, it was also notable that the province's 45,400 women union members now made up a small majority of the total union membership in the province.[21] Most of the new Federation members worked in the public sector. At the 2011 meetings, the largest single delegation (67 delegates) came from CUPE; the other largest delegations came from the new affiliates, the NBNU (31) and the NBU (23). The largest private sector delegation was from the CEP, a union that had suffered some of the biggest setbacks over the previous two decades. Overall, delegates from the public sector unions outnumbered those from the private sector about three to one, although not all reports recognized that some members of public sector unions were employed in privately operated workplaces.[22] Although the Federation had yet to elect a woman president, the lists of voting delegates also showed that the Federation was no longer dominated by male workers. The women outnumbered the men — by two. Moreover, the participation of francophone delegates remained strong, accounting for slightly more than one-third of the delegates.[23]

Meanwhile, in the face of a changing economy, there would be no substitute for organizing. With more than 300,000 workers in the provincial labour force, there was plenty of scope. At an earlier stage in provincial history, the public sector unions themselves had emerged as a response to the changing shape of employment and expectations of workers. The logic of history is that just as the organizing waves that created craft and industrial unionism in earlier days were followed by similar waves of unionization in the public sector, we are likely to see new initiatives, perhaps even new forms of labour organization, in the future. In meeting the challenges of the new century, unions will be drawing on their experience and exploring new kinds of multi-occupational and community-based organizing that take into account the diverse and often fluid class identities within the provincial economy. As they learn about the next generation of workers and their needs, established unions are in a position to share resources and knowledge in preparing the way for the next "new unionism" of the twenty-first century. In a time of transition, the house of labour is able to provide a form of social and cultural capital for working people in the province. As in the past, the Federation of Labour represents a tradition of continuity in maintaining standards, protecting rights, and sharing values.[24]

In the history of social reform, the unions are one of the more successful examples of how working-class citizens have found ways to establish durable organizations of opposition to the shortcomings of the existing economic system. "We suffer from a deficit of memory when it comes to working people and their achievements," writes political economist Thom Workman. "Forgetfulness about working-class achievements seems to be a sort of default setting for capitalist society."[25] In the daily reports of unemployment rates, labour disputes, and economic uncertainty, it is too easy to forget that labour organizations occupy a special place in the social order because

MICHEL BOUDREAU When the Federation president addressed a conference on labour history and public policy in 2009, Michel Boudreau underlined the achievements of organized labour in the past as well as the challenges facing workers today: "All citizens should know the part that organized labour has played in the history of our country and our province." Source: Courtesy of Oliver Flecknell.

they directly address the principal contradiction within the capitalist economy, namely the inequitable control and distribution of wealth. This position offers the unions far-reaching responsibilities. They may choose to protect the interests of a small number of fellow workers in their own place of work, and they may even turn a deaf ear to the appeals of other workers; but they are also in a position to build more inclusive solidarities and respond to the need for alternative forms of social and economic organization, both at home and abroad.

Returning to the early years of the twentieth century, we might consider the views of a veteran labour radical who grew up in Saint John and was still in school at the time the Federation of Labour was making its first appearance in history. After working in the sugar refinery and at other jobs, he went on down the road, first to the shipyards in Halifax and then to western Canada, where he joined the One Big Union during its heyday, and then to California where he joined the Industrial Workers of the World. Living in Chicago for much of his life, Fred Thompson became a custodian of the hopes and memories of his early days. "The labour union movement is an institutional development with indirect historical consequences of even greater importance than its direct bargaining achievements," wrote Thompson. "To accomplish its wage and related objectives, it is steadily impelled to push against managerial prerogatives. It is my expectation that it will continue to do this, and by doing this become the major institution for coordinating and directing our economic activities in a post-capitalist society."[26]

This kind of radical prediction was not likely to be endorsed by delegates to the conventions of the New Brunswick Federation of Labour. Practical utopias must find their roots in actually existing social movements, and the Federation has generally presented itself as a moderate organization that defends the affiliated members and advances the general interests of workers in the province. This has been described as a form of "social unionism" that has broader commitments than does "business unionism" but is not as fully committed to militancy as "mobilization unionism" or as dedicated to social change as "social movement unionism."[27] In a variety of circumstances over its history, the Federation of Labour has reflected all four of these visions of labour activism, but it has always been mindful that the house of labour cannot stand without the participation of its members and that its goals cannot be achieved without the support of allies. In recruiting and educating new members, including those who do not have the experience of breaking new ground and building a union from the bottom up, labour will need to draw on the experience of the past. The Federation itself originated and evolved in order to achieve greater social and economic rights for workers, and its leaders emerged from within their own ranks. Over the course of its history, the Federation has had some measurable success in achieving a better balance of power between workers and employers, and also in reforming provincial society in the direction of greater democracy. But as long as work and wages remain part of the human condition, their mission will not be completed, and it will often need to be defended.

As the Federation approaches its second century, the delegates are wearing buttons that convey basic messages learned over the course of more than one hundred years of provincial labour history. Some are single words with a general appeal —"Respect" and "Equity" and "Solidarity." Others deliver messages about harassment, scabs, racism, and campaigns for fair taxation and labour legislation. Still others spell out longer statements, such as "Non à l'eau pour le profit," "L'équité salariale, une question de justice," "Unions — The Folks That Brought You the Weekend" and "Unions — The Anti-Theft Device for Working People." Leaving that convention hall and returning to their workplaces and communities, union members will be carrying these ideas with them, and they will continue to show the same "stubborn strength" that brought their Federation through the first century of its history.

In the years ahead there will be changes in the structure of the economy, in the practices of employers, and in the policies of governments, but workers will continue to organize and support unions. They will do this in order to achieve and maintain secure employment, fair pay, and safe conditions in the workplace — and because they cannot depend on employers or governments to do this. As individual workers they will also hope, in ways both modest and ambitious, to achieve greater satisfaction and recognition in their working lives. And as citizens of the province they will work to defend the causes of social and economic democracy within the community and to win a better distribution of the rewards of life and work for all. Over the course of the century, unions have become part of the Canadian way of life and their Federation has helped to write a history of solidarity among the province's workers. As members look back through the history of labour in New Brunswick, they have every reason to know that the Federation of Labour will continue to be there to build the solidarities of the future.

Membership in the New Brunswick Federation of Labour, 1913–2011

1913	1,849	1938	3,509	1962	n.a.	1987	37,945
1914	2,000	1939	5,500	1963	18,005	1988	37,870
1915	1,600	1940	6,375	1964	19,164	1989	38,393
1916	2,000	1940	7,343	1965	21,774	1990	39,270
1917	2,000	1941	8,033	1966	23,196	1991	39,022
1918	3,500	1942	8,501	1967	23,807	1992	37,854
1919	7,000	1943	8,753	1968	27,882	1993	36,303
1920	7,000	1944	9,277	1969	28,655	1994	37,097
1921	4,564	1945	n.a.	1970	30,391	1995	35,979
1922	2,500	1946	10,477	1971	34,099	1996	35,024
1923	4,165	1947	10,408	1972	41,107	1997	34,098
1924	4,000	1948	11,082	1973	43,133	1998	31,019
1925	2,315	1949	11,131	1974	n.a.	1999	31,748
1926	2,500	1950	11,529	1975	44,545	2000	31,302
1927	2,500	1951	11,790	1976	45,306	2001	32,062
1928	2,593	1952	13,243	1977	46,497	2002	31,401
1929	3,000	1953	13,652	1978	46,762	2003	30,515
1930	4,500	1954	n.a.	1979	48,626	2004	29,337
1931	3,700	1955	14,628	1980	48,262	2005	35,080
1932	3,500	1956	15,949	1981	47,330	2006	n.a.
1933	3,186	1957	16,169	1982	38,689	2007	34,437
1934	2,911	1958	17,725	1983	39,636	2008	n.a.
1935	2,964	1959	17,140	1984	39,322	2009	39,473
1936	3,059	1960	n.a.	1985	39,566	2010	n.a.
1937	2,921	1961	17,440	1986	38,884	2011	47,163

SOURCES

For 1913 through 1930, federal Department of Labour reports and directories. For 1930 and through to the present, reports (usually prepared by the secretary-treasurer) contained in the NBFL convention proceedings. From 1940 to 1973, only net losses or gains were recorded, and membership numbers have been calculated from these data. There were two conventions in 1940, and no reports in 1945, 1974, 2006, 2008, and 2010. In 2001, suspension for non-payment of dues was not applied; the actual membership in good standing was 28,416.

Introduction: "Makers of History"

1 For classic works, see Eugene Forsey, *Trade Unions in Canada, 1812–1902* (Toronto: University of Toronto Press, 1982); and Harold A. Logan, *The History of Trade-Union Organization in Canada* (Chicago: University of Chicago Press, 1928). More recent general works include Desmond Morton, *Working People: An Illustrated History of the Canadian Labour Movement*, 5th ed. (Kingston and Montreal: McGill-Queen's University Press, 2007); and Errol Black and Jim Silver, *Building a Better World: An Introduction to Trade Unionism in Canada*, 2nd ed. (Halifax and Winnipeg: Fernwood Publishing, 2008).

2 Wilfrid Gribble, *Rhymes of Revolt* (Vancouver: n.p., 1913?), 21–24.

3 John Davidson, *The Bargain Theory of Wages* (New York and London: G. P. Putnam's Sons and the Knickerbocker Press, 1898), 256–57.

4 Greg Kealey, ed., *Canada Investigates Industrialism: The Royal Commission on the Relations of Labor and Capital, 1889* (Toronto: University of Toronto Press, 1973), 11.

5 Janice Cook, "Child Labour in Saint John: New Brunswick and the Campaign for Factory Legislation, 1880–1905," MA thesis, Department of History, University of New Brunswick, 1994.

6 The first of these histories was Paul Phillips, *No Power Greater: A Century of Labour in British Columbia* (Vancouver: B.C.

Federation of Labour, 1967), and the latest is Alvin Finkel et al., *Working People in Alberta: A History* (Edmonton: Athabasca University Press, 2012), but none are explicitly histories of provincial federations. The Québec Federation of Labour (Fédération des travailleurs et travailleuses du Québec) published a partial history (to 1965), *FTQ: Des milliers d'histoires qui façonnent l'histoire* (Montréal: FTQ, 1988), and Québec labour history has been well served by works such as Jacques Rouillard, *Histoire du syndicalisme au Québec des origines à nos jours* (Montréal: Boréal Express, 1989), and the updated edition, *Le Syndicalisme québécois: Deux siècles d'histoire* (2004).

7 The quotations are from oral history interviews conducted by the Labour History in New Brunswick (LHTNB) project and deposited at the Provincial Archives of New Brunswick, in Fredericton (LHTNB fonds, MC3477), and at the Centre d'études acadiennes Anselme-Chiasson (fonds LHTNB), in Moncton. In the case of interviews in French, I have provided an English translation of quoted material.

8 For one recent example, see Bonnie Huskins and Michael Boudreau, "'Getting By' in Postwar Saint John: Working-Class Families and New Brunswick's Informal Economy," in Michael Boudreau, Peter G. Toner, and Tony Tremblay, eds., *Exploring the Dimensions of Self-Sufficiency for New Brunswick*

(Fredericton: New Brunswick and Atlantic Studies Research and Development Centre, 2009), 77–99. For a selection of older articles, many of them from the pages of the journals *Acadiensis* and *Labour/Le Travail*, see David Frank and Greg Kealey, eds., *Labour and Working-Class History in Atlantic Canada: A Reader* (St. John's: ISER Books, 1995).

9 Howard Kimeldorf, "Bringing Unions Back In (or Why We Need a New Old Labor History)," *Labor History*. 32, no. 1 (Winter 1991): 91–103, with responses by Michael Kazin, Alice Kessler-Harris, David Montgomery, Bruce Nelson, and Daniel Nelson, 104–29.

10 Geoff Eley and Keith Nield, *The Future of Class in History: What's Left of the Social?* (Ann Arbor: University of Michigan Press, 2007), especially 55–56, 139–43. See also James R. Green, *Taking History to Heart: The Power of the Past in Building Social Movements* (Amherst: University of Massachusetts Press, 2000).

11 The SSHRC project is commonly referred to by the acronym LHTNB (Labour History in New Brunswick). For further information about the project, see http://www.lhtnb.ca, which includes features, documents, and lesson plans on several themes in provincial labour history, as well as links to other resources. Specific sources from this website are given in the notes below, but one resource of general interest is the searchable database of officers of the Federation of Labour since 1913. For a discussion of the project, see Carol Ferguson, "Re-Connecting with the History of Labour in New Brunswick: Historical Perspectives on Contemporary Issues/Nouveau regard sur l'histoire du travail au Nouveau-Brunswick:

Les enjeux contemporains vus dans une perspective historique," *Acadiensis* 37, no. 1 (Winter/Spring 2008): 76–85.

A brief note on the present text is also in order here. Except where warranted by the context, I have translated quotations from the French into English and provided a translation in the endnotes. While bearing in mind historical context and the demands of clarity, I have at times used abbreviated or informal forms for the names of union organizations (as well as the formal name). In the case of organizations that did not have names in English, a parenthetical translation has been provided when the organization is first mentioned.

12 New Brunswick lacks a modern provincial history. The most useful surveys of history in Atlantic Canada challenge older generalizations about regional conservatism. See E. R. Forbes and D. A. Muise, eds., *The Atlantic Provinces in Confederation* (Fredericton and Toronto: Acadiensis Press and University of Toronto Press, 1993); and Margaret Conrad and James K. Hiller, *Atlantic Canada: A History*, 2nd ed. (Toronto: Oxford University Press, 2010).

One: "An Accomplished Fact," 1913–1929

1 *Eastern Labor News*, 20 September 1913.

2 *Standard*, 17 September 1913; *Daily Telegraph*, 17 September 1913; *Eastern Labor News*, 20 September 1913.

3 *Eastern Labor News*, 1 June, 15 June, 29 June, and 7 September 1912. On Hatheway, see *Dictionary of Canadian Biography,* vol. 15; and Gerald H. Allaby, "New Brunswick Prophets of Radicalism, 1890–1914," MA

thesis, Department of History, University of New Brunswick, 1972.

4 *Eastern Labor News*, 29 March 1913. In September 1912, Sugrue was attending meetings of the Trades and Labour Congress of Canada in Guelph, Ontario, and did not participate in the Saint John meeting that made the first attempt to organize a federation. As a member of the provincial executive committee for New Brunswick, Sugrue reported in May 1913 on the earlier effort by provisional officers as follows: "Owing to the lack of interest of one of these officers nothing was accomplished": *Trades and Labour Congress Proceedings, 1913*, p. 35.

5 *Standard*, 2 September 1913; *Eastern Labor News*, 21 September 1912. For biographical details on Sugrue, see *Dictionary of Canadian Biography*, vol. 15.

6 "New Brunswick Federation of Labour Minutes," 20 January 1914, 1 July 1914, 11 January 1915, and 1 July 1915. At the latter meeting, the frequency of meetings was reviewed, and they met annually thereafter. Canadian Labour Congress President Claude Jodoin later stated that a charter dated 25 February 1914 was signed by J. C. Watters and Fred Bancroft: NBFL *Proceedings*, 1956. The earliest proceedings are in minutebooks but were published in a printed form beginning in 1918 and then in typewritten form in 1923; from 1918 onwards they are cited here as NBFL *Proceedings*. No official minutes for 1916 and 1917 were located, though accounts are found in other union records. According to the *Globe*, 20 January 1914, delegates proposed that the Bureau of Labour, created in 1908 under the provincial secretary, be placed under a separate official "who would be a member of the government and a representative of the labor interests in it." The *Standard*, 21 January 1914, reported that the proposed amendments to the Fair Wage Clause stated that contractors on public works be required to pay union wages.

7 This account is based on the study by Robert H. Babcock, "The Saint John Street Railwaymen's Strike and Riot, 1914," *Acadiensis* 11, no. 2 (Spring 1982): 3–27.

8 TLC *Proceedings, 1913*, p. 35. See also the *Standard*, 16 and 17 September 1912. Montréal had been agitating for the honour for several years.

9 James L. Sugrue to Provincial Secretary, 1 August 1914, and Provincial Secretary to George R. Fuller, 4 August 1914, box 52, Executive Council Papers, RS9, Provincial Archives of New Brunswick (hereafter PANB). No copies have been located, but a similar booklet was published for the Calgary meetings in 1911.

10 TLC *Proceedings, 1913*, p. 35; TLC *Proceedings, 1914*, p. 3.

11 Saint John delegates C. H. Stevens and C. E. Harrison supported more training for street railway workers; Seymour Powell of the Moncton boilermakers called for more technical education for apprentices; Edwin Thomas proposed laws to regulate private detective agencies. In addition, a written appeal from Ella Hatheway of Saint John, president of the Saint John Women's Suffrage Committee, was favourably received, and the congress passed a resolution in favour of the extension of votes to women.

12 O'Reilly's appeal to union members was based not only on ideas of solidarity but also on the

self-interest of union members: by organizing women, the male union members would protect themselves against "the possibility of unorganized women crowding men out of employment by the lower rate of wages they would accept." According to the *Globe*, O'Reilly "made a deep impression" on the delegates. See the *Globe*, 23 and 24 September 1914. The newspaper reports spell her name as O'Riley. For a brief biography, see *Notable American Women, 1607–1950: A Biographical Dictionary*, vol. 2 (Cambridge: Harvard University Press, 1971), 651–53.

13 *Globe*, 22 September 1914.

14 "NBFL Minutes," 11 January 1915; *Globe*, 12 January 1915.

15 NBFL *Proceedings*, 12 March 1918. See also the report of the meeting in Minutebook, 1907–30, Saint John Typographical Union No. 85, S118-6, New Brunswick Museum (hereafter NBM).

16 For the changing legislation, see *Statutes of New Brunswick*, 1903, c. 11; 1907, c. 26; 1908, c. 31; 1912, c. 32; and 1914, c. 34. For context, see William Y. Smith, "Axis of Administration: Saint John Reformers and Bureaucratic Centralization in New Brunswick, 1911–1925," MA thesis, Department of History, University of New Brunswick, 1984, 47–71; and Robert H. Babcock, "Blood on the Factory Floor: The Workers' Compensation Movement in Canada and the United States," in Raymond B. Blake and Jeff Keshen, eds., *Social Welfare Policy in Canada: Historical Readings* (Toronto: Copp Clark, 1995), 107–21.

17 See folders for 15 February and 7 June 1916, box 54, and for 3 January 1917, box 55, RS9, PANB.

18 Compensation claims were considered by an independent board, using a standard schedule and, most importantly, without regard to the cause of the accident as long as it arose from conditions of employment; workers and their families could expect standard benefits without reference to their ability to seek restitution in the courts. The costs were paid by a form of taxation based on payroll lists and occupational categories; indeed, by increasing the liability of employers for accidents at work, the premiums were expected to create an incentive for promoting safe conditions at work. For the developing context, see Eric Tucker, *Administering Danger in the Workplace: The Law and Politics of Occupational Health and Safety Regulation in Ontario, 1850–1914* (Toronto: University of Toronto Press, 1990).

19 "N.B. Fed. of Labor report," 17 May 1917 (a report of delegates to NBFL Convention, 14–15 May 1917), ILA 273 Minutebook, May 1917–October 1917, International Longshoremen's Association Papers, NBM. For the full list of resolutions presented to the government, see folder: 11 July 1917, box 56, RS9, PANB.

20 An interim report was dated 14 May 1917. See "Report of the Commission Appointed to Enquire into the Working of the Ontario and Nova Scotia Workmen's Compensation Act," *Journals of the House of Assembly*, 1917. Public hearings were held in Saint John, Fredericton, Woodstock, Moncton, Chatham, Bathurst, and Campbellton. At each location, one or more of the commissioners, usually including Sugrue, listened to evidence given by workers, employers, doctors, journalists, and

others. Local union leaders took a prominent part in making the case for the new laws.

21 ILA 273 Minutebook, 20 March 1918, NBM.

22 *Proceedings of the Legislative Assembly of New Brunswick*, 1918, 33–34, 260–61, 277–79. For the progress of the bill, see Bill 23, 1918, RS24, PANB. There was also a plan to provide a list of industrial diseases covered by the act. However, a critical reading of the Workmen's Compensation Act should also draw attention to limitations characteristic of contemporary legislation. Exclusions for willful misconduct and intoxication were uncontroversial. Benefits generally were to be closely assessed on the basis of the extent and duration of incapacity and a worker's past earnings as well as other possible sources of income. Contributory negligence could be taken into account, and payments could not exceed 55 percent of earnings; while death benefits could be as high as $3,500, disability benefits could not exceed $1,500. In the case of fatalities, surviving children received a benefit to the age of sixteen, and widows were entitled to $20 per month, a benefit to be terminated upon remarriage. In its first year of operations, the board considered a total of 2,746 claims and authorized payments of $89,619.27. See *First Annual Report of the Workmen's Compensation Board of the Province of New Brunswick* (1919), 7, 20.

23 Initially Sugrue was to be paid less than the other members, but he appealed this and his salary was raised to the level of the vice-chairman, $3,000 per annum; in 1920 the chair was paid $4,500 and the other members $3,500. See folder: 2 October 1918, box 58; folder: 1 May 1919, box 59; and folder:

17 April 1920, box 61, RS9, PANB.

24 The account here draws on an unpublished paper by George Vair, "The 1917 Plumbers Strike" as well as a diary in the John Bruce fonds, MG31 B8, vol. 2, Library and Archives Canada (hereafter LAC).

25 "The Reconstruction Programme of N.B. Federation of Labor," *Gleaner*, 21 March 1919. The document was prepared by three Saint John delegates, J. E. Tighe, F. A. Campbell, and E. L. Sage.

26 Ibid.

27 For biographical details on Melanson, see the entry at http://www.lhtnb.ca.

28 Text of speech by Margaret MacNintch, 1946, p. 5, Unity Lodge #10, Ladies' Auxiliary, International Association of Machinists, fonds 150P, Service des archives, Université du Québec à Montréal.

29 *Moncton's Labor Day Celebration, September 1st, 1919*, p. 32. The parade was followed by a programme of sports events at the athletic grounds that was notable for variety, including five different versions of the 100-yard dash — war veterans, union men, ladies, boys aged fifteen and under, and men weighing 225 pounds or more. There were also exhibition booths, a free picture show, horse racing at the speedway, and fireworks in the evening. It was not all fun and games. The labour council pursued regularly issues of importance to the city's workers, including the rising rents and prices in the city. In June 1919, they telegraphed support to Toronto metal trades workers who were preparing to go out in a general strike. A list of affiliates included municipal employees, as well as women workers who belonged to

the United Textile Workers of America. See documents and correspondence in MS5, B1, Moncton and District Labour Council fonds, MC1407, PANB.

30 *Chatham Gazette*, 22 August 1919, *Chatham World*, 23 August 1919; *Union Advocate*, 5 September and 30 September 1919. See also Kimberley Dunphy, "August 20, 1919: 'Strike Fever' on the Miramichi River?" unpublished paper, April 2005; and Joe McKendy, "On the waterfront, back in the day," *Globe and Mail*, 1 May 2007.

31 NBFL *Proceedings*, 1920. Both were important recruits for the union movement. Born at Chatham in 1881, Martin had worked as a clerk for the Snowball enterprises before going into business as a storekeeper on his own account; he was active in community affairs, served on the town council, and was well-known as a bandmaster who played cornet and violin. For his part Stuart, born near Minto in 1873, had been a founder of the Fredericton Socialist League in 1902 and the New Brunswick Teachers Association in 1903; he had come to Newcastle as a newspaper editor and then worked as a school principal and served on the town council. An exponent of the social gospel, Stuart considered socialism to be nothing less than applied Christianity. He hoped to see broad cooperation among reform groups in the province. He encouraged the Federation to welcome the affiliation of teachers, and he called for close political cooperation between farmer and labour candidates. See *Prominent People of the Maritime Provinces* (Saint John: Canadian Publicity Co., 1922), 124; W.D. Hamilton, *Dictionary of Miramichi Biography*

(Saint John, 1997), 225; and J.K. Chapman, "Henry Harvey Stuart (1873–1952): New Brunswick Reformer," *Acadiensis* 5, no. 2 (Spring 1976): 79–104.

32 "Convention Call" [1920], MC1407, PANB. Federation stationery at this time featured a broad motto: "Organize, Educate, Federate, Co-operate": see, for example, C.A. Melanson to W.E. Foster, 3 March 1920, folder: 17 April 1920, box 61, RS9, PANB.

33 Thorne was noted as one of the credentialed delegates who was not present at sessions on the first day: *Standard*, 12 January 1921.

34 In addition to Melanson, the 1921 delegate list included several names of Acadian origin, all from the urban centres of Moncton and Saint John.

35 NBFL *Proceedings*, 1918. The same session had also produced a Vocational School Act.

36 NBFL *Proceedings*, 1919, 1920. For the order-in-council extending the Compensation Act to workers in the woods, see Minutes of the Executive Council, 17 April 1919, film 426, RS6, PANB. In 1920 the Factory Act was brought under the Workmen's Compensation Board; however, there remained only one inspector for the whole province, and recommendations for a female inspector were not acted upon.

37 NBFL *Proceedings*, 1920; *Union Worker*, April 1920. Although the newspaper was not directly controlled by the unions, it received an endorsement from the Federation. The managing editor, A.D. Colwell, was a member of the typographical union and secretary of the Saint John Trades and Labour Council. The newspaper was supported by subscribers and advertisers, although the latter included

only a small number of locals in Saint John who purchased cards for the union directory. A report on the Federation meetings underlined the "calm and dignified manner in which President Melanson conducted the proceedings," and the high quality of discussion and resolutions was seen as an indication that union members were well qualified to participate in governing the province.

38 *Union Worker*, February 1920. While supportive of independent labour politics, the newspaper identified itself with moderate labourism: "Within the columns, there will be no room for One Big Union ideology, Red Anarchy, Socialism, Bolshevism. The columns will consist of articles written by men in the ranks of labour who have by persistent efforts and honest toil won places for themselves in the community."

39 For provincial election results, see *Elections in New Brunswick, 1784–1984* (Fredericton: Legislative Library, 1984). As leader of the ILA local, Martin was, according to a biographical notice in 1922, "selected by laborers as an absolute labor man." He collaborated regularly with the Federation leaders in legislative matters, and the Federation president in 1923, for instance, acknowledged the "cooperation and assistance he received from Brother J. S. Martin, Labor Member for Northumberland Co. who was ready at all times to provide all the assistance possible": NBFL *Proceedings*, 1923. After his term as an MLA, Martin continued to attend as a delegate and was elected a vice-president on several occasions. Less is known about Vanderbeck, who was born at Renous in 1864 and traced his roots back to New

Jersey Loyalists who settled at Fredericton in 1783. He worked for the Snowball interests, both as an overseer and mill manager. Like Martin, he was active in community affairs, serving on the county board of health; he too was known as a musician and "played a unique twelve-string guitar." See W. D. Hamilton, *Dictionary of Miramichi Biography* (Saint John, 1997), 390–91.

40 NBFL *Proceedings*, 1921. There was no political breakthrough in the subsequent 1921 Dominion election. In Westmorland, the local ILP endorsed Albert E. Trites as a Farmer-Labour candidate, and Fred A. Campbell of the street railway union ran as the labour candidate on the Farmer-Labour ticket in St. John–Albert. Both finished in third place, Trites with 3,059 votes and Campbell with 1,224 votes.

41 Credentialed delegates numbered 48 in 1922, 38 in 1923, 42 in 1924, 25 in 1925, 26 in 1926, and 33 in 1928 and 1929; actual attendance was usually somewhat lower.

42 Melanson later became the city's receiver of taxes. He remained a leading citizen in Moncton, serving, for example, as a director of *L'Évangéline*. His labour background was not forgotten. In 1944 he was appointed a member of the province's Civil Service Commission, and as late as 1956 he was welcomed at the Federation convention as one of the early pioneers.

43 For biographical details on Tighe, see the entry at http://www.lhtnb.ca. A more detailed account is forthcoming in the *Dictionary of Canadian Biography*, vol. 16.

44 The conflict is documented in file 161, vol. 327, Strikes and Lockouts Files, Records of

the Department of Labour, RG27, LAC, available on microfilm at the Harriet Irving Library, University of New Brunswick. For a recent treatment, in the context of the breakdown of a progressive consensus in Saint John, see Don Nerbas, "The Changing World of the Bourgeoisie in Saint John, New Brunswick in the 1920s," MA thesis, Department of History, University of New Brunswick, 2006, 113–20.

45 *Union Worker*, August 1921.

46 *Standard*, 12 January 1921. A debate arising from the executive report at the 1921 meetings also seemed to indicate the increased subordination of the Federation to the TLC. This involved a requirement that the Federation's legislative programme be submitted to the Trades and Labour Congress. See NBFL *Proceedings*, 1921 and *Telegraph*, 13 January 1921.

47 *Union Worker*, March 1920, September 1921; *Gleaner*, 18 March 1926.

48 The 1921 meetings had called for the creation of a full Department of Labour, with a minister as a member of cabinet. When this reform was not forthcoming, the Federation supported proposals to consolidate the administration of the Factory and Workmen's Compensation Acts under a single board, pending the establishment of a proper Department of Labour. There was also considerable discussion of the labour provisions of the Treaty of Versailles, and Federation delegates participated in national meetings to discuss how to implement these in Canada.

49 In recommending Sugrue, George Melvin had written: "Mrs. Sugrue as you no doubt know is the wife of Mr. J. L. Sugrue Commissioner

on the Workmen's Compensation Board, and through his wide knowledge and experience of the Labor Movement and what it stands for and advocates, has herself aquired [*sic*] considerable knowledge of these matters": Melvin to P. J. Veniot, 9 June 1921, folder: 12 September 1923, box 65, RS9, PANB.

50 Minutes of Executive Council, 12 September 1923, RS6, PANB; *Journals of the House of Assembly*, 1925, 22; *Labour Gazette*, April 1925, 331. No copy of the report has come to light.

51 NBFL *Proceedings*, 1927.

52 NBFL *Proceedings*, 1923. At this time Veniot also announced that he would appoint the desired Commission on Mothers' Allowance and Minimum Wage Acts. The 1923 minutes report that Veniot was the first provincial premier to speak at the Federation meetings and note that "he stated that while he could not promise that we would get every thing we asked for, yet the doors of the Government would always be open to our representatives."

53 *Labour Gazette*, February 1924, 135–37. The Federation's agitation focused in part on raising minimum payments for disabilities and fatalities.

54 The employers' position was badly undermined by the fact that McLean's own Bathurst Lumber Company had refused to pay assessments. As one union resolution pointed out, the situation had forced other sectors to carry the costs of accidents occurring at non-compliant enterprises. The company's attempt to evade the act was the subject of legal action by the board; an appeal to the Supreme Court of Canada was decided in favour of the board in March 1924. See *Labour*

Gazette, December 1923, 1455, and April 1924, 350.

55 *Gleaner*, 18 March 1926.

56 There were objections, however, to the appointment of a labour representative on a royal commission on the administration of compensation in the lumber industry without consultation with the Federation: *Gleaner*, 23 March 1927.

57 NBFL *Proceedings*, 1928; *Gleaner*, 9 March 1928.

58 Tighe returned as NBFL president in 1934–36. In 1929, Tighe's successor as president was Eugene R. Steeves, like Melanson a member of the machinists union in Moncton.

59 *Telegraph-Journal*, 29 August 1929. As in 1914, the province agreed to provide a grant to support the event, in this case $1,500: see folder: 18 July 1929, box 73, RS9, PANB. Also in 1929, the province approved advertising expenditures in connection with Moncton meetings of the Brotherhood of Locomotive Engineers and the Canadian Brotherhood of Railway Employees: see folder: 20 August 1929, box 73, RS9, PANB.

60 TLC *Proceedings*, 1929, 3, 137, 185. For the occasion there was also a substantial publication, a *History of Saint John Labor Unions, Compiled and Issued by the Saint John Trades and Labor Council and Subordinate Unions*, an additional indication of local historical consciousness.

61 TLC *Proceedings*, 1929, 6–7; *Evening Times-Globe*, 27 August 1929. On Thomas, see *Dictionary of National Biography, 1941–1950* (Oxford: Oxford University Press, 1959), 875–77.

62 *Gleaner*, 22 March 1927.

Two: "What We Were Promised," 1930–1939

1 The photograph was published in the *Evening Times-Globe*, 8 January 1931, 2. The original is in the New Brunswick Federation of Labour fonds, MC1819, PANB. A reproduction in *The Early Presidents of the New Brunswick Federation of Labour, 1913–1964* (Fredericton: LHTNB, 2011), 20–21, provides identification for most of the delegates in the photograph.

2 For a short biography of Steeves, see the entry for "Eugene R. Steeves" at http://www.lhtnb.ca.

3 *Moncton Transcript*, 16 January 1930.

4 NBFL *Proceedings*, 1931.

5 "Minutes of Executive Board," 17 October 1931, box 196, NBFL Papers, MC1819, PANB.

6 *Evening Times-Globe*, 7 January 1931.

7 *Evening Times-Globe*, 7 January 1931. There were worse cases the next year. In 1932 it was reported that a contractor for the New Brunswick Electric Power Commission at Musquash was paying 17 cents an hour for a ten-hour day and charging 80 cents a day for board — leaving the men with a pay of 9 cents an hour.

8 NBFL *Proceedings*, 1932. See also *Chatham Gazette*, 4 January, 6 January, and 8 January 1932. Meanwhile, the urgent conditions across the country led the federal government of R.B. Bennett to adopt a plan for relief camps to put large numbers of single men to work at the lowest possible wages on government projects under the supervision of the Department of National Defence. The first of these camps in New Brunswick opened at Upper Brockway in November 1932, and additional camps opened at Blissville,

Cambridge, and Havelock (to build emergency landing strips across central New Brunswick), Millidgeville (the Saint John Municipal Airport) and Colter's Siding (an artillery training base and forest research station). Over the next several years, almost 8,000 New Brunswick men, mainly in their twenties and thirties but some as young as thirteen and others over seventy, worked in the camps, mainly cutting wood, hauling stumps, and clearing land. In addition to food and shelter, they received a pay of 20 cents a day. There were provisions for medical care and even for classes, but troublemakers were quickly weeded out (the records show that 580 men were expelled for disciplinary reasons). There were few disturbances and no unions of the kind that made the camps in western Canada hotbeds of unrest. See Brian Christopher Gallant, "'Half a Loaf': The Unemployment Relief Camps in New Brunswick, 1932–1936," MA thesis, Department of History, University of New Brunswick, 2003.

9 See David Frank, "Minto 1932: The Origins and Significance of a New Brunswick Labour Landmark," *Acadiensis* 36, no. 2 (Spring 2007): 3–27. For a shorter treatment, see "Minto, 1932," http://www.lhtnb.ca.

10 Executive Board Minutes, 5 July and 26 July 1930 (contained in NBFL *Proceedings*, 1931); Executive Board Minutes, 17 October 1931; NBFL *Proceedings*, 1932; Melvin to Whitebone et al., 30 August 1932, box 103, MC1819, PANB; "Minutes of the Executive Board, 16 September 1932." See also Melvin to Richards, 28 July 1930, folder: 17 September 1931, and Melvin to Richards, 20 October 1931 (with resolution), folder: 16 November 1931, box

76, RS9, PANB. One of the first decisions of the board after Steeves's appointment was the refusal of support to the widows Grace Betts and Greta Gallant, whose husbands had perished in the rescue attempts at Minto in July 1932; it is unclear why Steeves failed to support the widows in this case, which was not finally decided in their favour until the conclusion of an appeal to the Supreme Court of Canada. See Frank, "Minto 1932," 19–24.

11 "Served Long and Ably," among clippings dated 17 February 1970, in Genealogical Files, Saint John Jewish Historical Museum. My thanks to curator Katherine Biggs-Craft for assistance in using files related to the Whitebone family history, which were in storage at the New Brunswick Museum at the time of my research. For brief accounts of Whitebone, see "Noted Labor Leader Mourned," available in these files; and "In Memoriam James A. Whitebone," *Canadian Labour*, March 1970, 29. Whitebone and his wife are buried in the Catholic Holy Cross Cemetery in Saint John. See also *The Canadian Who's Who*, vol. 6, *1952–1954* (Toronto: Trans-Canada Press, 1954), 1108.

12 Whitebone also achieved prominence in community affairs. He was elected to Common Council as an alderman in 1936 and in his first year on council advanced several labour causes, including a fair wage clause in city contracts and an eight-hour day for civic employees. See Saint John Common Council Minute Book, no. 57 (1936–39), PANB. He remained active in municipal politics for several decades and in 1960 served as acting mayor of the city. For a short biography, see "James A. Whitebone," http://www.lhtnb.ca.

13 NBFL *Proceedings*, 1933; *Gleaner*, 28 February, 1 March 1933.

14 *Gleaner*, 1 March 1933; NBFL *Proceedings*, 1933.

15 *Gleaner*, 2 March 1933; *Moncton Daily Times*, 2 March 1933; NBFL *Proceedings*, 1933. When officers of the Federation were chosen, Jamieson, closely associated with the CCF resolution, was elected first vice-president. The importance of the machinists in promoting the CCF is discussed by Patrick Marsh in "Machinists of Moncton: The Endeavours of Local 594, International Association of Machinists, 1916–1933," MA thesis, Department of History, University of New Brunswick, 2010, 86–95.

16 Executive Meeting, 29 April 1933; "Proceedings of Organization Meeting, New Brunswick Section of the Co-operative Commonwealth Federation," 23 June 1933 (included in NBFL *Proceedings*, 1934). Also elected were Watson Baird of Moncton as vice-president and G. M. Legget of Saint John as secretary-treasurer. Other executive members included Alcide LeBlanc, Richibucto; H. W. Gillies, McAdam; Alonzo Martin, Edmundston (who in 1935 was a district vice-president for the rival New Brunswick Council of Labour); and Mrs. D. B. Mitton, Moncton.

17 *Moncton Daily Times*, 24 June 1933. Woodsworth had also spoken to audiences at the Rialto Theatre in Saint John before arriving in Moncton: *Evening Times-Globe*, 22 June and 23 June 1933. With the formation of a New Brunswick section, the CCF lacked a presence in only two provinces, Nova Scotia and Prince Edward Island. A Prince Edward Island section was organized in 1936.

In August 1938, the first union in Canada to affiliate to the CCF was District 26, United Mine Workers of America, whose membership was predominantly in Nova Scotia but also included New Brunswick members by this time. See Ian McKay, "The Maritime CCF: Reflections on a Tradition," *New Maritimes*, July–August 1984, 4–9.

18 *Moncton Daily Times*, 25 September 1933; TLC *Proceedings, 1933*, 189–91. See also Marsh, "Machinists of Moncton," 75, 91–95. The Moncton delegates at the TLC also included E. H. Carson and B. L. Skidmore of the Brotherhood of Railway Carmen, Lodge 245, who won endorsement for a resolution supporting "the principle of national control of the banking system."

19 *The Pilot*, August 1933 and September 1933; Max Tarik to Bert Robinson, 21 August 1933, William McKelvie to Bert, 15 September 1933, box 8, Socialist Party of Canada, Ontario Papers, Woodsworth Memorial Collection, MC35, Thomas Fisher Rare Book Library, University of Toronto; Watson Baird, "Officers and Members . . ." (secretary-treasurer's report), 9 August 1935, vol. 89, Co-operative Commonwealth Federation Papers, MG28 IV-I, LAC. Even before the founding meeting in June, one of the delegates from Saint John complained that leaders of the Federation were "afraid of the words Socialization and Socialism": Tarik to Robinson, 26 May 1933, box 8, Socialist Party of Canada, Ontario Papers, Woodsworth Memorial Collection. By 1935 the original branches in Saint John and Moncton had been supplemented only by small branches in Beersville and Targettville, both in rural Kent County.

20 NBFL *Proceedings*, 1934; *Gleaner*, 13 February 1934.

21 *History of Federation of Labor of New Brunswick* (Saint John: New Brunswick Federation of Labour, [1934]). The unattributed cover art may well have been produced by teachers or students in graphic arts at the Saint John Vocational School. The image from 1934 remained in use on the covers of the Federation proceedings from 1936 to 1961. The production of the book itself caused controversy, as Tighe questioned Whitebone closely about the financial arrangements, under which a Saint John printer received 60 percent of the gross proceeds from the book. A year later, Secretary-Treasurer Melvin pronounced the book "a complete success, both as to the book itself, its contents, and the financial return to the Federation," which Melvin placed at $486.38. See *Gleaner*, 14 February 1933, NBFL *Proceedings*, 1934 and NBFL *Proceedings*, 1935.

22 NBFL *Proceedings*, 1935.

23 *Gleaner*, 20 February 1935.

24 NBFL *Proceedings*, 1936; *Gleaner*, 13 March 1936. Failure to participate meant that the citizens of New Brunswick were supporting a national programme from which they received no benefits, even though the provincial contribution at this time was only 25 percent of the cost.

25 NBFL *Proceedings*, 1937. Political tensions were apparent. Although Premier Dysart had accepted an invitation to speak, he did not do so; he also stated that the legislature would not be able to receive a delegation during the convention, which Whitebone described as "an insult to the Federation." Meanwhile, Opposition leader F. C. Squires curried favour with the delegates —"Labor is too important in the life of the country to be neglected"— and the convention received a telegram of greetings from the Maritime Section of the CCF in Saint John. In response to Liberal charges that "the Tory wolf has lain down with the labour lamb," Whitebone denied partisan affiliations. See *Gleaner*, 3 March 1937, and NBFL *Proceedings*, 1937. Meanwhile, the Maritime Section of the CCF sent the premier resolutions on education, minimum wages, and workers' right to organize: E. A. Dryden to A. A. Dysart, 16 October 1937, folder: 10 November 1937, box 84, RS9, PANB.

26 NBFL *Proceedings*, 1937.

27 NBFL *Proceedings*, 1937: see Resolutions 9, 10, 26, and 39.

28 The short draft bill was prepared by the Trades and Labour Congress and forwarded to provincial governments, accompanied by a four-page legal memorandum: see P. M. Draper and R. J. Tallon to Members of Provincial Legislative Assemblies in Canada, 15 February 1937, with accompanying documents, folder: 16 April 1937, box 83, RS9, PANB. While the draft bill asserted the lawfulness of collective bargaining, unlike the Wagner Act it did not provide for the enforcement of recognition and bargaining.

29 *Statutes of New Brunswick*, 1936, c. 51, and 1937, c. 39. The mandate was to hear complaints, conduct investigations, hold conferences for "voluntary adjustment," and if necessary issue orders for rates of wages and maximum hours covering specific groups of workers. For the early activities of the Fair Wage Officer, see *Labour Gazette*, June 1938, 652–53.

30 Executive Meeting, 31 March 1937; Melvin to W. F. Roberts, 13 April 1937, folder: 2 and 4 August 1937, box 83, RS9, PANB. In the same file, see other correspondence concerning these appointments, including Frank H. Gillespie to Roberts, 17 July 1937 and James D. Leger to J. B. McNair, 21 April 1937. The Fredericton Labour Council nominated James D. Leger in part on the grounds that "we believe it is imperative that a French speaking man should be appointed, as some 40% of our population are French, and also that the central part of the Province should be represented": Stanley Goodspeed to Roberts, 20 April 1937. The Federation had been concerned that the province would accept only one of their nominations, the second labour member to come from "some other labor body," an allusion to the emergence of the New Brunswick National Council of Labour, for which Gillespie served as Legislative Representative.

31 The account here is based mainly on Patrick H. Burden, "The New Brunswick Farmer-Labour Union, 1937–1941," MA thesis, Department of History, University of New Brunswick, 1983. Burden notes that the NBFLU advanced a critique of local economic development in which "big business" was accused of betraying the economic interests of the community and the potential of local resources. In Newcastle, the sympathetic T. H. Whalen, editor of *Farm and Labor*, favoured more attention to cooperative methods for sustaining rural life but also supported the worker's "right to a living wage," partly on the basis of his reading of the papal encyclical *Rerum novarum*.

32 Ibid., 36–43. Burden notes that many of the workers who participated were former members of the waterfront workers union of longshoremen and millworkers established as an ILA local in 1919. A failed sawmill strike in the summer of 1934 led to their withdrawal from the ILA, and by 1936 they were functioning as an Independent Labor Association and calling for wider local forms of organization. Burden also notes that no single union active in the province was prepared to meet the needs of lumber workers and states that "the focusing of the entire province's trade union movement through the lens of a Saint John-Moncton labour bureaucracy alienated and ignored lumber workers from a depressed region like the Miramichi," 36–37.

33 Greg McEachreon to A. A. Dysart, 26 February 1937, with resolution, folder: 16 April 1937, box 83, RS9, PANB. McEachreon, the South Nelson storekeeper who became president of the NBFLU, included "legislation of benefit to workers" and "collective bargaining" among the principal objectives of the new union.

34 Cited by Burden, "The New Brunswick Farmer-Labour Union, 1937–1941," 92.

35 NBFL *Proceedings*, 1938. A delegation from the NBFLU was present at the convention. Whitebone noted that the NBFLU had 2,000 members in Northumberland, Restigouche, Gloucester, and Albert counties; Burden reports that by the time of the first annual convention in June 1938, there were 2,500 members in 20 locals. Although Whitebone stated in 1938 that they had applied for affiliation, there were no delegates at subsequent conventions. Some Miramichi locals

gained union recognition from employers in the early years of the war, but few locals lasted beyond 1941. As Burden concluded, the NBFLU was "a creature of the Depression, a synthesis of various local strategies to deal with the depressed economic conditions" (95). For discussion of "amalgamation," see *NBFL Proceedings*, 1931.

36 Allen Seager, "Minto, New Brunswick: A Study in Canadian Class Relations Between the Wars," *Labour/Le Travailleur* 5 (Spring 1980): 81–132, especially 106–14. Much of the following discussion draws on this important study.

37 The local union president later stated that the vote was 762 in favour, 15 against, with two spoiled ballots: *NBFL Proceedings*, 1938.

38 Seager, "Minto, New Brunswick," 118–19. For the women's participation, see also the *Gleaner*, 2 December, 6 December, and 8 December 1937.

39 "The Truth About Minto," pamphlet, 1937.

40 For the conciliation board report, see *Labour Gazette*, July 1938, 725–31.

41 *NBFL Proceedings*, 1938; Seager, "Minto, New Brunswick," 123. Premier Dysart told the convention that he would not discuss the Minto situation at all as it was "sub judice": *Gleaner*, 27 January 1938. Whitebone was replaced by another senior Federation officer, John S. MacKinnon, who was also Secretary to the Fair Wage Board.

42 *Gleaner*, 27 January 1938; *NBFL Proceedings*, 1938. As Patrick Burden has noted, the Miramichi and Minto strikes of 1937 "contributed to a reevaluation of the province's labour relations policy" ("The New Brunswick Farmer-Labour Union, 1937–1941," 84–85).

43 *NBFL Proceedings*, 1938; *Gleaner*, 28 January 1938. For the Nova Scotia law, see *Statutes of Nova Scotia*, 1937, c. 6. The convention agreed to seek introduction of legislation as a private member's bill if necessary.

44 *Proceedings of the Legislative Assembly of New Brunswick*, 1938, 157–59, 211. The key provision regarding collective bargaining was only permissive: "It shall be lawful for employees to bargain collectively with their employer and to conduct such bargaining through their representatives duly elected by a majority vote of the employees affected or through the duly chosen officers of the organization to which the majority of such employees belong": *Statutes of New Brunswick*, 1938, c. 68, pt. 2. For a summary, see *Labour Gazette*, September 1938, 987–89. The irrelevance of the new law to resolving the Minto situation had already been identified by the conciliation board: "The statute does not compel recognition of any one union to the exclusion of others, nor does it compel collective bargaining with the officials of any one union": *Labour Gazette*, July 1938, 727. Seager assesses the government's initiative in introducing the bill as part of an attempt to restore the legitimacy of the provincial state in the face of its failure to assist workers at Minto: "After smashing the strike, the provincial authorities stepped back from the brink" ("Minto, New Brunswick," 129).

45 "The Labor and Industrial Relations Bill," folder 251, Frank and Libbie Park fonds, vol. 15, MG31 K9, LAC. The section protecting workers from intimidation received a more positive assessment. Park's critique of the Fair Wage Act was relatively straightforward: it

was an exercise in paternalism in which standards and conditions were at the discretion of officials and ministers: "The government is trying to do the Union's work for them. The result will be a weakening of the Unions just when the need for them is most apparent." As for the provisions for investigation and conciliation of disputes prior to a strike, it was a "complicated rigmarole" of administrative delays and discretionary decisions. Moreover, the provisions for fines in the event of illegal strikes were "a savage section and unworthy of this government or any government calling themselves Liberals."

46 *NBFL Proceedings*, 1939. Whitebone objected also to the inactivity of the Fair Wage Board: "Surely in this Province where low wages and long hours is the rule rather than the exception there is unlimited scope for investigation and adjustment of wages and working conditions, yet the Board apparently ceased to function some months ago."

47 *Evening Times-Globe*, 12 January 1939.

48 *NBFL Proceedings*, 1939.

49 Joseph Vandenbroeck to J.B. McNair, 2 September 1938, folder: 14 September 1938, box 85, RS9, PANB.

50 Joseph Vandenbroeck to Whitebone, 23 January 1940, box 103, MC1819, PANB. He noted that the 1939 convention had adopted their resolution calling for an amendment to meet the standards of the Nova Scotia law.

51 *Evening Times-Globe*, 10 January 1939.

52 *Evening Times-Globe*, 12 January 1939.

53 *NBFL Proceedings*, 1937–39. Whitebone's report in 1938 noted that "the membership of existing unions has been greatly augmented" and that in addition to the coal miners, new unions were organized among dairy workers, hospital workers, and other groups.

54 *NBFL Proceedings*, 1931, 1932.

55 *Canadian Unionist*, August 1935, 68; Frank Gillespie to A.R. Mosher, 22 July 1935, vol. 187, MG28 1103, Canadian Labour Congress Papers, LAC.

56 *Canadian Unionist*, February 1937, 224, June 1937, 12, and September 1937, 100. In 1938, however, the ACCL also issued charters to the Rothwell Mine Workers Union and the Miramichi Mine Workers Union — decisions that opened them to charges of endorsing company unionism in the wake of the Minto strike and the defeat of the United Mine Workers.

57 New Brunswick National Council of Labour, "Report of Proceedings at the Fifth Annual Meeting, Moncton, New Brunswick, June, 1939," vol. 187, MG28 1103, Canadian Labour Congress Papers, LAC. The council was not consistent in including the term "National" in their title.

58 The schism between craft and industrial unions resulted in the suspension of the CIO unions (including the UMWA) from the American Federation of Labor in 1936 and the formation of the new Congress of Industrial Organizations in 1938. In Canada, the TLC expelled the CIO unions in 1939, which led the CIO unions to join with the ACCL to create the Canadian Congress of Labour in 1940.

59 *NBFL Proceedings*, 1938, 1939. Whitebone's comment in 1939 was a direct criticism of immigration policies that refused the entry to Canada of Jewish refugees from fascism.

60 *NBFL Proceedings*, 1938; *Evening Times-Globe*, 12 January 1939.

Three: "A Province Fit for Heroes," 1940–1956

1 Untitled ms. dated 7 May 1945, "Radio Talks," box 103, MC1819, PANB. Other items in this file are identified as radio broadcasts on the stations CHSJ and CFBC.

2 This time Saint John delegates were not in a majority, although they were still the largest group with 25 of the 79 delegates. The domination of the southern cities was balanced by the appearance of 29 delegates from the north of the province, primarily members of unions in the pulp and paper industry and the railway trades. This included delegates from Dalhousie (15), Edmundston (6), Bathurst (5) and Atholville (3). Although longshoremen were the third largest group in 1940, they were outnumbered by the paper mill workers and the machinists. Despite this picture of diversification, the Federation had lost some ground, as the 37 locals participating in the 1940 convention represented 22.1 percent of the 167 union locals reported in the province for 1940.

3 *Moncton Transcript*, 10 January 1940; NBFL *Proceedings*, 1940 (January). Note that the NBFL held two conventions in 1940, one on 9–11 January and another on 29–31 October.

4 NBFL *Proceedings*, 1940 (October), 1941; *Gloucester Northern Light*, 16 October 1941; *Evening Times-Globe*, 31 October 1940.

5 NBFL *Proceedings*, 1941; *Evening Times-Globe*, 15 October 1941.

6 NBFL *Proceedings*, 1940 (October), 1941, 1942, and 1943.

7 Douglas Cruikshank and Gregory S. Kealey, "Strikes in Canada, 1891–1950," *Labour/Le Travail* 20 (Fall 1987): 85–145, data at 138.

8 NBFL *Proceedings*, 1944.

9 Certification Files, Industrial Relations Board Records, RS895, PANB. My thanks to Raymond Léger for sharing his research in these files.

10 NBFL *Proceedings*, 1941; see also *Gloucester Northern Light*, 16 October 1941.

11 NBFL *Proceedings*, 1942.

12 "Post War Reconstruction Brief Submitted by the New Brunswick Federation of Labor" (July 1943), included in the folder for NBFL *Proceedings*, 1942, MC1819, PANB. However, the Federation expected better results from the federal government than from the provincial governments. Past and present experience, Federation leaders believed, had shown that the way to ensure that all Canadians shared equally in standards of social security was to bring social legislation under the control of the federal government through amendments to the British North America Act.

13 *Evening Times-Globe*, 16 September 1943.

14 NBFL *Proceedings*, 1943.

15 For the platform, see the party advertisement in the *Moncton Times*, 23 August 1944. My thanks to students Wade Tower and Sharon Kitchen, who wrote papers on the 1944 election. Interestingly, one of the Saskatchewan CCF members elected in 1944, Beatrice Coates Trew, was a New Brunswicker who had gone west as a teacher.

16 For election results, see *Elections in New Brunswick, 1784–1984* (Fredericton: Legislative Library, 1984), 117–19, and for detailed reports, see *Telegraph-Journal*, 29 August 1944. Labour connections were determined from NBFL *Proceedings* and other sources. The province's only previous CCF candidate was Joseph C. Arrowsmith, who

received 712 votes in Saint John in 1939. There were twenty candidates in 1948 — including Gladys West in Queens, the wife of a former miner, who was the second woman to run in a New Brunswick provincial election. There were only twelve CCF candidates in 1952 and none at all in 1956 and 1960. In Edmundston, Marmen failed to gain election as an Independent or as a Liberal but was elected mayor in 1948.

17 *Evening Times-Globe*, 8 May 1975; NBFL *Proceedings*, 1942. See also the MLA biographical files at the Legislative Library. On the history of the department, which emerged as a small "Labour Bureau" (1910) and later became a branch within an expanded Department of Health and Labour (1936), see Delbert W. Gallagher, "The New Brunswick Department of Labor — History and Development," *Trades and Labor Congress Journal*, July 1955, 23–25.

18 Labour Relations Act, 1945, *Statutes of New Brunswick,* 1945, c. 41.

19 NBFL *Proceedings*, 1943.

20 During this period the number of women union members in the province increased from 748 in 1939 to 1,272 in 1946. See the data cited by Raymond Léger on pp. 23–24 of "L'évolution des syndicats au Nouveau-Brunswick de 1910 à 1950," *Égalité: Revue acadienne d'analyse politique*, 31 (printemps 1992): 19–40. See also Kimberley Dunphy, "The Feminization of the Labour Movement in New Brunswick: Women in the New Brunswick Federation of Labour, 1913–1984," MA thesis, Department of History, University of New Brunswick, 2009. The Moncton laundry workers and Saint John telephone operators were the most prominent groups represented by women delegates prior to 1956.

21 NBFL *Proceedings*, 1946; *Evening Times-Globe*, 15 October 1946.

22 In addition to the CCL unions, other, independent, unions were also taking advantage of the new labour laws to press their case for union representation. One notable example was the Restigouche Woodsmen's Union, which succeeded in gaining certification at several lumber operations in the north of the province in the early 1950s. See Léger, "L'évolution des syndicats au Nouveau-Brunswick," and Certification Files, RS 895, PANB.

23 Biographical information is drawn from a union souvenir booklet, *A Tribute to Angus MacLeod* (Saint John, 1971) and an obituary, in the *Telegraph-Journal*, 15 December 1980. See also Sue Calhoun, *Ole Boy: Memoirs of a Canadian Labour Leader, J. K. Bell* (Halifax: Nimbus Publishing, 1992), and Craig Chouinard, "Shipyard Struggles: The Origins of the Maritime Marine Workers' Federation in Saint John, N.B., 1939–1947," MA thesis, Department of History, University of New Brunswick, 1995.

24 *Industrial Union of Marine and Shipbuilding Workers of Canada, Local No. 3, Annual Labour Journal* (Saint John, 1944?), 1.

25 MacLeod was also an unabashed CCF supporter, stating in 1948, for instance, that "until the CCF comes to power, the ideas of labour, organized and unorganized will never be brought to fruition": *Maritime Commonwealth*, 27 May 1948. MacLeod was president of the New Brunswick Council of Labour in 1946–51 and again during its final year in 1956.

26 Cruikshank and Kealey, "Strikes in Canada," 138; *Report of the Department of Labour, New Brunswick, 1947.*

27 Patrick Burden, "The 600 Men Who Dig Coal Under a New Brunswick Forest," unpublished paper, University of New Brunswick, 1981. One feature of the strike was that the New Brunswick miners did not protest limited operations, under provincial supervision, to provide coal for the Grand Lake power plant.

28 Michael Briggs, "The Little Piggies That Didn't Go to the Market: The 1947 UPWA Nation-Wide Strike," unpublished paper, University of New Brunswick, 2006. Moncton railway workers participated in Canada's first national railway strike in 1950, which involved more than 4,000 local workers belonging to both TLC and CCL and unaffiliated railway unions. The one-week strike, which was ended by emergency legislation in Parliament, eventually produced improved wages as well as the 40-hour week. See Courtney McLaughlin-Butler, "The Nationwide Railway Strike of 1950: Moncton as a case study of local reactions," unpublished paper, University of New Brunswick, 2003.

29 File 7-55-412, vol. 1793 (1947) and file 53, vol. 463 (1948), RG27, Strikes and Lockouts Files, Department of Labour Records, LAC. See also Certification Files, RS895, PANB. The 1948 strike was recalled in an interview with Robert Moore, a young boy at the time, who remembered union songs played through a public address system on the front porch of his home on York Street. He also recalled that one of the union leaders was fired as soon as the strike was settled. See Robert Moore Interview, 2005, LHTNB fonds, MC3477, PANB.

30 Whitebone's hope for a national labour code was disappointed, and each province continued to set its own standards. Ottawa's Industrial Relations and Disputes Investigation Act (1948) carefully avoided interfering with provincial rights and applied only to the usual areas of federal jurisdiction in transportation and fuel production. See Peter S. McInnis, *Harnessing Labour Confrontation: Shaping the Postwar Settlement in Canada, 1943–1950* (Toronto: University of Toronto Press, 2002).

31 Labour Relations Act, *Statutes of New Brunswick,* 1945, c. 41, s. 10(2).

32 Quoted by W.B. Cunningham, *Compulsory Conciliation and Collective Bargaining: The New Brunswick Experience* (Fredericton/Montreal: Department of Labour/Industrial Relations Centre, McGill University, 1957), 17–18.

33 Ibid., 99.

34 NBFL *Proceedings,* 1946, 1947.

35 Memo of 7 January 1948, cited in Siobhan Laskey, "'Employees Under the Law': The Challenge of Industrial Legality in New Brunswick, 1945–1955," unpublished paper, University of New Brunswick, 2006, 17.

36 However, in 1951 municipalities were given the power to declare themselves employers under the act, an instance of the incremental practical reforms that led to the eventual enactment of public sector labour relations legislation.

37 Labour Relations Act, *Statutes of New Brunswick,* 1949, c. 20.

38 Laskey, "'Employees Under the Law,'" 5.

39 Ibid., 7–8.

40 *Labour Gazette,* May 1952, 613–15.

41 *Labour Gazette,* January 1956, 86–87.

42 Michael Wilcox, "Canada Veneers and Irving Oil: Labour and the Postwar Settlement in Saint John, New Brunswick, 1945–1949," MA thesis, Department of History, University of New Brunswick, 2007, 50–72.

43 For accounts of the CSU, see Jim Green, *Against the Tide: The Story of the Canadian Seamen's Union* (Toronto: Progress Books, 1986); and William Kaplan, *Everything That Floats: Pat Sullivan, Hal Banks, and the Seamen's Unions of Canada* (Toronto: University of Toronto Press, 1987). See also George Vair, "The 1949 Canadian Seamen's Union Strike (The Saint John Story)," available online at the website for the Frank and Ella Hatheway Labour Exhibit Centre, http://www.wfhathewaylabourexhibitcentre.ca.

44 NBFL *Proceedings*, 1947, 1948.

45 *Telegraph-Journal*, 1–29 April 1949; *Evening Times-Globe*, 2–11 May 1949; *Searchlight*, 26 May 1949; Green, *Against the Tide*, 230–32. As George Vair's account shows, the CSU held out longer in Saint John than in other ports, in large part thanks to the solidarity of the longshoremen. For his "illegal" actions in supporting the CSU, Crilley was expelled from the longshoremen's union and blacklisted on the waterfront. He shoveled snow on the CPR tracks the next winter before finding work as a freightchecker for the CNR and subsequently becoming an officer of the Canadian Brotherhood of Railway Employees; he was later a vice-president of the Federation.

46 NBFL *Proceedings*, 1949.

47 *Telegraph-Journal*, 15 July, 16 July, and 17 July, 15 September and 17 September 1952.

48 *Telegraph-Journal*, 17 September 1952.

49 NBFL *Proceedings*, 1952; *Telegraph-Journal*, 16 September, 17 September, and 18 September 1952.

50 NBFL *Proceedings*, 1952.

51 The political strategist Dalton Camp, a former Young Liberal who worked for the Flemming campaign in 1952, recognized that McNair had made a mistake and considers the union issue to have been a decisive factor in his defeat: Dalton Camp, *Gentlemen, Players and Politicians* (Toronto: McClelland and Stewart, 1970), 52. His campaign in 1952 included an attack by "L. C. House" on the Liberal Minister of Labour Samuel Mooers: *Telegraph-Journal*, 3 September 1952.

52 *Labour Gazette*, February 1953, 371; November 1953, 1638.

53 *Maritime Advocate and Busy East*, September 1953, 32; *Evening Times-Globe*, 25 May 1960. See also the MLA biographical files at the Legislative Library. Note that some sources state erroneously that Skaling was a president of the Federation of Labour; however, he had served as a vice-president. Skaling was prominently featured in a souvenir booklet published by his union: *International Union of Bricklayers and Allied Craftsmen, Local No. 1, N.B., 100th Anniversary, November, 1989*.

54 *Labour Gazette*, November 1954, 1592–95.

55 *Statutes of New Brunswick*, 1956, c. 9, p. 25; *Labour Gazette*, June 1956, 721–24.

56 NBFL *Proceedings*, 1956. See *Statutes of New Brunswick*, 1956, c. 42, p. 105, and c. 43, p. 106. Whitebone stated that the decision regarding policemen "is of the greatest importance to all of us inasmuch as other unions could have been placed in the same position by action of the courts had the Act not been

changed." Another amendment in 1956 limited the effect of ex parte injunctions in labour disputes to no more than five days.

57 Gregg addressed the convention each year from 1950 to 1956, with the exception of 1951, and Skaling addressed the convention each year from 1953 to 1956. In addition, the Federation benefited from government appointments. After the death in 1952 of former Federation president E.R. Steeves, who represented labour on the Workmen's Compensation Board, there was little delay in appointing Robert G. Jones of the International Molders and Foundry Workers Union, Local 236, Moncton, as a replacement. In addition, the government named Whitebone to the board of the New Brunswick Electric Power Commission.

58 NBFL *Proceedings*, 1954. The certification of unions continued apace during these years; a total of 138 new certification orders were issued in 1953–56. See Certification Files, RS895, PANB.

59 *Labour Gazette*, February 1955, 153; similar views were presented by the New Brunswick Council of Labour.

60 Chouinard, "Shipyard Struggles," 174–98; Calhoun, *Ole Boy*, 56–57. At its final convention in 1956, the New Brunswick Council of Labour passed a resolution calling on Maritime firms engaged in marketing oil products and exploiting natural resources to "contribute to our regional economy by building, repairing and registering ships in Canada": *New Brunswick Council of Labour Convention Proceedings*, 1956.

61 Mary McIntosh, "Community Resistance to De-Industrialization: Milltown, New Brunswick, 1952–1957," MA thesis, Department of History, University of New Brunswick, 1990. See also Bill Eagan, *Woven in Time: An Oral History of the Milltown (St. Croix) Cotton Mill* (Bayside, NB: Korby Publishing, 2004). Local 858 president Tom Jones was a vice-president of the New Brunswick Council of Labour.

62 NBFL *Proceedings*, 1954, 1955. Gad Horowitz, *Canadian Labour in Politics* (Toronto, University of Toronto Press, 1968), notes that Whitebone was among the minority of TLC executive officers who "opposed the rapid progress towards merger" (179), in part because he feared it would lead to an endorsement of the CCF, which the CCL supported.

63 NBFL *Proceedings*, 1955.

64 The fraternal delegates included Angus MacLeod and Ralph Evans of the New Brunswick Council of Labour as well as the regional director for the new CLC, Henry Harm, who was based in Moncton, and the two Saint John representatives, Harold Stafford (formerly of the TLC) and Bill Craig (formerly of the CCL).

65 In conversation with Nicole Lang, Blanchette has recalled that when he chaired convention sessions and committee meetings as a vice-president he took care to speak in both languages in order to encourage the participation of fellow francophones. He also recalled that President Whitebone was "un vrai anglais de Saint-Jean."

66 The women delegates were Agnes Dillon, Lola Pellerin, and Muriel Chandler, IBEW 1472 (Saint John) and Yvonne Cormier and Grace Derocher, Laundry Workers Federal Union, Local 570 (Moncton). See Dunphy, "Women in the New Brunswick Federation of Labour."

67 NBFL *Proceedings*, 1956.

68 Ibid.

69 Ibid. In similar fashion, Whitebone had addressed the convention of the New Brunswick Council of Labour several weeks earlier, which also endorsed plans for the merger: *New Brunswick Council of Labour Convention Proceedings*, 1956. In his final speech to the council, MacLeod stated: "History has taught us, if nothing else, that Labour can no more afford to let others have complete control of the political affairs of a country, than to allow our employers to have complete control of our economic affairs."

70 On the refinery strike, see file 151, vol. 514 (1955), Department of Labour Records, RG27, LAC. Prior to the strike, a labourer's wage was $1.06 an hour for a 48-hour week; the wage for "ordinary female labour" was 71 cents an hour; skilled and experienced workers received higher rates, with women receiving 5 cents an hour less in all categories. Under the new agreement, with reduced hours, rates increased to $1.18 and 77 cents for male and female labourers respectively. See also *Lantic Sugar Refinery, Saint John, N.B.* (a memorial volume, published circa 2000), 69–70. The local entered the Bakery and Confectionery Workers International Union in 1956, and Simonds later became director of organizing for the CLC.

71 NBFL *Proceedings*, 1956. Jodoin's address, at pp. 44–51, was the first speech reported verbatim in the Federation proceedings to include several paragraphs in French (pp. 47–48). His reference to the CLC's general objectives echoed the joint submission of the TLC and CCL to the Royal Commission on Canada's Economic Prospects in 1955, which also included "the preservation of a free, independent Canadian nation, even at some economic cost" and "the preservation of the historic communities which make up the Canadian nation": *Labour Gazette*, April 1956, 384–88.

72 NBFL *Proceedings*, 1954–56.

73 NBFL *Proceedings*, 1956.

74 Ibid. Harm was an example of the new generation of labour leaders and had a background in both TLC and CCL unions. An immigrant from Norway as a young man in the 1920s, he worked at the Dalhousie paper mill and was a member of the papermakers union there. During the war, he worked in the Pictou shipyards in Nova Scotia, where he joined the Industrial Union of Marine and Shipbuilding Workers. Subsequently, he became an organizer for the CCL. On Harm, see *Viewpoint: The Voice of Labor in Cape Breton*, January–April 1968, 12.

Four: "The New Unionism," 1957–1975

1 NBFL *Proceedings*, 1965, 33–41. Also included in one of the earliest recordings of convention proceedings, at SCD09213-BL3, MC1819, PANB. Robichaud's earlier comment (in French) was: "I consider the movement you have undertaken to be very important, and the interests of all the labourers and all the workers of New Brunswick are close to my heart."

2 Ibid.

3 Ibid.

4 On Robichaud, see Della M. M. Stanley, *Louis Robichaud: A Decade of Power* (Halifax: Nimbus Publishing, 1984), which describes him as a reformer with "socialistic"

tendencies: "Louis Robichaud was a pragmatist, moved more by his human sympathies than by any philosophical doctrines. He was a democrat, a socialist, a conservative and a liberal all wrapped into one." Robichaud's parents had worked in the cotton mills in Massachusetts before returning to the family home in Kent County to bring up their family. See also *L'ère Louis J. Robichaud, 1960–1970: Actes du colloque* (Moncton: Institut canadien de recherche sur le développement régional, 2001). In thanking the premier for his address in 1965, Federation President Lofty MacMillan "expressed satisfaction that it dealt with subjects very close to the Labour Movement to-day, especially in the Region and the Province": NBFL *Proceedings*, 1965.

5 John Hunter, "A Survey of Wage and Labour Conditions in the Province of New Brunswick," MA thesis, Department of Economics, University of New Brunswick, 1957.

6 In 1961, the average personal income in New Brunswick was 68.1 percent of the Canadian average; in 1970, it had increased to 71.5 percent but was still the third lowest in the country. See Ian Adams et al., *The Real Poverty Report* (Edmonton: Hurtig Publishers, 1971), 58–59.

7 *Canadian Labour*, October 1956, 13–15. For more context on this period, see E. R. Forbes and D. A. Muise, eds., *The Atlantic Provinces in Confederation* (Fredericton and Toronto: Acadiensis Press and University of Toronto Press, 1993), chaps. 11–13.

8 Again, my thanks to Raymond Léger for sharing his research in the files of the Industrial Relations Board and its predecessors, RS895, PANB.

9 Greg Allain, "L'évolution du syndicalisme au Canada et au Nouveau-Brunswick," *Égalité: Revue acadienne d'analyse politique* 31 (printemps 1992): 57–61.

10 *Campbellton Tribune*, 31 August 1960.

11 NBFL *Proceedings*, 1957. The constitution was discussed by a unity committee earlier in the year. The Federation would support the principles and policies of the CLC, and membership was limited to branches of unions affiliated to the CLC or to local unions and labour councils chartered by the CLC. An initial version was found "incompatible" with the CLC's requirements; however, no copy of this draft was located. At the convention, the only significant discussion of changes referred to the exclusion of sectoral councils (such as a Building Trades or a Waterfront Council). Interestingly, Whitebone headed his presidential report as a report to "the forty-fifth convention," but the 1958 convention was officially identified as the "first" convention of the "new" Federation.

12 NBFL *Proceedings*, 1957. The progress continued to be cautious, however. For instance, while the government in 1959 addressed "fair accommodation" and "fair employment" practices by expanding the earlier 1956 terms to prohibit discrimination on the grounds of "race, creed, colour, nationality, ancestry or place of origin," the category of gender was not included: *Statutes of New Brunswick*, 1959, c. 6, pp. 9–11.

13 NBFL *Proceedings*, 1957. MacLeod was nominated for the presidency in 1957 but did not stand. He was, however, named as one of two delegates to the 1958 meetings of the CLC.

14 NBFL *Proceedings*, 1959. The proceedings for this year were not published in the usual full format; however, the file in MC1819, PANB includes several records compiled by Whitebone at a later date, including a booklet containing the 1959 President's and Secretary-Treasurer's Reports. See also *Telegraph-Journal*, 12–17 September 1959, and *Le Madawaska* (Edmundston), 17 septembre 1959. For information on the Escuminac Disaster, see "Escuminac, 1959" at http://www.lhtnb.ca.

15 *Telegraph-Journal*, 15 September and 16 September 1959. On Knowles, see Susan Mann Trofimenkoff, *Stanley Knowles, The Man from Winnipeg North Centre* (Saskatoon: Western Producer Prairie Books, 1982). Prior to the 1959 convention, one of the Federation vice-presidents distributed a circular letter warning against endorsement of the "new party" and stating that "most of our people are organized for one purpose, namely, to improve their working conditions and wages. That is all." There was also an element of "redbaiting": "What happens to us if we should have a Labor Government in the palms of our hands and some groups who have trained in the Kremlin decide to worm their way into our organization with the intention of taking over our country?" See Charles H. Malchow to Affiliated Local Unions, Restigouche and Gloucester Counties, 24 July 1959, box 101, MC1819, PANB.

16 *Telegraph-Journal*, 17 September 1959. Resolutions adopted in 1959 called for an improvement in workers' compensation rates to provide 85 percent of a worker's pay and legislation to ensure that women workers received "equal pay with male workers for equal work." One of the longest resolutions called on the province to live up to its commitment to provide full collective bargaining rights to the union members working for the New Brunswick Liquor Control Board. In respect of collective bargaining for municipal employees, however, the Flemming government had amended the Labour Relations Act to reaffirm the ability of municipalities to exclude themselves from the provisions of the act: *Statutes of New Brunswick*, 1959, c. 56.

17 *Telegraph-Journal*, 17 September 1959.

18 *Telegraph-Journal*, 31 August 1960.

19 NBFL *Proceedings*, 1960.

20 *Evening Times-Globe*, 9 June, 22 June, and 25 June 1960.

21 Whitebone to Donald MacDonald, 10 June 1960 (with a clipping from the *Evening Times-Globe*, 9 June 1960), MacDonald to C.J., W.D., 13 June 1960, "Angus MacLeod, 1960," vol. 263, CLC Papers, MG28 1103, LAC. Whitebone evidently also wrote to several Federation stalwarts, provoking a number of comments about unpaid bills and drinking at meetings as well as MacLeod's inconsistency in abandoning the CCF for the Liberals. Rolland Blanchette noted: "I am still opposed to a new political party, we have enough enemies of labour now without creating some more." See Blanchette to Whitebone, 17 June 1960, and Michael J. Kenny to Whitebone, n.d. [June 1960], box 103, MC1819, PANB.

22 In the 1963 election, Saint John voters produced a more strategic result, electing two members from each party. Whitebone himself remained active in municipal politics in Saint John, where he was first elected to council in

1936. After the 1958 election, he was named deputy mayor and, following the death of the incumbent in 1960, acting mayor. Whitebone was a candidate for mayor in his own right in 1960 but did not succeed. See clipping 23 October 1958, box 103, MC1819, PANB; see also Ellen E. Bowen, *The Mayors of Saint John, 1785–1985* (Saint John: Saint John Public Library, 1985).

23 NBFL *Proceedings*, 1960; *Telegraph-Journal*, 30 August and 31 August 1960; *Campbellton Tribune*, 31 August 1960. The auditor's report recommended that all cheques require the signature of two officers, and that all payments by affiliates be made directly to the Federation accounts rather than the officers. MacLeod continued to serve the members of his home union at the Saint John shipyards until his official retirement in 1971, when he was celebrated as a union pioneer with a selfless sense of duty. For his part, MacLeod stated that he had always acted without need for formal recognition: "I'm one of those who believe that the trade union movement owes me nothing. I owe them everything that I've got." He lived until 1980, when the *Telegraph-Journal*, 15 December 1980, described him as "a tough and dedicated man working for the things he believed in."

24 NBFL *Proceedings*, 1960; *Telegraph-Journal*, 1 September 1960. The results were Whitebone 85, Booker 28, Ferlatte 27. Ferlatte and Booker were both among the six district vice-presidents elected at this time. For biographical information on Ferlatte, see Morden Lazarus, *Up from the Ranks: Trade Union VIP's past and present* (Toronto: Co-operative Press Associates, 1977), 41; on Booker,

see the *Gleaner*, 3 April 2009. Interviews with both Ferlatte and Booker are included in the LHTNB fonds, MC3477, PANB.

25 NBFL *Proceedings*, 1961; *Telegraph-Journal*, 30 August 1961.

26 The resolution stated: "Whereas the principles and policies as enunciated by the New Democratic Party coincide in almost every respect with those laid down and supported in the past by this Federation, be it therefore resolved that this New Brunswick Federation of Labour adopt the policy of the Canadian Labour Congress and endorse the principles and policies of the New Democratic Party without direct affiliation."

27 *Telegraph-Journal*, 31 August 1961. One historian has noted that CLC officers in 1961 considered placing the Federation under "administration." At the CLC convention in 1962, Whitebone was not re-elected as vice-president for the Atlantic Region and was replaced by a strong NDP supporter, John Simonds of the Bakery and Confectionery Workers. See Gad Horowitz, *Canadian Labour in Politics* (Toronto, University of Toronto Press, 1968), 230–32. The NDP ran no candidates in the 1963 provincial election and only three in 1967, as well as one in a by-election in 1966.

28 *Statutes of New Brunswick*, 1960–61, c. 7, pp. 55–57; NBFL *Proceedings*, 1961, 1965; *Moncton Transcript*, 28 August 1961. As of 1 January 1965, the hourly rates were $1.05 in construction, mining, and forestry, 75 cents in retail and manufacturing and food processing, and 65 cents in the service sector: see Department of Labour, *Annual Report* (1965), 16, 61–74.

29 *NBFL Proceedings*, 1961; *Statutes of New Brunswick*, 1960–61. Less noted, and of less direct concern to the Federation at the time, was the addition of nurses to the list of workers excluded from the provisions of the Act.

30 *NBFL Proceedings*, 1961; *Moncton Transcript*, 29 August 1961. Whitebone was re-elected as president in 1961, by a vote of 82 to 50. The opposing candidate was the NUPE delegate Booker, who was re-elected as vice-president for Carleton, York and Sunbury.

31 *NBFL Proceedings*, 1962; *Labour Gazette,* December 1962, 1359–61.

32 *NBFL Proceedings*, 1962, 1963. In 1963 the Federation considered a resolution to condemn the federal government for the adoption of nuclear weapons, which was defeated by a vote of 59 to 44. Two years later, however, the 1965 convention endorsed a resolution warning that the ongoing war in Vietnam could escalate into a global nuclear conflict and supporting a negotiated settlement.

33 *NBFL Proceedings*, 1964. Whitebone noted that extensive amendments to the Labour Relations Act had been considered by the province in 1964 but that these were withdrawn after the Federation insisted on the opportunity to review them. Whitebone also played his own part in Robichaud's programme of reform, when he accepted an appointment to a provincial royal commission on the modernization of liquor licensing laws, a reform that Whitebone considered to be a matter of public safety.

34 Hodges was a pioneer in other areas as well. In 1959 he was a founder of the Saint John branch of the New Brunswick Association for the Advancement of Coloured People and later held appointments to the Labour Relations Board and the Human Rights Commission. See Mac Trueman, "Heroes of Black History," *New Brunswick Reader*, 25 May 1996, and *Evening Times-Globe*, 23 July 1999.

35 *NBFL Proceedings*, 1962–64; Kimberley Dunphy, "The Feminization of the Labour Movement in New Brunswick: Women in the New Brunswick Federation of Labour, 1913–1984," MA thesis, Department of History, University of New Brunswick, 2009, 36–38, 278. For an interview with Dorothy Power Lawson, see the LHTNB fonds, MC3477, PANB.

36 *NBFL Proceedings*, 1967–73; Dunphy, "Women in the New Brunswick Federation of Labour," 53–60. There had been only three women delegates to the 1957 convention (and only two in 1958). In 1967, Hartman did not support the creation of special offices for women within the labour movement. Hartman also spoke to the convention in 1968, focusing on collective bargaining for public employees. Hartman was an influential pioneer in "labour feminism" and from 1975 to 1983 served as president of CUPE, the first woman elected president of a major union in Canada. For a biography, see Susan Crean, *Grace Hartman: A Woman for Her Time* (Vancouver: New Star Books, 1995).

37 Richard LeBlanc, "Le fonctionnement et la structure du Conseil du Travail d'Edmundston et Région et l'évolution de l'état langagier de 1947 à nos jours," *Revue de la Société historique du Madawaska* 32, nos. 3–4 (juillet–décembre 2004): 23–37.

38 Aurèle Ferlatte interview, LHTNB fonds, MC3477, PANB; Hem C. Jain, "Impact of

Ethnic Differences in the Work Force in Industrial Relations: A Case Study," *Relations industrielles/Industrial relations* 24, no. 2 (1969): 383–402. Another study from this period found no significant differences between the attitudes of English and French workers at an unidentified manufacturing firm: 47 percent of the anglophone and 56 percent of the francophone employees were dissatisfied with their wages. The study also noted that francophone workers were paid $600 less per annum than other workers. See Vinay Kothari, "A Cross-Cultural Study of Worker Attitudes in a Bicultural Economic Environment," *Relations industrielles/Industrial relations* 28, no. 1 (1973): 150–65.

39 Dunphy, "Women in the New Brunswick Federation of Labour," 49–50; NBFL *Proceedings*, 1967, and for the recording, SCD09214-BR3, MC1819, PANB. See also the interview in the LHTNB fonds, MC3477, PANB. Blanchard ran as a candidate for the leadership of the Progressive Conservative party in 1969, describing herself at the time as a workers' candidate: "Je pense que je représente la classe ouvrière"; see *Mathilda, la passionnaria acadienne* (Montréal: Office national du film du Canada, 1997). On Blanchard, see also "Pattern-Breakers of New Brunswick," *Chatelaine*, July 1977, 32; and *L'Acadie Nouvelle*, 2 juillet, 3 juillet, and 6 juillet 2007.

Laberge's remark was: "I think there are more French-Canadian delegates here at this convention than we have English-speaking delegates at the Quebec Federation of Labour congress, and yet we have simultaneous translation. I know that your officers are thinking about this very seriously and that the only obstacle up to this point has been simply the question of costs."

40 NBFL *Proceedings*, 1972, and the recording, SCD09216-BR1, MC1819, PANB. See also *Campbellton Tribune*, 7 June 1972. The offensive statement was not reported in the proceedings or captured on tape, but see *Telegraph-Journal*, 7 June 1972. In 1977 Blanchard was elected regional vice-president for Gloucester County, making her the first woman to serve as a vice-president since the early 1920s. It is estimated that by this time at least 30 percent of the delegates at Federation meetings were Acadians. Although the province's Official Languages Act was enacted in 1969, it was not fully proclaimed and implemented until 1977.

41 Mark McLaughlin, University of New Brunswick, provided this information in an unpublished paper presented at a conference in 2009, "Labour Force Responses to Modernization in the New Brunswick Woods, 1945–1982." He goes on to note that the forest companies also turned to mechanization to address labour shortages. The chainsaw was introduced in the 1950s and became common in the 1960s, and mechanical harvesters in the 1970s severely reduced the demand for woods labour. In another development, Local 306 of the International Woodworkers of America organized workers at several sawmill and plywood operations on the Miramichi and won a long strike at the Burchill Brothers mill in 1964: see Andrew Neufeld and Andrew Parnaby, *The IWA in Canada: The Life and Times of an Industrial Union* (Vancouver: IWA Canada/New Star Books, 2000), 166–68.

42 Wayne Roberts, *Cracking the Canadian Formula: The Making of the Energy and Chemical Workers Union* (Toronto: Between the Lines, 1990), 84–89. The Roberts account is based on union records. A number of documents from the industrial relations process are presented in Hem C. Jain, *Canadian Cases in Labour Relations and Collective Bargaining* (Toronto: Longman Canada, 1973), 49–85.

43 Raymond Léger, *The First 25 Years: [RWDSU] Local 1065, 1959–1984* (Saint John, 1984), 2–7.

44 *Local 821 SCFP 1960–85* (pamphlet, c. 1985); Lofty MacMillan, with Emery Hyslop and Peter McGahan, *The Boy from Port Hood: The Autobiography of John Francis "Lofty" MacMillan* (Fredericton: New Ireland Press, 1996), 115–26. Membership in the local increased from 80 members in 1960 to 317 in 1975, and the lowest pay classification increased from $27.23 a week in 1960 to $113.91 in 1975. See also the fiftieth-anniversary history, *1960–2010: Cinquante ans de solidarité: L'histoire de la section locale 821 du Syndicat canadien de la fonction publique* (Moncton: SCFP 821, 2011). Among local union leaders who emerged from the hospital unions were key figures such as Jean Thébeau in Moncton and Joan Blacquier in Newcastle, who both later became CUPE staff representatives.

45 "A Submission of CUPE-CLC and its New Brunswick Division to the Special Committee Appointed to Study the Byrne Royal Commission Report," Appendix, NBFL *Proceedings*, 1964. At the CUPE founding convention of in Winnipeg in 1963, which created the new union by a merger of the National Union of Public Employees and the National Union of Public Service Employees, there were eight delegates from New Brunswick, three of them women; they represented city workers and school board and hospital employees from Saint John, Campbellton, Dalhousie, and Moncton. See Canadian Union of Public Employees, *Proceedings of the Founding Convention, 1963*, 33.

46 NBFL *Proceedings*, 1964. The *Report of the Royal Commission on Finance and Municipal Taxation* was commonly known as the Byrne Commission Report after its chair, Bathurst lawyer Edward Byrne.

47 MacMillan received 84 votes. Frank Murray, a delegate from Local 502, IBEW in Saint John, received 11 votes, and S. W. MacDonald, a delegate from Local 1974, IAM in Bathurst, 50 votes. NBFL *Proceedings*, 1964.

48 MacMillan was, like Whitebone, one of labour's standard bearers in municipal politics and served on Common Council for four years. In the 1958 election, he and Whitebone topped the polls among the elected councillors. There was an element of rivalry there, as MacMillan was declared the first-place finisher on election night but their positions were reversed in the official count. In addition to MacMillan, *The Boy from Port Hood*, see Raymond Léger, "Remembering a Giant: Lofty MacMillan, 1917–2006," *Our Times*, April–May 2006, 36–37.

49 NBFL *Proceedings*, 1964. The CUPE submission to the Special Committee argued that a set of basic principles should be asserted, including the right to join unions and the right to collective bargaining. Moreover, while the Byrne Report paid considerable attention to Sweden as a model in organizing public

services, it had failed to note that Sweden had one of the strongest union movements in the world and that public employees enjoyed full union rights. If the system was to be borrowed "as a package," CUPE's submission argued, "this package should include trade union rights."

50 NBFL *Proceedings*, 1965; *Telegraph-Journal*, 1 September 1965.

51 MacMillan, *The Boy from Port Hood*, 134–35.

52 *Statutes of New Brunswick*, 1967, c. 29, repealed s. 34, which specified that married women could not be employed unless widowed or lacking competent male support.

53 NBFL *Proceedings*, 1966, 1967. Meanwhile, under pressure from workers employed by the federal government, Parliament was proceeding towards adoption of the Public Service Staff Relations Act, which became law in 1967.

54 In a book on public sector labour relations, Frankel had little to say about the situation in Québec and the Atlantic provinces: "There are staff associations in all of these provinces; but they are weak in numbers, little respected by their Governments, and quite ineffective": see *Staff Relations in the Civil Service: The Canadian Experience* (Montreal: McGill University Press, 1962), 205–6. For additional context, see Lisa Pasolli, "Bureaucratizing the Atlantic Revolution: The 'Saskatchewan Mafia' in the New Brunswick Civil Service, 1960–1970," *Acadiensis* 38, no. 1 (Winter/Spring 2009): 126–50.

55 See *Report of the Royal Commission on Employer-Employee Relations in the Public Services of New Brunswick* (1967), 15–16.

This important document was published in both languages.

56 *Proceedings of the Legislative Assembly of New Brunswick* (1968), 647–48, 662–89, 709.

57 Public Service Labour Relations Act, *Statutes of New Brunswick*, 1968, c. 88; Léger, "Remembering a Giant," 37. The same prohibition on the use of strikebreakers did not appear in the Labour Relations Act. In situations where negotiations failed to lead to collective agreements, workers would have the choice of sending the dispute to arbitration or holding a strike vote. Nonetheless, all bargaining units would have the option to identify "designated employees" required to remain at work in the interests of public health, safety, and security. One interesting provision in the new law stated that no organizations that discriminated against members on the grounds of sex, race, origins, colour, or religion could be certified; nor could the board accept an organization seeking "the overthrow of constituted authority."

58 MacMillan, *The Boy from Port Hood*, 140; Industrial Relations Act, *Statutes of New Brunswick*, 1971, c. 9. Members of the New Brunswick Association of Registered Nurses agitated for improved wages and conditions throughout the 1960s, culminating in a mass-resignation campaign in 1969. Once they had received certification, the nurses concluded province-wide collective agreements in 1970 and 1971. See Linda Kealey, "No More 'Yes Girls': Labour Activism among New Brunswick Nurses, 1964–1981," *Acadiensis* 37, no. 2 (Summer/Autumn 2008): 3–17; and Roxanne Reeves, "Collective Bargaining

for New Brunswick Nurses by New Brunswick Nurses, 1965–1969: In Unity There Is Strength," MA thesis, Department of History, University of New Brunswick, 2006. Meanwhile, the province's teachers, who organized in separate but complementary groups representing teachers in the English and French school systems, received certification in 1972. The provincial Civil Service Association, which had existed since 1954, was denied certification in 1970 because their members included managers, but once reorganized under a new name in 1971, the New Brunswick Public Employees Association was recognized as the bargaining agent for some 5,000 civil servants. See Courtney MacIsaac and Lisa Pasolli, "NBPEA to NBU: Association to Union, 1970–2004," research report, June 2007.

59 The most perceptive discussion, which identifies the paradoxes of Robichaud's populism and the conditions of dependency, is James L. Kenny, "A New Dependency: State, Local Capital, and the Development of New Brunswick's Base Metal Industry, 1960–70," *Canadian Historical Review* 78, no. 1 (March 1997): 1–39.

60 NBFL *Proceedings*, 1965. For the dispute discussed here, see vol. 3112, reel T-3416, file 340, Department of Labour Records, RG27, LAC. Additional disputes at Belledune are documented in vol. 3115, reel T-3418, file 11; vol. 3116, reel T-3419, file 107; vol. 3117, reel T-3419, file 166; and vol. 3122, reel T-3421, file 442.

61 For biographical information, see Lazarus, *Up from the Ranks*, 67–68; *Telegraph-Journal*, 28 June 2000; and box 119, MC1819,

PANB. At some point after the 1966 convention, the vice-presidency for Gloucester and Restigouche was divided to create separate representation for Gloucester County. For many years the steel union was involved in a long-running conflict with a rival union with a more "leftist" reputation, the International Union of Mine, Mill and Smelter Workers, which also entered New Brunswick at this time and was represented by organizer Ed Levert. In 1966, Mine-Mill Local 1043 was locked in a long struggle for a union contract at the Nigadoo copper mine. Although Mine-Mill was excluded from the CLC and the Federation, MacMillan insisted on supporting this struggle, reporting to the 1967 convention: "The Federation took a stand that no employer in the mining field or otherwise would come into this province and impose substandard wages and conditions on fellow New Brunswickers, regardless of their trade union affiliation." As the Steel representative, he added, LePage had "exemplified real trade union principles during this period." At this stage a merger between Steel and Mine-Mill was near completion, and Levert came to work for Steel.

62 NBFL *Proceedings*, 1967.

63 NBFL *Proceedings*, 1968. An undated flyer in the Federation records, from a later stage in his presidency, promoted LePage in these terms: "decisive — dedicated — reliable — honest — respected — bilingual."

64 NBFL *Proceedings*, 1968, 1969; *Northern Light* (Bathurst), 13 June and 20 June 1968. See *Statutes of New Brunswick*, 1968, c. 85. The plan did not come into effect in the province until 1 January 1971. Meanwhile, the

Federation continued to call for the inclusion of optical, dental, chiropractic, and prescription drug coverage, as recommended by Justice Hall. One of the Federation's contributions to the debate was to advise against a provision for doctors to "opt in" rather than "opt out"; they also proposed an advisory committee, to include representation from organized labour and the medical profession among others, to report annually on the effectiveness of the plan. See "Submission by the New Brunswick Federation of Labour with regard to Bill#1, Medical Services Act" (June 1968). For the context, see Alvin Finkel, *Social Policy and Practice in Canada: A History* (Waterloo: Wilfrid Laurier University Press, 2006), 169–92.

65 The discussion here is based on Patrick Webber, "'For a Socialist New Brunswick': The New Brunswick Waffle, 1967–1972," *Acadiensis* 38, no. 1 (Winter/Spring 2009): 75–103. See also his "'For a Socialist New Brunswick': The New Brunswick Waffle, 1967–1972," MA thesis, Department of History, University of New Brunswick, 2008, which reproduces the manifesto on pp. 165–68. Support for the New Brunswick Waffle was largely based in the province's universities and new left, though one influential supporter was party President Pat Callaghan, a working-class immigrant from Scotland who was schooled in the traditions of the British Labour Party. Richardson continued as provincial NDP leader for several more years and was elected secretary-treasurer of the Federation of Labour in 1981.

66 NBFL *Proceedings*, 1972; *Telegraph-Journal*, 7 June 1972.

67 *Northern Light*, 12 January 1972; *L'Évangéline*, 14 janvier 1972. This account also draws on documents in box 111, MC1819, PANB. Although listed, Ralliement Créditiste leader Réal Caouette did not attend. See also James Kenny, "'Let the Workers Speak!': The Bathurst Day of Concern, 16 January 1972," unpublished paper, 2007, and Kenny, "Women and the Modernizing State: The Case of Northeast New Brunswick, 1964–72," in Janet Guildford and Suzanne Morton, eds., *Making Up the State: Women in Twentieth-Century Atlantic Canada* (Fredericton: Acadiensis Press, 2010), 175–77.

68 See *Northern Light*, 12 January and 19 January 1972; *L'Évangéline*, 14–18 janvier 1972; NBFL *Proceedings*, 1972.

69 LePage, "Address to the Day of Concern," box 111, MC1819, PANB. As Kenny has pointed out, such critiques largely accepted the premises of "state modernization policies" and, as became apparent, failed to appreciate the local mix of "ethnic, class and generational consciousness."

70 *Northern Light*, 19 January 1972; *L'Évangéline*, 17–18 janvier 1972. By September, Hatfield and Marchand were able to announce additional funding to support local industry under an amended federal-provincial agreement.

71 Richard Wilbur, *The Rise of French New Brunswick* (Halifax: Formac Publishing, 1989), 247, and, more generally, chaps. 15 and 16. The Parti Acadien at this time endorsed social and economic policies similar to those of the NDP. Party leader Euclide Chiasson, a professor at the Collège de Bathurst, received 1,011 votes in Nigadoo-

Chaleur in the 1974 provincial election, but none of the party's thirteen candidates was elected. See Roger Ouellette, *Le Parti Acadien: De la fondation à la disparition, 1972–1982* (Moncton: Chaire d'études acadiennes, 1992).

72 *Northern Light*, 15 February, 22 February, and 1 March 1972; "Report to the Executive Officers . . . re problems in Northeastern New Brunswick," 28 March 1972. Similar concerns were expressed in a letter in the *Northern Light*, 19 January 1972, which stated: "No: it was not the hour and the place to air Acadian grievances. We have enough tribulations facing us on the North Shore at the moment — now we should face them as a divided people!?!"

73 NBFL *Proceedings*, 1971–73. On Hatfield, see Richard Starr, *Richard Hatfield: The Seventeen Year Saga* (Halifax: Formac, 1987). As the party's house leader in 1968, Hatfield had supported Robichaud's initiatives in labour and social legislation. However, in the Hatfield years there was a shift away from ministers of labour who had a labour background, and in 1975 the name of the Department of Labour itself was changed to Labour and Manpower New Brunswick. With affiliations and administrative work both increasing, the Federation in 1972 decided to employ a full-time executive secretary. After interviewing three candidates, the executive hired John Murphy, a young graduate of Mount Allison University with a union background, who continued to serve the Federation over the next three decades.

74 NBFL *Proceedings*, 1975. At the 1973 meetings there was also continued impatience with the slowness of the Federation's progress towards bilingualism. Moreover, to LePage's embarrassment, the Resolutions Committee endorsed a resolution from the Canadian Seafood Workers Union in favour of full bilingualism for all Federation employees, which was vocally supported by Blanchard before it was defeated. By 1975 there was measurable progress, as policy documents and resolutions were presented in both languages, as were the financial statements. In another controversial debate in 1973, delegates from CUPE won support for a resolution condemning the Canadian Labour Congress for considering the admission of the New Brunswick Public Employees Association as an affiliate; in their view the NBPEA, the former Civil Service Association, was a weak organization with inferior contracts whose members in the civil service properly belonged within the jurisdiction of CUPE. See *Evening Times-Globe*, 4–6 June 1973.

75 NBFL *Proceedings*, 1975; *Moncton Daily Times*, 3 June 1975; *Telegraph-Journal*, 3 June 1975. The Department of Labour reported a total of 122,328 "man-days" of lost work in 1974, of which 70,300 were accounted for by continuing trouble at Brunswick Mines. There were 9 legal strikes and 32 illegal walkouts. The Federation offered financial support in four major disputes: six-week strikes at Eastern Bakeries and the New Brunswick Telephone Company, an 11-week strike at International Paper in Dalhousie — and a strike at Cirtex, a small knitting operation in Caraquet, where workers had already been out for six months.

76 These were discussed at the special policy meetings in 1974 that took place instead of the annual meeting and formed elements of a broader labour agenda seeking to redirect the wealth and productivity of the country towards shared social purposes. Consumers and farmers both needed protection from the multinational food corporations, it was argued. Housing was a right for all Canadians and could be strengthened by supporting cooperative housing plans. Pensions should be available to workers at age sixty, and all private plans should have minimum standards and be governed jointly by workers and employers. As for wages and incomes, the most important statement in the policy document was that the share of the national income going to profits was higher than at any time since 1951 and that labour's share of the national income had been in decline since 1966. Moreover, the chronic problem of low wages and high prices in New Brunswick was now being aggravated by rapid inflation, and real earnings were falling rapidly. The minimum wage needed to be raised to $3.50 per hour, with regular adjustments to take rising prices into account, and the same principle should also be applied to social security benefits. Meanwhile, unions must be prepared to reopen contracts in order to achieve cost-of-living adjustments and should expect more difficult rounds of collective bargaining ahead.

77 NBFL *Proceedings*, 1975; *Telegraph-Journal*, 6 June 1975.

78 *Moncton Times*, 3 June 1975; *Telegraph-Journal*, 3 June and 4 June 1975. His speech (which was preceded by a short film) is in the recorded proceedings at the PANB, SCD09217-AL4 and SCD09217-BLI. In the march through the streets, Chávez was accompanied not only by LePage but also by Constable Lorne Saunders of the Moncton police, the newly elected head of CUPE New Brunswick. At the convention the next day, LePage reported to delegates that he had received a telephone call from Dominion Stores head office stating there would be no change in policy: *Moncton Times*, 5 June 1975.

79 Allain, "L'évolution du syndicalisme," 59–61. The rate of union membership among men increased in these five years from 31.3 to 35.7 percent, and among women from 15.8 to 23.2 percent. Provincial union membership peaked at 33.8 percent in 1974.

80 NBFL *Proceedings*, 1975. The largest single delegation in attendance at the 1975 convention was from CUPE, with delegates from 32 locals in all parts of the province. The second largest were delegates from 14 locals of the Canadian Paperworkers Union, the new organization that had emerged from several pre-existing unions to form a distinct Canadian union in 1974. They too came from most parts of the province: Edmundston, Saint John, Bathurst, Dalhousie, Atholville, Nackawic, St. George, Newcastle, and Nelson. Other large delegations came from the Canadian Food and Allied Workers, the International Brotherhood of Electrical Workers, the United Brotherhood of Carpenters and Joiners, the United Steelworkers, and the Canadian Brotherhood of Railway, Transport and General Workers.

81 *Telegraph-Journal*, 7 June 1975.

Five: "On the Line," 1976–1997

1 The account here is based on George Vair, *The Struggle Against Wage Controls: The Saint John Story, 1975–1976* (St. John's: Canadian Committee on Labour History, 2006). Unless indicated otherwise, relevant quotations are from this book.

2 "Day of Protest 1976," box 201, MC1819, PANB. Several unions, such as the firefighters and police, declared support but did not quit work. In addition, unions such as the New Brunswick Nurses Union, who were not affiliated to the Federation, stated their support and encouraged off-duty members to participate.

3 Canada Labour Code, *Statutes of Canada, 1972*, c. 18. See also David Frank, "Why Us? The Campaign Against Wage Controls in Saint John, New Brunswick, 1975–76," in Marie Hammond-Callaghan and Matthew Hayday, eds., *Mobilizations, Protests and Engagements: Canadian Perspectives on Social Movements* (Halifax and Winnipeg: Fernwood Publishing, 2008), 211–21.

4 In addition to Vair, see Paul Young Interview, LHTNB fonds, MC3477, PANB.

5 *NBFL Proceedings*, 1976.

6 *NBFL Proceedings*, 1977. Apart from the loss of pay, there was one report of direct reprisals, as the municipal administration in Campbellton attempted to dismiss more than 40 workers. The city backed down when CUPE threatened that all local members of the union, including hospital staff and firefighters, would walk out in support.

7 *NBFL Proceedings*, 1977; *Telegraph-Journal*, 17 May 1977.

8 *NBFL Proceedings*, 1977; *Telegraph-Journal*, 17 May 1977. See also "Cirtex strike, 1975–77," box 88, MC1819, PANB.

9 *Telegraph-Journal*, 7 June 1978; *Moncton Times*, 9 June 1978. By the end of 1981, however, the company announced plans to close the plant: *Atlantic Insight*, November 1981, 18.

10 NBFL *Proceedings*, 1978, 1979; *Telegraph-Journal*, 6 June 1978; *Moncton Times*, 6 June 1978. The following year the delegates, most of whom had heard former federal NDP leader David Lewis speak at a pre-convention conference, adopted a resolution to support the NDP in the 1979 election, which took place a week later. The NDP showed a small surge in New Brunswick at this time, with the federal vote increasing from 8.7 percent in 1974 to 15.3 percent in 1979 and 16.8 percent in 1980. Provincial results were weaker; the NDP more than doubled its 1974 vote to 6.5 percent in the 1978 election; the Parti Acadien received 3.5 percent of the vote.

11 *Moncton Times*, 8 June 1978; *Telegraph-Journal*, 8 June 1978; *Moncton Times*, 15 May 1979; *Telegraph-Journal*, 15 May 1979. In a public statement, LePage rejected Blanchard's claims that the Federation was "anti-Acadian" and dominated by big unions: *Moncton Times*, 9 June and 10 June 1978.

12 NBFL *Proceedings*, 1980, 1981; *Telegraph-Journal*, 12 June 1980. LePage was also celebrated at a testimonial dinner in Bathurst on 6 September, which was attended by Premier Hatfield.

13 NBFL *Proceedings*, 1980; "Phil Booker for President" [1980], box 117, MC1819, PANB; and *Telegraph-Journal*, 11 June and 16 June 1980. See also Phillip Booker Interview, LHTNB fonds, MC3477, PANB. It was

reported later that Booker defeated Hanley by a relatively close margin of 20 votes.

14 Eleanor O'Donnell MacLean, *Leading the Way: An Unauthorized Guide to the Sobey Empire* (GATT-Fly Atlantic: Halifax, [1985]), 26–30; NBFL *Proceedings*, 1981; and *Moncton Times*, 13 May 1981.

15 NBFL *Proceedings*, 1981; *Telegraph-Journal*, 13 May 1981. The proposal to withdraw from government bodies was defeated, but delegates endorsed a resolution to discontinue preparing an annual brief for the provincial government.

16 NBFL *Proceedings*, 1981; *Moncton Times*, 12 May, 14 May, and 16 May 1981; *Telegraph-Journal*, 15 May 1981. See also boxes 68 and 116, MC1819, PANB. By the time of the suspension, the affected unions were already planning to establish the rival Canadian Federation of Labour, which functioned from 1982 to 1997. The affected unions included the International Brotherhood of Electrical Workers, the United Brotherhood of Carpenters and Joiners, the United Association of Journeymen and Apprentices of the Plumbing and Pipefitting Industry, the International Association of Bridge, Structural and Ornamental Ironworkers, the International Union of Operating Engineers, the Laborers' International Union of North America, the International Brotherhood of Painters and Allied Trades, the Sheet Metal Workers International Association, the International Brotherhood of Boilermakers, Iron Shipbuilders, Blacksmiths, Forgers and Helpers, the International Union of Bricklayers and Allied Craftsmen, the International Union of Elevator Constructors, and the International Association of Heat and Frost Insulators and Asbestos Workers. There were specific interunion rivalries in Québec and British Columbia at stake in the dispute, as was resistance to CLC guidelines to provide more autonomy for Canadian branches of international unions, which the unions considered to be an inaccurate assessment of conditions and undue interference in their internal affairs.

17 "Hanley for President," box 117, MC1819, PANB. See also *Telegraph-Journal*, 16 May 1981 and 22 March 2006; and *Atlantic Insight*, October 1981, 40–41. The 1972 quotation is from Robert Laxer, *Canada's Unions* (Toronto: James Lorimer, 1976), 309–10.

18 For a treatment, including illustrations and documents, see the website feature "Hot Cargo, 1979," http://www.lhtnb.ca. The event has been described as "the single most dramatic example of Canadian trade union solidarity with workers in the Third World." There was a second episode in 1982, when the Federation supported the decision of Local 273, International Longshoremen's Association to refuse to handle nuclear supplies for Argentina. Many years later, after the restoration of democracy in Argentina, the Argentine government presented a medal to the workers of Saint John.

19 *Moncton Times*, 14 May 1981; *Telegraph-Journal*, 14 May, 15 May, and 16 May 1981. George Vair considered Hanley an excellent organizer and orator who could think well on his feet: "He had sort of this uncanny sense of how far he could push the envelope and then would know when to pull back": *Telegraph-Journal*, 22 March 2006.

20 NBFL *Proceedings*, 1982; *Telegraph-Journal*,

15 June 1982. See also Leo Panitch and Donald Swartz, *From Consent to Coercion: The Assault on Trade Union Freedoms*, 3rd ed. (Aurora: Garamond Press, 2003), Appendix II.

21 NBFL *Proceedings*, 1982; *Gleaner*, 29 May–2 July 1981; "Nackawic CPU 219 Dispute, 1981," box 88, MC1819, PANB; "St. Anne Nackawic Pulp & Paper vs. CPU," *Judgements of the Supreme Court of Canada*, 1 SCR 704 [June 1986], http://scc.lexum.org. See also Beth Bilson, "Fencing Off Collective Bargaining: A Comment on *St. Anne Nackawic*," *Saskatchewan Law Review* 52, no. 1 (1988): 143–59, which notes that the decision paradoxically confirmed the jurisdiction of the Industrial Relations Board in labour disputes while also continuing to accept the use of court injunctions.

22 This discussion draws on Sue Calhoun, *A Word to Say: The Story of the Maritime Fishermen's Union* (Halifax: Nimbus Publishing, 1991), 77–159. The election of a young local schoolteacher, Jean Gauvin, as a government member in Shippagan-les-Îles in 1978 was also important in the political breakthrough; Gauvin pledged to support unionization for the fishermen and was able to advance this agenda when Hatfield named him minister of fisheries. At the federal level, Calhoun notes that after Roméo LeBlanc, who had a grudging admiration for the MFU activists, returned to office as federal fisheries minister in 1980, he allocated most of the herring stock to the inshore fishers. Several of the MFU organizers had a background as radical leftists. Thériault, for instance, had left the Parti Acadien in 1977 and supported the Montréal-based Workers' Communist Party

before it dissolved in 1982. When the Moncton Union Centre banned the MFU from using the building that housed the Federation and other union offices, the issue was taken up at the 1980 Federation convention. A mild resolution of protest was defeated, and delegates voted to move the Federation "to an office where all its affiliates are welcome." This ultimatum forced the centre to lift the ban on the MFU: NBFL *Proceedings*, 1980.

23 *Telegraph-Journal*, 16 June 1982.

24 NBFL *Proceedings*, 1982; "Elect McCarthy for President," box 117, and biographical information in box 126, MC1819, PANB; *Le Madawaska*, 9 juin, 16 juin, and 23 juin 1982; and *Telegraph-Journal*, 19 June 1982.

25 *Directory of Labour Organizations in New Brunswick*, 1985.

26 NBFL *Proceedings*, 1982, 1984; *Telegraph-Journal*, 15 June 1982. Moreover, when women activists looked for allies among the social movements in the province, they found experienced leaders in the ranks of the unions. When a provincial ad hoc committee of women's organizations called for a New Brunswick Advisory Council on the Status of Women in the 1970s, Dorothy Power Lawson played a leading part as co-chair. Once the advisory council was established in 1977, the Federation requested representation, and as a result Moncton union activist Kathryn-Ann Leger was appointed in 1981. See also Janet Guildford, "Persistence on the Periphery: Advisory Councils on the Status of Women in Atlantic Canada to 2000," in Janet Guildford and Suzanne Morton, eds., *Making Up the State: Women in Twentieth-Century Atlantic Canada* (Fredericton: Acadiensis Press, 2010), 232–37.

27 Kimberley Dunphy, "The Feminization of the Labour Movement in New Brunswick: Women in the New Brunswick Federation of Labour, 1913–1984," MA thesis, Department of History, University of New Brunswick, 2009, 75, 136–41, provides an account of the strike based on union records, now in MC3653, PANB, as well as her attendance at the local's twenty-fifth anniversary event in 2006. See also interviews with Joan Blacquier and Mary Moss, LHTNB fonds, MC3477, PANB.

28 Dunphy, "Women in the New Brunswick Federation of Labour, 1913–1984." 78–82; NBFL Proceedings, 1984; and Telegraph-Journal, 20 June 1984. After Beaulieu's election, three of the eight vice-presidents were women.

29 NBFL Proceedings, 1984, 1986; and Dunphy, "Women in the New Brunswick Federation of Labour, 1913–1984," 78. However, the change, as approved in 1986 and later included in the Federation Constitution, gave the official name as "Fédération des travailleuses et travailleurs du Nouveau-Brunswick."

30 Tim McCarthy to Pierre Juneau, 9 December 1985, box 161, MC1819, PANB.

31 NBFL Proceedings, 1987; Times-Transcript, 27 May 1987. The quotations are from the 1986 response paper and the 1987 press release, among other documents in box 161, MC1819, PANB.

32 Although Executive Secretary John Murphy had limited French-language abilities, the Federation's office secretary Alice LeBlanc was bilingual, and in 1986 it was estimated that 40 percent of her work was in French. In addition, a part-time secretary and a translator were employed as needed. Information is included in "Official Languages and Services Profile," box 126, MC1819, PANB, prepared in order to qualify for matching funds from the secretary of state for the provision of bilingual services. Limited funds to support bilingual services were also provided by the provincial Department of Labour.

33 "Francophone Concerns in 1985–86," box 141, MC1819, PANB.

34 NBFL Proceedings, 1986.

35 Times-Transcript, 14 May 1986.

36 Le Madawaska, 5 juin 1985. The comment reads: "The delegates were obviously delighted to have spent three days in the Republic of Madawaska."

37 "To all citizens of the Chaleur region who believe in justice — honesty — rights and freedom." The preceding statement reads: "Because our husbands are limited by an injunction in what actions they can take, we have decided to replace them, and we intend to maintain our picket line and block access to the sites until we obtain positive results."

38 Michel Roy, "Law, Class, and State: A Critical Analysis of the Labour Relations Regime in New Brunswick," unpublished paper, Carleton University, 1993. This study draws on local union documents as well as The Northern Light and L'Acadie Nouvelle.

39 Telegraph-Journal, 31 May 1985.

40 When the Public Service Alliance of Canada and other unions launched a legal appeal, the Supreme Court of Canada ruled that "freedom of association" under the new Canadian Charter of Rights and Freedoms did not protect the right to strike or the right to collective bargaining. See Panitch and Swartz, From Consent to Coercion, 32–37, 51–83. This decision was reversed in 2007.

41 *NBFL Proceedings*, 1985. See also *Evening Times-Globe*, 28 May 1985. At earlier conventions, McCarthy opposed withdrawing from the province's Industrial Relations Council, established by the Hatfield government to encourage consultation between unions, employers, and government; by 1985, however, he was convinced that the council was irrelevant, as major employers were adopting aggressive anti-union attitudes. McCarthy's recommendation to withdraw was carried unanimously.

42 *NBFL Proceedings*, 1986; *Times-Transcript*, 14 May 1986. The plan included a call for "labour history education in particular to inform new and younger members about the roots of the fights we are now waging."

43 "Your Voice Could Save 2000 Jobs," box 115, MC1819, PANB.

44 The discussion is based on documents in box 115, MC1819, PANB, which includes the texts of petitions, flyers, and the speech by Bourgeois. See also an extended submission on the impact of the closures prepared by Local 594, IAM, in 1986, "Why the Moncton Shops Must Stay." For these events, see also *NBFL Proceedings*, 1986, and *Telegraph-Journal*, 15 May 1986. For background on Bourgeois, see *The Machinist*, February 1984 and March 1985.

45 The account here is based on Raymond Léger, *423 Days on the Picket Line*, RWDSU Local 1065 (RWDSU, Saint John [1990]). See also *NBFL Proceedings*, 1988.

46 *NBFL Proceedings*, 1987; *Times-Transcript*, 25 May and 28 May 1987.

47 *NBFL Proceedings*, 1987, 1988; *Times-Transcript*, 17 May 1988.

48 *NBFL Proceedings*, 1987. See also *NBFL Proceedings*, 1988; and Richard Wilbur, "New Brunswick," in Leo Heaps, ed., *Our Canada* (Toronto: James Lorimer, 1991), 156–58. As it happened, there was no balance at all in the new legislature, as the Liberals took all 58 seats. For provincial election results in this period, see "Elections in New Brunswick/Les Élections au Nouveau-Brunswick, 1984–2006," prepared by the New Brunswick Legislative Library, available at http://electionsnb.ca/publications-e.asp.

49 *NBFL Proceedings*, 1986, especially Document No. 2, "Free Trade: A New Brunswick Perspective." See also *Telegraph-Journal*, 14 May 1986.

50 "NBFL Statement by Tim McCarthy, 13 July 1988," box 87, MC1819, PANB. See also other documents in this file as well as *Times-Transcript*, 9 May, 11 May, 12 May, and 16 May 1988; *Telegraph-Journal*, 9 May, 14 May, and 16 May 1988; *Globe and Mail*, 14 May 1988; and *NBFL Proceedings*, 1988. The case dragged on for several years, at considerable expense to both Murphy and the Federation, before it was dismissed by the courts in 1992.

51 *NBFL Proceedings*, 1985.

52 *NBFL Proceedings*, 1977, 1979, 1987, 1990, 1991, 1992; *Telegraph-Journal*, 19 May 1977, 28 May 1987.

53 The document was widely distributed as a broadsheet with both English and French texts through churches and study groups. See also John R. Williams, ed., *Canadian Churches and Social Justice* (Toronto: Anglican Book Centre and James Lorimer, 1984), 77–87.

54 NBFL *Proceedings*, 1983; *Telegraph-Journal*, 19 May 1983. One of the commission members, Bishop William Power of Antigonish, was invited to address the convention on this theme. For this and other documents, see Gregory Baum and Duncan Cameron, eds., *Ethics and Economics: Canada's Catholic Bishops on the Economic Crisis* (Toronto: James Lorimer, 1984).

55 NBFL *Proceedings*, 1991.

56 *Telegraph-Journal*, 6 June 1991. Later in the year there was an evening to honour McCarthy, where the Federation announced the establishment of the Tim McCarthy Environment Prize, to be given annually to union members or family members involved in helping to protect the environment. See NBFL *Proceedings*, 1992.

57 NBFL *Proceedings*, 1992. See also "John McEwen," Biographies File, box 126, MC1819, PANB; and *Times-Transcript*, 6 August 2004.

58 See Philip Lee, *Frank: The Life and Politics Frank McKenna* (Fredericton: Goose Lane Editions, 2001), who notes: "The government promoted low wages and labour legislation that was favourable to business" (185).

59 For background, see Jacques Poitras, "Leader on the Left," *New Brunswick Reader*, 8 October 2005.

60 *Telegraph-Journal*, 30 May 1989.

61 NBFL *Proceedings*, 1988–91. Meanwhile, the province had removed the right to strike from municipal and regional police officers and enacted special provisions for labour relations at designated "major projects" in the construction industry.

62 *Gleaner*, 18 April 1991. See also *Telegraph-Journal*, 18 April 1991; and Lee, *Frank*, 201–5.

63 *Telegraph-Journal*, 4 June and 6 June 1991.

See also NBFL *Proceedings*, 1991.

64 COR received 21.2 percent of the vote, and the NDP 10.8 percent. On the rise of COR, see Matthew Baglole, "'Many Closet Supporters Will Come Forward': New Brunswick's Confederation of Regions Party," in Hammond-Callaghan and Hayday, eds., *Mobilizations, Protests and Engagements*, 164–85. For the NDP, in a federal by-election in December 1990 there had been a hint of the potential to elect a union candidate in Acadian New Brunswick. Former MFU president Guy Cormier, a Cap-Pelé fisherman, won 12,587 votes, an impressive 37.37 percent of the total, when he stood against Jean Chrétien in the Beauséjour riding, where the future prime minister was taking advantage of a "safe" Liberal seat to return to the House of Commons as the Liberal leader. It was mainly a two-way race, as the Progressive Conservatives did not field a candidate; COR received 2,783 votes. See "History of Federal Ridings since 1867," http://www.parl.gc.ca.

65 A joint complaint against the 1991 legislation was filed by the Canadian Labour Congress, the National Union of Provincial Government Employees, and the New Brunswick Government Employees Union. The ILO ultimately encouraged the province to "take measures, in consultation with the trade unions concerned, with a view to restoring a collective bargaining and arbitration system which enjoys the fullest confidence of the parties." See Report No. 284, Case No. 1605, http://www.ilo.org/.

66 "Coalition of Public Employees Media Scripts," as cited by Caroline Mann, "'In McKenna No Trust': Labour's Response to

the Expenditure Management Act of 1992 in New Brunswick." See also Roxanne Reeves, "'Nurses in Mourning': New Brunswick Nurses' Reaction to the 1991–1992 McKenna Wage Freeze." The account here draws on these two unpublished papers prepared at the University of New Brunswick in 2005. See also Linda Kealey, "'A Bitter Pill to Swallow': New Brunswick Nurses, Professional Identity, and Collective Bargaining, 1991–92," in Guildford and Morton, eds., *Making Up the State*, 217–27; and William Vinh-Doyle, *Catching Up, Fighting Back: The New Brunswick Council of Hospital Unions* (Fredericton: CUPE 1252, 2010), 49–58.

67 New Brunswick Government Employees Union, "Response to 'The New Brunswick Tax Structure: A Review,'" 1992, and "Federation Clarifies Role in Coalition," New Brunswick Teachers Federation News Release, 27 April 1992, box 88, MC1819, PANB.

68 Kealey, "'A Bitter Pill,'" 223–24.

69 Kealey, "'A Bitter Pill.'" See also the website feature "The Nurses vs. McKenna, 1991–1992," http://www.lhtnb.ca.

70 NBFL *Proceedings*, 1992.

71 *Telegraph-Journal*, 1 June 1992. The list of observers included nineteen members of the media, more than twice as many as in 1991.

72 *Times-Transcript*, 2 June 1992.

73 Vinh-Doyle, *Catching Up, Fighting Back*, 53–57. Lofty MacMillan later commented on his experience attending rallies around the province at this time: "Many staff from CUPE and other unions have told me 'the members are not like they were in your day,' 'not so militant.' This was a pack of nonsense, for I found the rank and file ready to fight once they had the

leadership": MacMillan to Ron Caplan, 18 November 1994 (copy in author's possession).

74 *Times-Transcript*, 4 June 1992.

75 *Telegraph-Journal*, 4 June 1992.

76 *Times-Transcript*, 4 June 1992.

77 Quoted in Lee, *Frank*, 262–63.

78 Lee, *Frank*, 216–18.

79 See Panitch and Swartz, *From Consent to Coercion*, 129–31: "CUPE claimed, with some justification, that it had won a major victory. And there can be no doubt that what it did achieve was the result of the union actually having waged a serious struggle to defend its members' bargaining rights. In this light, the strike was certainly not a defeat, but neither was it the kind of victory that Canadian workers so badly needed, a victory that would stand as a clear symbol that the practice of permanent exceptionalism could be successfully countered."

80 The following year, CUPE NB President Bob Hickes formally expressed the appreciation of his union for the Federation's support in the struggles of the previous year: NBFL *Proceedings*, 1993.

81 NBFL *Proceedings*, 1993.

82 NBFL *Proceedings*, 1994. When the government at this time brought the Industrial Relations Act and the Public Service Labour Relations Act under the jurisdiction of a single board, labour's recommendations for a chair were ignored; the new Labour and Employment Board commenced operations under a McKenna insider, Paul Lordon, who had served him as a deputy minister and was one of his original law partners in Chatham.

83 "If a group of employees take a strike vote and 70 percent of them vote against a strike, the

30 percent who voted for a strike cannot go out on strike." See RWDSU Local 1065 Brief, July 1995, pp. 5, 7, 9. The anti-scab legislation was one of five themes in the "Make It Fair" campaign undertaken by the four Federations of Labour in the Atlantic Region. Other objectives for reforming provincial labour codes included improved certification standards, an option for binding first-contract arbitration, stronger successor rights, and speedier arbitration of contract grievances.

84 In the September provincial election, the Liberals were returned with a strong majority; the COR Party collapsed, however, allowing the Conservatives to return as the Official Opposition. Weir was easily re-elected in Saint John Harbour, and the NDP had strong second-place showings in Saint John Champlain (physician Paula Tippett) and in Dalhousie-Restigouche East (union veteran Aurèle Ferlatte).

85 NBFL Proceedings, 1995.

86 NBFL Proceedings, 1993, 1994, 1995. The other two labour seats went to the nurses and the building trades, but none of the labour representatives from the Health and Safety Commission was included among the appointments. The province later agreed to expand the board and provide a second seat, for which the Federation named Blair Doucet: NBFL Proceedings, 1997. See also CUPE Research Department, "Presentation to the Independent Review Panel, New Brunswick Workplace, Health, Safety and Compensation Commission" (2007). In the two-year period from 1992 to 1994, unsuccessful claims increased from almost 70 percent to more than 80 percent.

87 The date referred to the original enactment in 1914 of workers' compensation laws in Ontario, which had helped set the standard for provincial laws across the country. The Day of Mourning was adopted by the ILO as International Workers' Memorial Day and is marked in more than a hundred countries around the world.

88 In 1993 the Federation's Health and Safety Committee reported that work-related injuries in the province currently accounted for twenty fatalities each year as well as the equivalent in injuries of 1,800 full-time jobs lost.

89 For a fuller discussion, see David Frank and Nicole Lang, *Labour Landmarks in New Brunswick / Lieux historiques ouvriers au Nouveau-Brunswick* (Edmonton: Canadian Committee on Labour History / Comité canadien sur l'histoire du travail, 2010), 65–75. The book also discusses a variety of other labour monuments, including memorials established by individual unions such as the firefighters and the longshoremen.

90 NBFL Proceedings, 1995. Clavette had previously observed that only two-thirds of the union locals affiliated to the CLC also participated in the Federation, and the 1993 convention endorsed an "affiliation campaign" to promote participation in both the Federation and labour councils. Clavette also noted that the return of several of the expelled unions to the CLC, including the Carpenters and the Labourers, held promise for strengthening the Federation, as did provisions for the direct affiliation of nurses, teachers, and other groups.

91 "Bob Hickes Resumé," CUPE NB, 2011. McEwen subsequently became chair of the Workers' Investment Fund.

92 *Gleaner*, 22 July and 25 July 1995.

93 *Telegraph-Journal*, 14 August 1996.

94 Erin Steuter, "Roll-back at the Irving Refinery: The Real Meaning of 'Expecting Excellence' in the Workplace," *On the Table: A Review of Work and Society* 2 (November 1997): 6–8.

95 Steuter, "Roll-back at the Irving Refinery," 6–8. Steuter also noted that media coverage of the strike threatened to have a lasting influence: "The fact that media presented the results of the strike as perfectly reasonable and normal encourages defeatism in the face of corporate and governmental intimidation." See also Steuter, "The Irvings Cover Themselves: Media Representations of the Irving Oil Refinery Strike, 1994–1996." *Canadian Journal of Communication* 24, no. 4 (1999): 629–47, and Erin Steuter and Geoff Martin, "The Myth of the Competitive Challenge: The Irving Oil Refinery Strike, 1994–1996," *Studies in Political Economy* 63 (Autumn 2000): 111–32.

96 *NBFL Proceedings*, 1996. The theme of the convention, "Social Programs: Worth the Fight!" was appropriate, Hickes said, but gave him no satisfaction: "Unfortunately, hitting the theme bang on does not make me happy. If anything it makes me mad. I hope it makes my brothers and sisters mad too." For context, see Alvin Finkel, *Social Policy and Practice in Canada: A History* (Waterloo: Wilfrid Laurier University Press, 2006), chap. 12.

97 *L'Acadie Nouvelle,* 5 février and 30 avril 1996; Richard Wilbur, "New Brunswick," *Canadian Annual Review of Politics and Public Affairs, 1996* (Toronto: University of Toronto Press, 2002), 160–61; and Jean-Claude Basque, "Chômage: Résistance aux politiques anti-travailleurs et travailleuses

en Acadie," paper presented at l'Atelier sur l'histoire du travail au Nouveau-Brunswick, Fredericton, 29 May 2011.

98 The NDP vote increased to 18.4 percent in the province. This election was also a breakthrough for the NDP in neighbouring Nova Scotia, where the party won six seats and 30.4 percent of the vote.

99 *NBFL Proceedings*, 1997.

100 Hickes and Boyce to McKenna, 12 March 1997, box 23, MC1819, PANB.

101 "Mission Statement of N.B. Common Front for Social Justice," February 1997, box 23, MC1819, PANB. This included objectives such as promoting the value and dignity of human work, creating a more dynamic democracy, maintaining and improving social programmes, challenging policies of privatization, deregulation and the withdrawal of the state, establishing a fair and equitable tax system, and safeguarding "that which makes the Canadian and New Brunswick identity so distinct."

Epilogue: "Honour the Past. Build the Future"

1 *NBFL Proceedings*, 2011. Boudreau was elected president in 2005 and has held office since then. As a worker at the Villa du Repos Nursing Home in Moncton, he became president of CUPE Local 2079 in 1988 and president of the New Brunswick Council of Nursing Home Unions in 1998. He was also an elected school trustee (1989–92) and vice-president of the Moncton and District Labour Council (1990–92). "Elect Michel Boudreau for President" (2005) (copy in author's possession).

2 *NBFL Proceedings*, 2011. For the decisions, see *Canadian Union of Public Employees*

vs. *Province of New Brunswick*, Court of Queen's Bench, New Brunswick, 17 June 2009; the legislation was amended in 2010. See also "Health Services and Support — Facilities Subsector Bargaining Assn. v. British Columbia," *Judgements of the Supreme Court of Canada*, 2007 SCC 27, [2007] 2 S.C.R. 391, http://scc.lexum.org. For a cautionary discussion of the Supreme Court decision, see Eric Tucker, "The Constitutional Right to Bargain Collectively: The Ironies of Labour History in the Supreme Court of Canada," *Labour/Le Travail* 61 (Spring 2008): 151–80.

3 Thom Workman, *Social Torment: Globalization in Atlantic Canada* (Halifax: Fernwood Publishing, 2003), 58–65, 75–91. See also the issues of *On the Table: A Review of Work and Society* from 1997 to 2000.

4 "Unionization in Canada: A Retrospective" (Summer 1999), and "Unionization 2010" (October 2010), *Perspectives on Labour and Income in Canada* (Statistics Canada). Supplementary data on unionization in New Brunswick was provided by Sharanjit Uppal, Labour Statistics Division, Statistics Canada, 6 December 2011.

5 It later became part of Post-Secondary Education and Training, then Post-Secondary Education, Training and Labour.

6 NBFL *Proceedings*, 2001. See also Blair Doucet Interview, 7 July 2006, LHTNB fonds, MC3477, PANB and *Northern Light*, 10 February 2009. Doucet died in 2009. One of his achievements as president was the establishment of an annual summer camp for high school students, later renamed the Blair Doucet Youth Summer Camp.

7 For results in this period, see "Elections in New Brunswick/Les Élections au Nouveau-Brunswick, 1984–2006," prepared by the New Brunswick Legislative Library, available at http://electionsnb.ca/publications-e.asp.

8 *Telegraph-Journal*, 26 May 1999.

9 William Vinh-Doyle, *Catching Up, Fighting Back: The New Brunswick Council of Hospital Unions* (Fredericton: CUPE 1252, 2010), 66–72.

10 NBFL *Proceedings*, 2003, 2005, 2007.

11 Press Release, 8 October 2004, box 23, MC1819, PANB.

12 For results, see "Thirty-Seventh General Election, September 27, 2010, Report of the Chief Electoral Officer," available at http://electionsnb.ca/publications-e.asp.

13 For federal election results in this period, see "Past Elections," http://www.elections.ca.

14 Under this arrangement, six at-large officers were elected by ballot at the convention: president, first vice-president, second vice-president, secretary-treasurer (with a requirement that at least one of these four be a woman and another a francophone), plus a women's vice-president and youth vice-president. Three trustees were also elected by the convention, and there was a representative for each labour council. In addition, the reform created two vice-presidencies for each union with more than 5,000 members, one for unions with more than 1,000 members, and two to be shared by unions with fewer than 1,000 members.

15 Doucet Interview; NBFL *Proceedings*, 2003. The Federation's executive secretary, John Murphy, retired in 2005 after thirty-three years of dedicated service.

16 *NBFL Proceedings*, 2005.

17 Statement by New Brunswick Coalition of Unions, 9 February 2004, box, 23, MC1819, PANB.

18 *NBFL Proceedings*, 2005.

19 Courtney MacIsaac and Lisa Pasolli, "NBPEA to NBU: Association to Union, 1970–2004," research report, June 2007. See also *NBFL Proceedings*, 2007, 2009. History rarely proceeds in a straight line, however, and before the end of the year in 2011, the NBU unexpectedly decided to suspend their participation; it was not clear if this would be a temporary adjustment or a lasting setback to provincial solidarity.

20 Linda Kealey, "No More 'Yes Girls': Labour Activism Among New Brunswick Nurses, 1964–1981," *Acadiensis* 37, no. 2 (Summer–Autumn 2008): 3–17. See also "How Nurses Learned to Wear Two Hats: Professional and Unionists," http://www.lhtnb.ca. Other well-established professional unions that joined the Federation at this time included the faculty associations at St. Thomas University (2009) and the University of New Brunswick (2011).

21 *NBFL Proceedings*, 2011. However, the Federation's breach with the building trades had not been repaired at the provincial level, although several of these unions had rejoined the CLC. Another large group of unionized employees outside the Federation were the teaching staff in the province's schools. Interestingly, the renewal of the Federation through new affiliations was a news development largely missed by the provincial media, whose absence from the Federation conventions had been notable since the 1990s. As the sources for this book often show, for many years local

and provincial newspaper reporters had attended the full convention and filed stories on a variety of debates and developments. For a comment, see "Numbers Make a Difference," *Our Times: Canada's Independent Labour Magazine*, July–August 2005, 14–15.

22 The secretary-treasurer reported a total of 375 affiliated local unions and seven labour councils, as well as the Federation of Union Retirees. As usual at conventions, not all unions sent delegates (and one labour council was not represented). Moreover, most unions were eligible for more representation; in 2011 the UFCW filled 10 of 14 possible seats, but the CAW filled only 7 of 25. As in the past, attendance was affected by factors such as the location of the convention; locals also weighed the costs of sending delegates to national or international meetings of their own union. Absences nonetheless deprived members of opportunities to participate in the solidarities represented by the Federation at the provincial level. The concept of "open" conventions in which unions encourage non-voting delegates to attend has the potential to introduce more members, especially less experienced members, to labour activism at the provincial level.

23 *NBFL Proceedings*, 2011. Among the total of 166 voting delegates, there were 84 women and 82 men; it is estimated that there were 57 francophone delegates.

24 One by-product of deindustrialization and downsizing is the loss of identity for workers who consider themselves to be closely attached to the union in their trade, occupation, industry, or community. The challenge has appeared before, and at least in the case of senior citizens, organizations of union retirees

offer one means of continued participation in the solidarities of labour. For a discussion of workers' attachment to community and workplace, see Steven High, "The Forestry Crisis: Public Policy & Richard Florida's Clock of History," *Our Times: Canada's Independent Labour Magazine*, December 2009–January 2010, 26–33.

25 Thom Workman, *If You're in My Way, I'm Walking: The Assault on Working People Since 1970* (Halifax and Winnipeg: Fernwood Publishing, 2009), 136.

26 Fred W. Thompson, *Fellow Worker: The Life of Fred Thompson* (Chicago: Charles H. Kerr Publishing, 1993), 84. Other New Brunswickers who left the province at a young age also became prominent in labour history in other places. Émile Boudreau, born near Petit-Rocher in 1915, worked in the mines in Québec and became a leading figure in the Steelworkers and the Fédération des travailleurs et travailleuses du Québec. Buzz Hargrove, born at Bath in 1944, went to work in the auto plants in Ontario and was president of the Canadian Auto Workers from 1992 to 2008. For their autobiographies, see Boudreau, *Un enfant de la grande depression: Autobiographie* (Outremont, Québec, Lanctôt éditeurs, 1998) and Hargrove, *Labour of Love: The Fight to Create a More Humane Canada* (Toronto: Macfarlane Walter and Ross, 1998).

27 David Camfield, *Canadian Labour in Crisis: Reinventing the Workers' Movement* (Halifax and Winnipeg: Fernwood Publishing, 2011), 50–52.

INDEX

NOTE: Page numbers in boldface refer to photographs.

Canadian Union of Public Employees (CUPE), 116,
122–27, 132, 156–57, 162, 189–96, 202–3, 222,
255n45, 267n79. *See also* hospital workers; National
Union of Public Employees; public employees;
public sector general strike (1992); school boards
capital punishment, 142
Caraquet, 27, 85, 118, 153, 164–65
Carland, Everett, 28
Carlin, William, 88
carpenters, 18, 79, 82, 119–20, 145, 158, 262n16
Carr, Shirley, 180, 184
Carter, Terry, 220
casual workers, 26, 187, 213–14, 216–17
Catholic social teachings, 122, 185, 206–7, 218, 266n54
Catholic unions (Québec), 38, 68
Charlebois, Réjean, 130
Charles, Prince of Wales, 207
Charter of Rights and Freedoms. *See* Canadian
Charter of Rights and Freedoms (1982)
Chávez, César, 143–44, **145**
Chestnut Canoe: strike (1948), 83, 246n29
Chiasson, Euclide, 258–59n71
child labour, 7–8, 16, 29, 49, 77
Chrétien, Jean, 202, 266n64
Cirtex Knitting: strike (1976), 153, 155
Civil Service Association of New Brunswick, 126–27,
257n58. *See also* New Brunswick Public Employees
Association
Clavette, Maurice, 174
Coalition of Public Employees (1991–92), 190, 192,
196, 220
coal miners, 36, 38, 76; Minto mine tragedy (1932),
48–49; strikes, in 1937–38, 61–67; in 1947, 82–83,
246n27
Coca-Cola (Brunswick Bottling): strike (1987–88),
179–81
Cochrane, Dennis, 179, 183
Coleman, Ed, 200
collective bargaining, 4, 7–9, 37, 58–59, 64–66, 75–76,
90, 148–49, 193–94, 197; first contract legislation,
176, 208; John Davidson on (1898), 7, 213; municipal workers, bargaining rights for, 113, 251n16;
provincial public employees, bargaining rights for,
65–66, 84–85, 89–91, 122–29. *See also* Canadian
Charter of Rights and Freedoms; Industrial Relations
Act; Labour and Industrial Relations Act; Labour
Relations Act; Public Service Labour Relations Act
Common Front for Social Justice, 206, 208–9,

212–13, 269n101
Communications, Energy and Paperworkers Union (CEP),
203–4, 222. *See also* Canadian Paperworkers Union
communists, 68, 87, 251n15, 263n22
Community-University Research Alliance, 13, 230n11
Confederation of Regions Party, 191
Conservation Council of New Brunswick, 185, 209
consumer protection, 260n76
Co-operative Commonwealth Federation (CCF),
51–54, 71, 77–79, 91, 110, 239nn15–19, 240n25,
244–45nn15, 16, 248n62
Cormier, Guy, 266n64
Cormier, Stella, 11
Craig, Bill, 248n64
Crawford, George, 26, 43
Creaghan, Paul, 152
Crilley, Frank, 88, 88, 116, 132
Crothers, T. W., 24
Cyr, Pierrette, **169**

Daley, Fred, 25
Dalhousie, 57–59, 110–11. *See also* Campbellton-
Dalhousie and District Labour Council
Daly, John, 11
Dalzell, Vance, 53
Darcy, Judy, 190, 194, 196
Davidson, Bob, 190, 193
Davidson, John, 7
Davis, Harry, 88
daycare, 117, 170, 205
Day of Concern, Bathurst (1972), 135–40
Day of Mourning, 200–201, 268n87
Day of Protest (1976), 147–52. *See also* wage controls
(1976)
Department of Labour (New Brunswick), 79, 84, 141–42,
215, 236n48, 245n17, 259n73
DeWare, Mabel, 154–55, 158
Donovan, Ian, 200
Donovan, J. J., 16–17
Doucet, Blair, 174, 186, 202, 215, **216**, 217, 219–20, 270n6
dry dock (Saint John). *See* shipyards (Saint John)
Dufour, Linda, 167
Duguay, Roger, 218
Dysart, A. C., 56, 60–61, 64, 242n41

Edmundston, 57, 79, 95, 107, 114, 174; Edmundston
and District Trades and Labour Council, 117
employment insurance. *See* unemployment insurance